GETTING UNSTUCK

UNRAVELING THE KNOT OF
DEPRESSION, ATTENTION, AND TRAUMA

Don Kerson M.D.

Copyright © 2009 Don Kerson, M.D.
All rights reserved
Published in the United States of America by
Greenpoint Psychiatric Press
861 Manhattan Avenue
Brooklyn, New York 11222
Library of Congress Cataloging-in-Publication Data
Kerson, Don
Getting unstuck:
unraveling the knot of depression,
attention and trauma /
Don Kerson. — 1st ed.
p.   cm.
Includes bibliographical references and index
ISBN-13: 978-0-9769867-2-0
LCCN: 2007937242
1. Depression, Mental Popular Works.
2. Attention-deficit disorder Popular works.
3. Attention-deficit disorder in adults Popular works. Dissociation
(Psychology). I. Title

Printed and bound in the United States of America

FIRST EDITION

DEDICATION

This work of so many years could never have been possible without the unstinting support and encouragement of my wife Dr. Roslynn Glicksman, whom it is simply impossible to thank adequately.

I am also grateful to my parents, and to all the other members of my extended family whom I have studied carefully over the years to learn just how it is that smart, hyperactive people make their way in the world.

Finally, if predictably, I need to thank the many hundreds of patients I have had the privilege to treat over the past twenty years of psychiatric practice. Without their trust and confidence I could never have put together the ideas you will soon be reading.

TABLE OF CONTENTS

Figures

CHAPTER 1

What Does It Mean to be Stuck?

Being stuck means not moving.
Being stuck means not being able to get things done.
Being stuck means not growing.

Being stuck means feeling frustrated, unsatisfied, unfulfilled, lost, confused, blocked.

It's not that stuck people lack the knowledge or understanding of what to do about their circumstances. Stuck people know what to do. They just can't get themselves to do it.

Being stuck does not result from ignorance or laziness. Rather, it results from a lack of self-control. It results from not doing what should be done, and from doing what should not be done. It results from problems with focus, planning and execution. Stuck people are inefficient. They function below their capabilities. They don't maximize their resources or opportunities. They can't seem to plan or follow through when it comes to the behaviors required to move forward in life.

No one likes to be stuck, although an awful lot of people are so. If you're stuck, you most likely want to change and most likely want to get going, working, moving, growing.

Most likely you want to know how to get unstuck. If you do, keep reading. I've shown others how, and I can show you, too.

WHO SHOULD READ THIS BOOK

If you are an educated individual — a college graduate, say, or a person who has studied and mastered moderately challenging academic material — and yet, even after considerable intelligent self-examination and reasonable efforts at obtaining professional help, you remain stuck and confused, then you should read this book.

If you are a professional of almost any sort - a social worker, psychologist, therapist or counselor, teacher, coach, cop - and you work with good-hearted, well-meaning folks who seem to be trying hard but just can't get anywhere, then you should read this book.

If you are the parent, the spouse, the partner, the lover, the sibling, the colleague, or even just the good friend of a stuck person, then you, too, should read this book.

If you fit into any of the above categories, you will want to read this book because inside it you will find, for the first time ever, some straight answers about what's really going on with us in this fast-paced, complex, unforgiving world, and what we can and should be doing to help ourselves.

WHAT'S INSIDE THIS BOOK

Inside this book, you'll find discussions about what I call the Four Threes:

- Three conditions
- Three remedies
- Three journeys
- Three tools

The three conditions are depression, dissociation, and attention deficit disorder (ADD). In my practice, I have found that these three interconnected conditions are the primary causes of people becoming stuck.

The three remedies are information, medication, and integration.

The three journeys are three types of guided visualization (inner child, inner parent, and inner guide). They can be used to heal the effects of all sorts of trauma on the ever-developing organization of the self.

The three tools are time maps, pessimistically planned transitions, and request-handling algorithms. These are techniques for time and task management.

MY INTENTIONS

I began to write this book - perhaps almost a decade ago - out of a wish to train other mental health practitioners in the use of the hypnotherapeutic techniques I had been customizing for my patients with ADD and depression. Once the book began to take shape, however, I found myself using it routinely to speed up my work with my patients. I've been giving it to my patients in various forms for five years now, and I have no doubt that it accelerates their progress enormously. It provides an organizational overview both of the problems that they bring to me and of the solutions I am prepared to provide.

Fundamentally, this book is designed to assist in the quest for a more satisfying and productive life. It's a book about what gets in our way as individuals, as professionals, and as a society and culture, and about what we can do to remedy it. Specifically, it's a book about the complicated relationship between three different conditions that influence human experience — depression, ADD, and trauma — and ways to deal with them. The central contention of this volume is that "being stuck" is an end state that is common to all three of these disorders, and further, that effective treatment depends entirely on separating out and addressing all the components that are present at any one time.

The three conditions operate at three different layers of causation: Attention is neurophysiological, having to do with the structure of the brain; depression is biochemical, having to do with wear and tear at the neurotransmitter level; and trauma is dissociative, having to do with the storage and flow of information within the structures of the self.

In addition to guiding and informing individuals who suffer from any combination of the three conditions, my wish and my mission are to influence my profession and to change how we, as a society, approach these issues. Therefore, you will find herein a subtler and more useful way of looking at attentional issues in mental health (ADD is still both underdiagnosed in adults and simplistically and/or ineffectively treated in all age groups), as well as an emphasis on the interactions between the different conditions and the different levels of causation. Ultimately, my wish is to attempt to redress the unfortunate disintegration of medication and therapy, to influence how practitioners are trained, and, at the very least, to spread these ideas and practices as widely as I can. I believe Americans are waiting impatiently for an approach to their mental health problems that makes sense and that works.

It is not at all accidental that in this book, I discuss the three conditions together, something that, to my knowledge, has never been done before. For the past decade, I have been a specialist in the treatment of adults with ADD. At the same time, I have treated a large number of patients with depression who were sent to me by the insurance companies with which I participate. Many of the people who came to me for help with ADD were also depressed, and a large number of those who suffered from depression also had ADD — ADD that almost never had been properly diagnosed or treated. Both these sets of patients often had underlying post-traumatic dissociations.

When we compare the three conditions, we see that their clinical presentations are often strikingly similar — so similar, in fact, that the conditions are often confused with one another. The three conditions, by different mechanisms, all lead to the same condition of being stuck.

Let's take a moment to compare the three conditions.

THE THREE CONDITIONS

Attention Deficit Disorder

What is now called attention deficit disorder is a hardware problem, an inherited neurophysiological condition that is estimated by authoritative sources to affect 3 to 7 percent of the population.

Although ADD is usually associated with children, it is being increasingly recognized as a widespread problem among adults as well. The three classic symptoms of ADD in children are distractibility, impulsivity, and hyperactivity. In adults, the hallmark symptoms also include procrastination and disorganization. Probably ADD can be more accurately described as an inherited relative underactivity of inhibitory centers in the front of the brain. This means that people with ADD who need to focus on an attentionally demanding task may have difficulty turning off or preventing the activation of competing areas of the brain. This translates in practical terms into a tendency toward underreflectiveness, a preference for action, and a delay in the development of executive functioning.

Executive functioning is defined as the ability to plan across time in order to optimize outcomes. Poor executive functioning is the most common presenting complaint of adults with ADD (read inherited under-reflectiveness). ADD is extremely variable in its presentation, in the degree to which it impairs any given sphere of life, but difficulty in executive functioning, problems with planning and follow through, should always raise our suspicions that attentional problems may be present even if previously undetected.

Although official estimates vary, I have come to believe that the prevalence of ADD has been grossly underestimated. Rather than the 3 to 7 percent usually discussed, I believe closer to 10 or 12 percent of the population suffers with ADD. I see attentional issues as an iceberg, more than half of which is still submerged below the surface, unseen, undetected, and unaddressed. This is for two important reasons: (1) because the condition is poorly named, and (2) because hyperactivity can be invisible. The disorder is poorly named because many people have no absolute deficit in attention. Rather, they have a problem modulating their attention — that is, turning it on, keeping it on, and turning it off. Many people with ADD focus quite well, just not selectively or consistently enough to please everyone they need to please.

When I say that hyperactivity can be invisible, I am making another very important point. If, in ADD, inhibitory systems in the brain are relatively underactive, it follows that some other part of the brain is going to be underinhibited, or overactive. The question is which part.

When the underinhibited part of the brain involves verbal or gross motor activity, ADD is recognized fairly early. However, if it involves systems that are tactile, visual, musical, sexual, emotional, or something else more internal, the patient will very rarely be diagnosed, but the effect on the development of adequate executive functioning may be the same.

Because I believe ADD is an inherited set of nervous system tendencies, it cannot be cured. People with ADD, especially those who do not know themselves well, quite often become stuck. Fortunately, the effects of ADD can often be mitigated almost entirely by a judicious combination of wisdom, medication, and the acquisition of compensatory skills.

Depression
Depression, also called affective disorders, is the label we commonly use to connote neurotransmitter disorders, which are metabolic or biochemical disorders of the brain. It affects an estimated 20 to 25 percent of the population.

Bipolar disorder, obsessive-compulsive disorder (OCD), and many of the anxiety disorders, as well as the more obvious depressive conditions are all neurotransmitter disorders. These are all wear-and-tear problems, a little like running out of brake or transmission fluid in a car. They are biochemical imbalances in the brain caused by some individualized combination of poor lifestyle, stress, and hereditary susceptibility. Any of these conditions can also alter attention, but they also show themselves in a range of other changes in things like sleep pattern, appetite, energy level, and nervous and emotional reactivity. Depression is an enormous cause of being stuck. Again, fortunately, if it is properly diagnosed by subtype (there are four major types), it is almost always reversible with medication and/or therapy.

Dissociation
Dissociation is the way in which a wide range of traumatic childhood experiences are stored and expressed in adulthood. It has to

do with the ability of the brain to perform more than one function at a time and to vary and adjust the flow of information about these functions in and out of conscious awareness. Dissociative disorders are not widely understood, but they are extremely common. We know that extreme trauma can profoundly affect individuals. The post-traumatic stress disorders (PTSDs) of combat troops and September 11 survivors are examples. The category includes not only people who were overtly battered or sexually abused as children, but also those who were more subtly but still chronically traumatized, such as the children of alcoholics, drug addicts, or mentally ill parents; the children of bitter divorces or frequent relocations; and people who grew up with Asperger's syndrome, ADD, or learning disabilities. What become dissociated are what are commonly called the left (verbal) brain and the right (visual) brain.

What we know nowadays is that persistent childhood trauma interferes with the natural process of learning how to manage consciousness and self-consciousness; creating, if you will, programming problems in the brain that affect the way individuals learn to process information and organize the self and the mind.

Throughout history, every culture, to a greater or lesser degree, has recognized the dual nature of the human mind — the rational versus the emotional, the judging versus the experiencing. In modern times, we recognize that this duality has a basis in the left and the right hemispheres of the cerebral cortex. The essential difference between the two hemispheres is in how they process and store information. The right brain is primary, experiential, before words, visual, bodily, emotional, pattern-seeing, in the moment. The left brain, which comes into play later, is verbal, planning, naming, labeling, comparing, judging, one step removed from experience. In order to become most fully human, our best selves, we must integrate these aspects of the mind/brain, these two selves. When children are taught to reject or despise themselves, for whatever reason, that process of integration is disturbed and altered. The flow of information back and forth between the planning left brain and the feeling/doing/knowing right brain becomes stilted and inefficient.

Dissociation — the divorce of intent from action, of the left brain from the right brain — is a concept central to the understanding of being stuck. Although dissociation in its more obvious forms (for example, traumatic amnesia, battle fatigue, and dissociative identity disorder, which is also called multiple personality disorder) is a widely recognized syndrome, it is usually overlooked when diagnosing and treating adults who can't get things done. Many adults who are correctly diagnosed with ADD suffer less from the underlying neurophysiological problem than from the dissociative effects of a lifetime of interaction with a world that is not in sync with their rhythms or methods of relating. It is this consistently negative and variably but persistently traumatic interaction that interferes with their ability to master and integrate the various parts of the self. As already mentioned, ADD is only one of many traumatizing childhood experiences that can create dissociation and "stuckness."

RUNNING THE NUMBERS

If you find yourself remaining stuck even after considerable intelligent self-examination and reasonable efforts at professional help, the chances are exceedingly high that you are suffering from one (and probably more than one) of the three extremely common conditions we have been discussing — depression, ADD, and dissociation. When I say that the chances are exceedingly high, I am not exaggerating. In my perhaps biased view, at least 10 percent of the population is affected by attention deficit disorder as I define it. Neurotransmitter abnormalities, commonly known as depressive and anxiety disorders, collectively affect 25 percent of the population. Dissociative disorders, caused by a myriad of conditions and situations, altogether easily affect 25 percent of the population. Add up those numbers and, even accounting for overlap, you'll see that it's safe to say that more than one in three Americans are affected by one or more of these three conditions.

These are pretty astounding numbers when you think about them. If we extrapolate simply from figures of 10 percent for ADD and 25 percent for neurotransmitter abnormalities, we come up with 2.5 percent of our population having ADD and depression. That's 7.5 million Americans. But in reality, it's way more than that, because ADD leads to depression, and ADD leads to dissociation, and dissociation leads to depression as well. When all is said and done, tens of millions of Americans suffer from some combination of these interacting conditions.

A BROKEN SYSTEM

Unfortunately, the mental health system is just as fragmented as the patients it seeks to treat. Therapists largely are neither prescribers nor diagnosticians. Prescribers are primarily general practitioners and the overwhelming majority of psychiatrists don't even do therapy at all anymore anyway. Nowhere nearly enough psychiatrists are being trained, and those that are being trained are not being trained broadly enough. Although it is possible to receive skilled treatment for depression with both medication and therapy, the therapist and the diagnostician/prescriber usually are not the same person. Treatment for dissociation is provided largely by hypnotherapists, who neither prescribe nor diagnose, and has been focused almost exclusively on the more severe cases-post-traumatic stress disorder (when the acute trauma occurred in adulthood), and multiple personality disorder (when the acute trauma occurred in childhood). Almost no literature at all exists on psychotherapy for adults with ADD, and the literature that does exist on children and adolescents with ADD focuses almost exclusively on medication.

PROFESSIONAL CONFUSION

What is obvious is that confusion about stuck people is pervasive. Doesn't everyone have trouble getting things done? Doesn't everyone have trouble with self-control? Most stuck people are half-convinced themselves that they're just lazy, selfish bastards who need a good kick in the pants. Does ADD even exist? If so, exactly what is it? Should medicine be used? Under what circumstances? What else can be done? Is there a specific effective treatment? Is therapy just more coddling?

The whole thing is a mess. Excellent treatments do, in fact, exist for a wide range of aspects of mental functioning. It's just exceedingly difficult to know how and where to find them.

To illustrate the point, consider the following exchange. In June 2000, *The New York Times* ran an article discussing the heightened awareness of attentional difficulties in adults and describing some strategies for coping with ADD in the workplace. It defined the syndrome as a biochemical imbalance that results in six symptoms-procrastination, impulsiveness, disorganization, hyperactivity, lack of motivation, and inability to manage time.

Within days, a cranky psychiatrist shot back a testy response in which he labeled the condition as merely a collection of bad habits that, if legitimized as a diagnosis, would surely lead to wholesale drug dependence and the collapse of the mental health reimbursement system.

I may be overstating the psychiatrist's position, but, if nothing else, this exchange demonstrates vividly how confused and conflicted we are today about the diagnosis and treatment of attentional problems and of stuck folks in general. First off, *The Times* was mistaken in a very important way when it labeled ADD as a chemical imbalance. Depression is a biochemical imbalance that can, sometimes at least, be rebalanced. ADD is something else entirely. It is a neurophysiological condition, an inherited variation in brain structure. Although it can be made virtually invisible by medication or the acquisition of compensatory skills, it can never be cured because it is not an illness.

WHAT'S REALLY GOING ON

If the aforementioned psychiatrist is any indication, it's no wonder that so many stuck people have difficulty finding sympathetic, let alone effective, treatment. I'm not sure exactly how classifying a common set of human problems as bad habits helps people to function better. (What does he propose to do for the folks with "bad habits"?) In any case *The Times* article does nicely summarize, with its six symptoms, pretty much what I am trying to get at by using the umbrella term "stuck."

ADD is real, that's for certain. I know because I have it, because my children all have it, and because I have seen thousands of people with it over the past decade. It's easy to talk about bad habits or bad character. It's easy to call people lazy, selfish, unmotivated, irresponsible, or unreliable. What's more useful is to start with the idea that, given the opportunity, most people want to do well, to "be good." If they're not doing well, there's a reason, and if we want to help them do better, it behooves us to find out what that reason is. To do that, we need to abandon old approaches that just don't work. We need to start dealing with the complex layers of causation that make people stuck.

Getting unstuck involves looking at the complex weave of depression, ADD, and dissociation. Three factors that operate at three different levels and that all must be examined if a speedy and effective treatment is to be devised. These factors can appear in isolation or in various combinations, sequentially or simultaneously, confounding both psychiatrists wedded to an ADD diagnosis and those biased against it — and disappointing patients who seek their help. No wonder so much confusion and controversy surround effective treatment for dysfunctional adults.

What we are about to discuss in this book is not the treatment of three separate conditions. Rather, more accurately, it is the treatment of seven different conditions:

- Post-traumatic left-right brain dissociation (henceforth referred to simply as dissociation)
- Biochemically-based neurotransmitter disorder (henceforth referred to simply as depression)
- Neurophysiologically-mediated attention deficit disorder (ADD)
- ADD plus dissociation
- Depression plus dissociation
- ADD plus depression
- ADD plus depression plus dissociation

THE THREE REMEDIES

Information

The past thirty years have witnessed enormous progress in the field of psychiatry in accurately defining treatable clinical entities. We now know a great deal about the nature, course and treatment of most common conditions, and I believe that it is of vital importance to a successful treatment that this information be shared with the patient. Large parts of this book are my efforts to put together in one place the materials that I thought would help my patients better understand their conditions. Chapters 3, 4, and 5 contain a great deal of what I try to explain to my patients about their conditions so that they may most effectively assist in their treatment. Throughout the text are references to books that I have found especially useful. These books are collected in a Reference List at the end of the text. Please consider *Getting Unstuck* a starting point in your exploration of these topics, and read for yourself the books in the "Recommended Reading List" that apply to you the most. All of the books to which I refer have much greater depth that I can convey in my brief references, and all will reward further reading.

Medication

Medication for ADD is actually a relatively simple issue. Two medications (Dexedrine and methylphenidate. both in a multitude of preparations) account for the overwhelming majority of prescriptions. Three other drugs, two of them also antidepressants (Strattera, Wellbutrin, and desipramine) make up almost all the rest. Medication for the full range of neurotransmitter, depressive, and anxious disorders is a much more complicated issue. I commonly use a palette of as many as fifteen to twenty drugs.

Depression continues to be ineffectively treated for two common reasons. First, some or all of the depressive subtypes that may be present in a person at any given time are inadequately identified or addressed, and second, the effects of attentional issues on the nature and course of the depression are inadequately appreciated.

Medication is, of course, rarely the only answer, but resisting its role is equally futile. Much wonderful therapy — directive, interpersonal, eclectic, or psychodynamic — is wasted when it is performed on folks whose neurotransmitter problems are interfering with their ability to turn thought and conversation into action. I have repeatedly witnessed what I call the slingshot effect — when bright people with a lot of therapy under their belts finally get a sufficiently subtle diagnosis that allows the prescription of the proper mix of medications, and boom, they take off like rockets because now, they can finally use all that great stuff they've been learning and talking about all that time.

By the time you finish reading this book, you should be able to easily identify the various medication-responsive neurotransmitter-based symptom clusters (there are four major types), and just as easily see the presence of prefrontal cortex-mediated underreflectiveness (ADD) in its many disguises.

Integration

What I believe distinguishes my approach from many others is my emphasis on right-left brain integration as a complicating factor in the treatment of both depressive and attentional disorders. All human beings struggle with the challenge of integrating their left and right brains. The same right-brain utilization techniques that can be used to change the course and the effects of various mental and nervous diseases and emotional disturbances (the traditional bailiwick of psychiatrists) are the very stuff of the human potential movement in all its varied glory, the very tools of personal growth that have been sold by one wise man or another, from Tony Robbins to Werner Erhardt, from Krishnamurti to the Bhagwan Shree Rajneesh to Norman Vincent Peale and back again. It's all the same stuff. It's all yin and yang. It's all always about integration of the parts. Always.

In the second half of this book, after we have spent some time defining and describing the three interwoven conditions, we'll look at a range of exercises designed to move along the process of learning to make our parts work as a whole, and we'll see how they can assist us in addressing the reasons for being stuck.

———◆◆◆◆◆———

Ultimately, what I am hoping for is that you, the reader, will find in this book a better way of thinking about, analyzing, and ultimately treating the factors that are keeping you stuck. I am hoping that this volume will be the impetus for a grand collaboration between patients and their therapists, between teachers and their students, between the members of all sorts of families, who will share the book with each other, and use the ideas found within it to spur each other forward in the never-ending quest to be more completely themselves.

Now, let's see just how this all works.

CHAPTER 2

STUCKNESS

CHAPTER OVERVIEW

Stuckness: A General Profile

You don't take care of yourself physically, occupationally, financially, socially, or emotionally.

You know what steps you can and ought to take to make your life better, but you don't take them, and you don't know why.

Your emotions get in your way; you lose perspective.

You have an uneasy relationship with time: You can't get organized, and you can't prioritize.

You don't get things done efficiently or at all.

You're not in control — not of your intentions, not of your feelings, not of your relationships, not of your behavior.

Bottom line: You know what to do, but you can't get yourself to do it.

15

Stuckness is best defined as a cluster of traits that boil down to an inability to get things done, and that show up in different ways depending on whether the underlying cause is ADD, dissociation, or depression. The clearest way to begin to understand the different types of stuckness is to look at some actual cases.

ALBERTO: ADD AND DISSOCIATION

Alberto, a young man in his late twenties, was a New York City schoolteacher and frustrated filmmaker. He came to me after a disappointing experience with a psychologist who didn't know much about ADD. Alberto had diagnosed himself, but when he asked the psychologist for more specific guidance, the doctor didn't have much to offer.

We got along well from the start. I agreed with Alberto's self-diagnosis, and he appreciated that I was knowledgeable about ADD, thanks both to my practice and to my firsthand experience. I prescribed stimulants, first Ritalin and later Adderall, and he felt that the medicine helped him concentrate better. Since using time effectively is such a big issue for adults with ADD, I gave him a couple of standard time-management reliability scripts that I use with my patients (for an example, see Chapter 8 and Appendix B). I also showed him how to make contact with his generic inner self through basic trance induction and deep relaxation. He seemed to use these tools pretty well, so we started a more standard sort of therapy, talking a lot about his relationship with his parents, who were in the middle of a messy divorce, and about his girlfriend, whom he would soon marry.

Alberto had been taking classes for his master's degree, which he needed in order to keep his teaching job. He'd had intermittent difficulties in graduate school, repeating several classes and taking some incompletes, although just as often his work had been fine and he had been generally liked by the faculty. After I prescribed the stimulants, he felt confident that he would get his degree in time to keep his job. He had only two classes to go, and he finished the first one in the fall semester without much difficulty.

At the end of the first seven months of therapy, we both thought things were going pretty well. Alberto was happy and moving forward on a number of fronts. We'd been meeting twice a month, but circumstances forced us to miss a few visits in February and March. Then, seemingly out of nowhere, Alberto showed up for his late April visit in a panic. He was about to flunk his last class, and he was two weeks late on a take-home exam. He kept planning to do it, but it just didn't get done. He couldn't believe this was happening to him again. He thought he was over all this stuff. Instead, it was just like adolescence. He was totally bummed. He was going to lose his damn job. For crying out loud, he was afraid even to go see the teacher. And on and on.

What was happening here? Alberto was an intelligent man. He had, at least on the surface, every motivation to pass that last class and secure his livelihood. He was taking medication, and he felt it was working. All the pieces seemed to be in place, but he still was not focused. He was avoiding something vital. Why wasn't he doing his paper?

Alberto is important not only because he is such a typical example of the frustrating procrastination that plagues the attentionally impaired, but also because he clearly demonstrates that even in the same individual, attentional difficulties can flow from several sources. First, of course, are the attentional problems that are neurophysiological in origin, inherited in the structure of the brain. This is ADD, a condition we recognize in children as young as two or three years old. ADD manifests as being out-of-sync; not being in the same rhythms as everyone else, changing activities too frequently, or too infrequently, needing extra guidance, having trouble with routines, talking too much, showing an overall lack of reflection. Our best theorists think of ADD as a weakness in the inhibitory system, the system that's supposed to keep us from reacting too soon or too much. The purpose of stimulant medications is to beef up that system. But Alberto was already taking a stimulant in the form of Adderall, so what else was there? Why couldn't he finish his paper?

I asked him to calm down for a second, and to close his eyes and focus on his breathing. I'd done this with Alberto before. He was fairly talented at trance techniques, and he quickly became absorbed within himself. His handsome face began to relax as he slipped into a trance. His breathing changed and his jaws slackened in the telltale signs that he was focused inward.

I spoke, my voice soft and rhythmic.

> You remember the staircase, don't you, Alberto?
> I've had you go down the staircase before, haven't I?
> A black spiral staircase
> That goes down,
> Down,
> Down,
> Deeper and deeper into yourself.
> When you get to the bottom of the stairs,
> There's an archway,
> And through the archway
> Is a cavern,
> The cavern of yourself.
> And you may already begin to be curious
> About all the interesting things you may find there.
> As you enter the cavern,
> Off to one side is a table,
> An oval table,
> With two chairs.
> Now even in this restful state, Alberto,
> You can nod your head, can't you?
> *Alberto nods.*
> And you are relaxed, aren't you, Alberto?
> *Alberto nods.*
> And can you see the table and the chairs yet?
> *Alberto nods.*
> Sit in one of the chairs, Alberto,
> And see that sitting in the opposite chair

Is also you,
The "inner you."
Can you see him?
Alberto nods.
We've met him before, haven't we?
*Alberto nods. He had met him before, although it was about six
months earlier.*
Remember that he's your inner self,
Your visual self,
Your body self,
Your movement self,
Your spatial self,
Your musical self,
Your sexual self,
Your spiritual self,
Your emotional self,
Your social self,

The self that sees faces and understands what they are saying
Without words,
All your nonverbal knowledge,
So many kinds,
All your experiential knowledge.
You plan;
He acts.
You name and label and judge;
He is.
And he files it all so differently than you do.
Can you see him?
Alberto nods.
Do you know him?
Alberto nods.
Does he know you?
Alberto nods.
Are you friends?

Alberto nods.
Even in this restful state, Alberto,
You can nod your head, can't you?
And you can even speak
Without changing this lovely state of focus and relaxation,
Can't you, Alberto?
Alberto says, "Yes," in a soft voice.
Are you friends?
Alberto says, "Yes."
Will he speak to you?
Alberto says, "Yes."
Is he angry with you?

Alberto says, "A little."
Why is he angry?
Is it because you've been pushing him around,
Telling him what to do,
Not consulting him,
Acting like he doesn't exist?
He's busted his ass for you for years.
You can't scare him anymore.
You've got to explain things,
Get his consent,
Before you make plans.
If he's on board,
You'll do it.
If he isn't,
You won't.
He'll tell you,
If you bother to ask,
Won't he?
Alberto nods.
Has he been listening to me?
Alberto nods.
Do I have it right?

Alberto says, "Yes."
Then talk to him,
Work it out,
Negotiate respectfully.
You've done that.
You do it all the time.
Alberto nods.
So take some quiet time
And talk it over with him,
Come to an understanding,
Agree on a plan.

Alberto wanted me to write his teacher a letter documenting his ADD, so I turned to the computer and began to type, basically ignoring him, occasionally murmuring, "That's right" or "Um-hmm." After about ten minutes, I finished the letter and turned back to Alberto. I asked him if he'd had a good conversation with himself. He said yes. I asked him if he had worked out whether he intended to get his paper done. He said yes. We brought him out of trance, and as he awoke, he said that it had been a very profound experience, that he had really talked to himself, and that the "inner Alberto" had told him that he had to make more time for creative projects if he expected himself to keep fulfilling all his "duties." He now felt confident that he could get his work done.

Alberto went straight home and wrote the paper in one sitting. I continued to see him for another year, during which time he left teaching altogether, taught himself several computer languages, and got a new job in networking at a much higher salary.

What happened to Alberto during his trance?

I would say that what occurred in Alberto that evening was a reassociation (the correction of a dissociation) between the two most important parts of almost every person — the verbal, labeling, judging, left-brain part of the self and the nonverbal, experiential, right-brain part of the self. Part of Alberto — his everyday self — knew full well that he needed to do his paper, that he should do it. His inner self, however, was tired, irritated, and operating independently on his own schedule for his own reasons. Alberto had been going back and forth between his two selves, getting nowhere and growing more and more frustrated, until he finally used a trance to get them to talk to each other and sort things out.

In other words, at that moment in time, Alberto's attentional impairment, his inability to get things done, was due not to his underlying ADD but to a second factor, dissociation.

BORIS: A COMPLEX DEPRESSION

Boris was sixteen. He was supposed to be in the eleventh grade, but there was no way he would graduate even nearly on time. For the last several years, he'd been failing his classes, doing no homework, missing lots of days. After two years of high school, he'd gotten only a few credits, maybe six months' worth, and finally he told the guidance counselor he "can't concentrate."

Boris lived alone with his mom, an earnest and concerned Polish immigrant who had worked as a cleaning woman but was now retired on disability. Boris himself was a big, chubby guy with slightly accented speech and scraggly hair. When I met him, he told me what he had told the guidance counselor. He said that he was restless in class, couldn't even attempt to do his homework, and hadn't done it for years. School, he said, was pointless and boring and not worth the trouble. In fact, for the several months just before he came to me, he had barely been going at all — twice a week at best. He gave me notes from his school administrators, who were bewildered, and from his mother, who was worried, all asking that he be evaluated for ADD.

As it happened, Boris didn't have ADD. He had a whopping depression. He hadn't been complaining about being depressed, which was what was misleading. If anything, he just seemed like a complacent, know-it-all, slacker type. He had a rueful, self-deprecating sense of humor, and he said he wasn't sad exactly. However, he said that nothing interested him, even things he used to love, such as playing computer games and Rollerblading. He also said that he felt very grouchy, although he kept it to himself most of the time, and that he was tired all the time. He had trouble falling asleep, but once he did, he could sleep all day, and he often did.

I looked for ADD in Boris, but I didn't see it, even though poor focus and concentration were important parts of his presentation. What really made ADD unlikely here was the time frame of his attentional difficulties. Boris developed his symptoms gradually over a two-year period, after functioning well in school until seventh grade, paying attention appropriately and getting good grades. ADD is a lifelong condition, and Boris had no trace of attentional issues before the age of thirteen or so.

What Boris did have was a subtype of depression, an imbalance in serotonin and dopamine, two important neurotransmitters, that is at least partly hereditary. I prescribed Celexa, a drug that increases serotonin levels, and Wellbutrin, which increases dopamine levels. Within several months, Boris was a different person, happy, energetic, and enthusiastic. He decided he'd had it with high school, so he dropped out, got a job, and started working toward an equivalency diploma so that he could go to college. Now he's paying attention to things he enjoys and moving forward with his life.

The point of Boris's story is that depression is highly variable in its presentation. People who suffer from it are not always sad. Often, as seen here, depression presents as attentional impairment, an inability to get things done. To Boris's teachers and his mother, his problem looked like ADD. In fact, his was a case of attentional difficulties caused solely by depression, with no ADD involvement at all.

CATHY: DISSOCIATION, DEPRESSION, AND ADD

Cathy was a smallish young woman with dark curly hair. She was intelligent, well spoken, and, at the moment, quite miserable. She worked for an Internet start-up in New York, and for the past three months, she'd been dating a consultant who was down from

Boston on a long-term assignment with her company. Five days before she came to see me, he had told her he wanted to damp things down a bit. Two days later, he had reversed himself, but it was too late. The damage had been done.

The damage was that Cathy felt herself slipping into an all-too-familiar state. Twice before, when she'd broken up with a guy, she felt the same way. The last time, she took Prozac for three or four months. Now, she couldn't sleep and she couldn't eat. All she could think about was this guy and what a loser she was and how she was going to be alone. At the same time, she was horrified that she was falling into this state, didn't understand it at all, knew that it shouldn't be such a big deal. One of her biggest concerns was that she couldn't concentrate. She was disorganized and unproductive at work, and that was not like her. She was usually a real go-getter, very focused and motivated. She felt herself spiraling out of control, she was afraid she was going crazy, and she wanted to start taking Prozac again, right away, before things got worse.

I listened to Cathy for a while, and then I asked her if she was a visual person, if she could see things easily in her mind's eye. She nodded, and we decided to do some guided visualization.

With Cathy, I used a basic inner-child technique to explore the intensely frightening feelings of hopelessness and isolation that were overwhelming her. (For the complete transcript, see Appendix I.) The technique is startlingly simple. I simply asked Cathy to focus in on her feelings and then to see a girl who also felt that way. Without fail, patients see themselves at a very particular age, giving them access to a powerful but at least somewhat hidden part of themselves.

What was fascinating about Cathy, and why I bring her up, is that the trance revealed a bright but sad, hyperactive five-year-old who was just beginning a long journey of recognizing and dealing with the fact that she was somehow different from the other children, different in ways that would, if she weren't careful, separate her, alienate her, and leave her rejected and abandoned.

No one who knew Cathy as a successful young woman would

have guessed that she had ADD because she was smart enough, determined enough, and well loved enough to learn how to unleash her hyperactivity productively, making it largely invisible. After she emerged from her trance, we talked about ADD. The long and the short of it was that she had it, but because she was an intelligent girl from a loving family and, because she had quite purposefully learned to motivate and control herself, she had never been diagnosed. Purely attentional difficulties weren't noticeable in her at all as long as she was careful to commit only to work that truly interested her.

Cathy was representative of a very large group of poorly understood and often poorly treated individuals whose ADD is not prominent but who develop depression later in life. Often, as I will point out repeatedly in this book, the stress of compensating for ADD in a demanding world is enough to create several types of depression.

In Cathy, the path was even more circuitous. In her, the painful aspects of a childhood complicated by mild ADD and her resulting fear of inadequacy, isolation, and abandonment had been split off and sequestered, and were now rarely a part of her everyday experience. Despite its rare appearance, this part of her continued to exist unhealed, and when it woke up and emerged forcefully, she became stuck there. What needs to be said here is that because this part of her had been out of her consciousness all these years, sequestered so that her sadness and agitation would not interfere with her meeting the many developmental challenges she faced, this split off part had not been sharing in and experiencing the growth that all the other, nonsequestered Cathys had been going through. For that reason, the five-year-old Cathy was frozen helpless and stuck. She didn't even know about all the other Cathys that existed, let alone what they might be able to do for her in this particularly upsetting mess.

Once Cathy became stuck in her agitated, helpless, five-year-old persona, she was constantly hyperaroused, in a fight-or-flight state, which can quickly lead to an acquired stress depression if not addressed. Thankfully, addressing this was not at all difficult to do, as shown in the most important part of her trance.

  Okay,
  Look into the little girl's eyes.
  Take her on your lap.
  Stroke her hair.
  Tell her she's a good girl.
  She is a good girl, isn't she?
  Cathy nods.
  She tries so hard.
  She means so well.
  Tell her she's a good girl.

  This girl was quiet,
  She felt okay,
  She was sort of sleeping.
  Cathy nods.
  But now, she's woken up.
  Cathy nods.
  And she needs your help,
  Your love,
  Your acceptance.
  She's sweet, isn't she?
  Cathy nods.
  She deserves love and understanding.
  Every child deserves love and understanding,

  Don't they?
  Cathy nods.
  Can you give her your love?
  Cathy nods.
  Think of your love like a radiant energy,
  An aura surrounding you.
  Envelop the girl in your love.
  Turn up the volume.
  Turn up the heat.

Can the little girl feel your love?
Cathy nods.
That feels better, doesn't it?
When she feels better, Cathy,
You feel better, too.
So, look her in the eye.
Tell her you accept her.
Tell her you'll be there for her.
Look her in the eye and say,
Now . . .
Cathy says, "Now . . ."
We're in this together.
Cathy says, "Now we're in this together."
Tell her you'll be back.
Give her a hug.
Cathy says, "Now we're in this together."

The salient act here, discussed in much more depth in Chapter 7, was Cathy's accepting and loving her hurt parts and allowing them access to the grownup coping abilities contained in her other, more mature selves. Shortly after her first session, Cathy found her sleep patterns and appetite returning to normal. Over the next week or so, she had some "bad trances" during which she felt like a trapped, naughty little girl, but it took only three sessions and a phone call or two for Cathy to assimilate the rationale and use of the inner-child trance to rapidly soothe her agitated state and escape from her state of fear. By then, she had also broken off her relationship with the consultant, and she was once again feeling fine and functioning normally.

Cathy's case demonstrates the complex way in which ADD, depression, and dissociation can interact to create problems. She came to me worried about depression, a depression that was creating an acute attentional impairment, making her overattend to her boyfriend and underattend to her work. She had a history consistent with ADD, but ADD was not the immediate cause of these problems. Cathy was upsetting herself so thoroughly that she was on the verge of a depression that would have required medication to reverse, but the depression was not the direct cause of her attentional problems, as it had been with Boris. More like Alberto, Cathy wasn't functioning because of a dissociation, a lack of connection between her cut-off, immature, suffering, right-brained self and her more logical, older, outer, left-brained self. Her case is an excellent illustration of how ADD and dissociation can combine to create conditions that can lead to depression.

I am well aware that with Cathy, as with Alberto, I am referring casually to a model of the self and its constituent parts that is not, on its face, obvious or self-explanatory. For a fuller description of this model, please see Chapter 5.

———————◆◆◆◆◆———————

The stories of Alberto, Boris, and Cathy put flesh and bones on the different causes of being stuck. When we are confronting serious dysfunction, when we aren't "getting it done," we need to consider the complex weave of ADD, depression, and dissociation if we are to locate the source of our attentional difficulties and address them effectively. The three chapters that follow are intended to more fully differentiate and delineate these levels of causation.

CHAPTER 3

ATTENTION DEFICIT DISORDER

CHAPTER OVERVIEW

ADD-Based Stuckness

You're underreflective. You have trouble thinking things through.

You're overactive, mentally if not physically, and often verbally as well.

You're overreactive to stimuli, both external (distractibility) and internal (impulsivity).

You feel that authority figures do not empathize with you.

You have a history of unreliability and poor planning when it comes to time, money, and obligations.

You've been told that you're an underachiever, that you don't really try, and that you're insensitive or thoughtless, even though you feel that you try hard all the time.

You have lots of ideas but follow through on them poorly.

You have difficulty structuring your time and spending time alone productively.

You have difficulty motivating yourself.

You're often moody, irritable, restless, and impatient.

You're very sensitive to the level and type of stimulation.

You have a family history of ADD.

Bottom line: You know what to do, but not when you need to do it.

ADD, as a cause of stuckness, is most accurately understood to be a relative underactivity of inhibitory centers in the front of the brain, as one end of the normal neurophysiological spectrum concerned with the relative balance between reflection and action. It is also an important but somewhat confusing variable in a wide range of life difficulties, one that remains largely unrecognized and, even if recognized, poorly understood and poorly addressed.

BADLY NAMED AND POORLY DEFINED

ADD is confusing for a number of reasons. It has a very varied presentation, and it often coexists in complicated ways with a wide range of other conditions. More to the point, both its name and its current diagnostic criteria are unintentionally more than somewhat misleading.

Its name is misleading because, despite a huge body of psychological research looking for it, an absolute or measurable deficit in pure attention has never been shown to exist. Context is everything. Under the proper circumstances, attention in children and adults with ADD can be more than adequate. In fact, overfocus can be as much of a problem for people with ADD as can underfocus. Attention Regulation Disorder or Attention

Modulation Disorder might be more accurate names. It's not just paying attention that is at issue, its facility in the shifting of attention, paying attention to the right thing at the right time. The diagnostic criteria are misleading because they overemphasize dysfunction at key developmental junctures. Children who compensate well never get noticed. Individuals with a wide range of balancing gifts are routinely overlooked in both educational and therapeutic contexts.

Some portion of the confusion about ADD is due to the inherent limitations in the delicate process of negotiation and validation that has, over the last thirty-five years, spurred the rapid growth of reliable, modern psychiatric diagnosis. *The Diagnostic and Statistical Manual of Psychiatry*, vol. 3 (DSM-III) and *The Diagnostic and Statistical Manual of Psychiatry*, vol. 4 (DSM-IV) are essentially identical when it comes to ADD, and although it is my understanding that the next edition will be improved, it is the criteria the DSM presents that have both informed and clouded the debates about ADD over the past twenty-five years.

The inherent limitations to which I refer include the fact that the diagnostic criteria are intentionally atheoretical (without theory). This is because, in the absence of definitive proof, the drafters and revisers of the criteria avoid expressing bias concerning the underlying causes of the condition, instead focusing entirely on external, observable behaviors. This complete focus on behavior misses large groups of people who are more mildly affected and better at compensating, and therefore leads to an underestimation of the presence of ADD in the adult population.

TOWARD A BETTER DEFINITION

My goal here is to make our understanding of ADD broad enough so that we can be as inclusive as possible, so that everyone whose life is affected by this chameleonlike condition will be recognized and advised or treated.

Thankfully, we are no longer confined to an atheoretical approach. We now know much better what ADD really is, both on the level of brain physiology and on the level of external human behavior. Two newer measures of brain metabolism, single photon emission computed tomography (SPECT) and neurometric electroencephalography (EEG), have been used to show convincingly that ADD is correlated with electrical and metabolic underactivity in an area of the brain called the prefrontal cortex during tasks that require certain kinds of concentration. Thanks at least in part to an encyclopedic review of the psychological literature by Russell Barkley, Ph.D., in *ADHD and the Nature of Self-Control* (New York: Guilford, 1997), we can also see more clearly how that underactivity translates on the cognitive psychological level into a delay in the development of executive functioning and all that such a delay entails.

Since the first observations of difficult boys over a hundred years ago, the same three behaviors have been consistently described: hyperactivity, impulsivity, and something that was originally called distractibility but evolved into being called inattentiveness, from which the misnomer "attention deficit disorder" came. Over the years of repeated attempts at more accurate psychiatric classification, hyperactivity, and impulsivity have been separated from pure inattentiveness. In the current version of the criteria for diagnosing ADD, hyperactivity and impulsivity are considered one syndrome cluster, inattentiveness is considered a second syndrome cluster, and each of these syndrome clusters has nine separate criteria.

When examined critically, the nine criteria for distractibility/inattentiveness actually involve only three separate ideas. The first has to do with the nature and quality of attention: The attention span is short and spotty, and the attention is both difficult to attract and easy to derail. The second idea has to do with the storage and retrieval of information: There is a lack of something that could be called presence of mind or working memory, resulting in disorganization and poor follow-through. The third idea has to do with the avoidance of mental work. The nine criteria for hyperactivity and impulsivity are again conceptually repetitive, containing only two basic ideas: moving too much and talking too much.

These five ideas — the short spotty difficult to attract or maintain nature of attention, poor information storage and retrieval, distaste for purely mental activity, moving too much and talking too much — have been useful guideposts to the more obvious cases of ADD. However, they exclude the large number of people whose brains function in the same underlying manner but who have compensated better or whose dysfunctions are subtler.

One of the more prominent proponents of SPECT imaging technology, Daniel Amen, M.D., in his broadly useful book *Healing ADD: The Breakthrough Program That Allows You to See and Heal the 6 Types of ADD* (New York: Berkley, 2002), proposes a slightly different group of five core symptoms: short attention span for routine tasks, distractibility, problems with spatial and temporal organization, difficulty with follow-through, and poor internal supervision.

Dr. Amen's list begins to stretch us beyond the shackles of the atheoretical DSM-IV largely because he recognizes that attention is poor only in particular situations, under certain circumstances. We can argue about the most useful ways to address whatever those particular situations might be for any one person, but if we don't recognize that an attention deficit is not an absolute thing, that it is not a measurable lack that exists uniformly across all situations, then we will certainly overlook many affected individuals.

Comprehensible keys to understanding the patterns of attention in individuals with ADD do, in fact, exist, and we can learn to choose situations that enhance our attention and to avoid those that impair it. Bright, accomplished hyperactive individuals have been discovering these keys for themselves and unleashing their hyperactive energies productively for generations. The bias inherent in the idea of a deficit has led countless patients of mine and their previous clinicians to ignore or rule out ADD simply because the patients at times were able to successfully pay attention to complex things that mattered to them.

The DSM criteria are too general and do not accurately describe the nature of attention in ADD. It is not always short, and it is not always spotty. Ask the parents of children with ADD how well their children pay attention to videogames or their favorite TV shows. Ask them how easily their children seem to remember and get stuck on things they want, such as sweets or a particular friend, or do not want, such as staying in a place that's uncomfortable. People with ADD are not consistently unable to focus. They are unable to focus on things that other people want them to focus on. They have trouble moving from their own agenda to someone else's agenda. People with ADD can display an enormous difference in the way they attend to something when the wish or need for that attention comes from the inside out, from the person himself or herself, rather than from the outside in.

This is one of the reasons that people with ADD can have so many problems with parents, spouses, and children. They seem selfish because of the disparity between the tenacious way they can hold on to their own wishes and the apparently cavalier manner in which they often treat the wishes of others.

People with ADD are not uniformly unable to pay attention in all situations. As I have already said, and will repeat, it is far more accurate to think of ADD as a problem of attention regulation rather than of absolute deficit, as a condition in which people cannot pay attention consistently enough across the board to meet society's (and their own) expectations of someone of their level of intelligence. People with ADD have variable focus, and, although that focus may seem unpredictable to a stranger, it is not, in fact, random. It has discernible patterns, and once the patterns are observed and understood, they can be mastered and regulated.

EXECUTIVE FUNCTIONING

If we compare the two short lists of criteria presented in the previous section, we can see that the DSM gives significant weight to physical and verbal hyperactivity, while Dr. Amen puts more emphasis on various aspects of what both he and Barkley call executive functioning: poor follow-through, poor internal regulation, and poor spatial and temporal organization. The DSM criteria do not specifically mention executive function, but speak instead about the avoidance of mental work. The prefrontal cortex has long been known to be involved both in behavioral inhibition and in the broad array of mental activities that are collectively termed executive functions. In *ADHD and the Nature of Self-Control*, Dr. Barkley defines behavioral inhibition as the ability to stop oneself from behaving. He translates that into three overt features attributable to inadequate behavioral inhibition: (1) difficulty in preventing any reflex response, (2) easy derailment from and subsequent difficulty in resuming an activity, and (3) the inability to stop or alter behavior in response to feedback about that behavior. He goes on to sum up the overall behavioral effect of this deficiency in inhibitory systems as a "developmental delay in reflection," defining "reflection" as "persistent analytical thoughtfulness." Reflection, as opposed to action, occurs when the myriad of reflexive behaviors are simultaneously inhibited enough to allow planful thought. Lack of reflection leads to the underdevelopment of executive functioning.

Effective executive functioning can be viewed as the opposite of being stuck. For Dr. Barkley and other academics, executive functioning is useful self-regulation, self-control that allows us to make the most of our opportunities, to select for positive outcomes and to avoid negative ones. A big part of executive functioning is something called cross-temporal planning. Cross-temporal planning is a shorthand technical term for the process of forecasting possible futures and then comparing them with past experiences in order to formulate strategies and make choices in the hope of influencing outcomes — in other words, making plans and following through on them.

It is not hard to see how inadequate reflection can contribute to poor planning and follow-through in a wide range of important human activities. Inadequate reflection is another way of thinking about impulsive behavior. Although impulsively moving and talking a great deal are not necessarily problems in themselves, they almost certainly can become social problems.

Children or adults who move or talk too much, in rhythms that do not match the rhythms of their peers, are not adequately reflecting upon the effect of their behavior on those around them, quite often to their lasting detriment.

Inadequate behavioral inhibition and consequent underreflectiveness may be the central differences that define ADD, but reflectiveness exists on a broad continuum. To quote Dr. Barkley, "ADD represents a lower end of a continuum of a normal trait or set of traits that comprises behavioral inhibition and the self-regulation associated with it."

This is a critical point. ADD is not an illness. Illnesses in the medical sense are episodic, or deteriorating, or a distinct alteration from a previously established level of physiological functioning. ADD is none of those things. Depression and the other neurotransmitter abnormalities are illnesses, but ADD is not. Rather, ADD is at one end of a spectrum of normal inherited neurophysiological tendencies.

One of the things I like about Dr. Barkley's approach to the issue is that he makes a clear distinction between the primary deficit (atypical reflective tendencies) and what can be called the accumulated skill deficits resulting from inadequate focus over time, the secondary attentional impairment (poor organization, poor time management, unreliable information and task processing, mental-task avoidance, poor mood, and motivation management) that develops when underreflectiveness, poorly understood and unempathically dealt with by authority figures, interferes with the maturation and development of executive functioning.

DISORGANIZATION: A SURMOUNTABLE DELAY

Reflective inhibitory abilities undergo a natural maturation in everyone, people with ADD included, until about age thirty. Many people who suffer with overactivity and disinhibition in childhood gain adequate self-control in early adulthood through normal maturation. Some lose it again in the face of later, more complex organizational challenges. These opposing trends, and the inconsistent performance they generate, are part of what makes ADD so controversial and confusing.

In several ways, ADD is much more like dyslexia than depression. Many children with dyslexia overcome their deficit entirely — that is, despite whatever specific neurological variations exist (and continue to exist) in their brains, they are somehow able to train their brains enough so they can become adequately proficient at the complex end task involved, which in this case is reading. With executive functioning and disorganization, proficiency is also an attainable endpoint. ADD is like dyslexia also in that it is only revealed when specific sorts of demands are made upon the individual. A person with dyslexia has no difficulty whatsoever in a nonliterate society. Apart from a relatively circumscribed deficit, a dyslexic is entirely healthy. Similarly, in societies where private reflection is relatively unnecessary, where life is simple and highly structured (tribal or agrarian, perhaps), ADD is not necessarily a problem.

What makes self-regulation different from reading and ADD different from dyslexia is that increasing success at self-regulation often leads to further demands for more of the same. Years ago, this concept, when applied to corporate culture, was called the Peter Principle: We rise to our level of incompetence. This is a concept quite familiar to high-functioning hyperactives.

UNDERREFLECTIVE EQUALS HYPERACTIVE

Beginning with DSM-III, it was noted that some children had poor executive functioning and inattentiveness/distractibility without appearing to be hyperactive, and a subtype, ADD without hyperactivity, was born. Over time, a general consensus was reached that the fundamental nature of the disorder was attentional, with hyperactivity a less-central concern.

I question this imbalance in emphasis as inaccurate and counterproductive. It is not generally possible to think about an underactivity or immaturity in inhibitory systems without asking exactly how, in any particular individual, this lack of inhibition affects the various other subsystems and areas of activity in the brain. A decrease in inhibitory activity means an increase in excitatory activity somewhere else. In other words, no muscle contracts without another one relaxing. Every action has an equal and opposite reaction. There is no underreflectiveness without hyperactivity. No yin without the yang.

The important question to ask, for a specific affected person, is which systems are hyperactive. Clearly, only some systems are obvious to external observers. In addition to the classic gross motor restlessness that is so often seen, I have found purely verbal, interpersonal/emotional, sexual/tactile, and imaginative hyperactivity to be frequently present. I have even seen a few cases in which gustatory or musical hyperactivity existed. In my view, it is the variety of the brain areas and functions that can be more or less affected by, or more or less in balance with, the underactive prefrontal/reflective areas that accounts for a lot of the diagnostic confusion, for the range of presentations in individuals, all of whom may suffer from some neurophysiologically-mediated developmental delay in executive functioning.

People who have been labeled as having ADD without hyperactivity are often, in my experience, simply hyperactive in different ways. A not-very-physical daydreamer's mind may bounce around very quickly, but this may not be obvious to anyone else. Many girls are hyperactive primarily in a verbal way, and some restlessness may be due to tactile or auditory hypersensitivity or hyperactivity. People who have social/interpersonal/emotional hyperactivity may suffer from paralyzing shyness and self-consciousness, especially if they are also hyperactive in obsessive or socially phobic brain areas. On the other hand, if they are also verbally hyperactive, they may be among the most socially and emotionally successful people you can imagine. Almost any human ability can be thought of as hyperactive, and I hope it will become apparent as we go along that, in my view, learning to understand and utilize whatever hyperactivities exist is a wise, powerful move indeed.

MOTIVATION AND ATTENTION

We are now defining the core difference in the brain of a person with ADD as a relative underdevelopment of prefrontal cortex inhibitory areas, influencing both rhythms of action and reflection and the development of adequate executive functioning. Let's emphasize the first word of this statement, "relative." As I keep saying, people with ADD are not incapable of reflection. They are less facile at it and naturally less likely to do it, but they can do it — and do it a lot — if the situation is right and if the motivation is right. Yes, if the motivation is right. Which leads us to perhaps the most important thing I can say about ADD that remains to be said: ADD is about an atypical relationship between motivation and attention.

I have already said that despite appearances to the contrary, there is, in fact, a discernible pattern to attention in people with ADD. That pattern involves motivation. Simply put, what we consistently observe is that individuals whose reflective inhibitory abilities are at the lower end of the spectrum require more motivation to achieve adequate attention in any given setting than do "average" individuals.

I don't think anyone will deny that motivation in general, as a psychological, self-improvement sort of topic, has been explored (and marketed, mind you) exhaustively, from many angles, and yet it remains elusive, slippery. Clearly influenced both from without and from within, by the self and by others, motivation has something to do with intensity of desire, with cultivation of interest, with rewards and punishments. We may not be able to easily measure motivation or define it exactly, but we know it when we see it, and we certainly know it when we feel it.

I would offer the idea that motivation is, in fact, a neuroelectrical phenomenon, a reflection of our ability to turn on or off various aspects of our functioning and the various neural substrates that underlie those aspects. The therapeutic implications of this understanding are discussed at length in Chapter 9, but for now, let's say that if motivation is electrical activity, we can understand why it compensates for a sluggish prefrontal cortex.

The prefrontal cortex is itself a map of the whole brain, and when any part of the brain is stimulated, the prefrontal cortex is likewise stimulated. Obviously, then, the more pieces of our brain that are being used at once in a coordinated fashion, the more stimulation for the prefrontal cortex and — aha! — we have threshold, we have liftoff, we have behavioral inhibition, we have focus.

The people who compensated well in childhood and young adulthood are those who, consciously or unconsciously, discovered how to cultivate and use their own motivation, discovered how to be connoisseurs of interest and desire, discovered how to turn on their brains adequately.

It is my contention that the current criteria substantially undercount affected individuals because they miss those who cope most sucessfully. The DSM-IV criteria state that there must be "clear evidence of clinically significant impairment" in "two different settings." Many affected individuals, particularly brighter ones, will not meet that test at typical junctures. Too many professionals believe the misconception that people who have ADD are impaired across the board and unlikely to succeed to any degree at anything very much at all. This is patently untrue. When hyperactive people do manage to focus their considerable energy (and many do), they are often among the most productive, interesting, and creative people around.

In practice, adults with ADD, the overwhelming majority of whom were never diagnosed in childhood, exhibit unevenness; unlikely, incongruous blocks to progress; frustration; and "stuckness" in the face of the developmental crises of early and middle adulthood. (They also often exhibit depression, but we'll discuss that later.) They are people who got by for a long time. When they were younger, they perhaps underachieved, or achieved unevenly, but they compensated well enough, or cultivated their motivation well enough, so that they were not recognized at the usual junctures for the usual reasons.

Often, adults who had mild or moderate tendencies toward underreflectiveness in earlier life find themselves at an impasse. They may previously have functioned adequately, absorbing motivational knowledge unconsciously, but now they need to relearn that motivational knowledge consciously to meet the ever-more-complex challenges of a successful, modern adult life. Many people on the lower end of the normal spectrum of inhibitory abilities, especially those who compensated well, are unlikely to recognize or accept their underlying natures until their compensations fail in the face of increasing organizational and self-regulatory demands.

When the importance of motivation in understanding attentional patterns is appreciated, two ideas (avoidance of mental work and poor information handling/poor presence of mind) presented under the category of inattentiveness in the DSM criteria can be seen for the variably present secondary symptoms they are. Specifically, the tendencies to be forgetful, to lose things, to fail to follow through, and to avoid mental tasks are all things that may or may not be present in adults with ADD. Their presence depends solely on whether or not adults have assimilated enough knowledge about themselves and about how to master and influence their motivation. Many techniques are available for enhancing motivation, desire, and memory, and although people with ADD may find it somewhat harder to master the art of creating and maintaining habits of mind on their own, mastering these skills is actually relatively easy with proper guidance. We will describe some of these techniques in detail in Chapters 6 through 10.

What we see here, and what we shall see repeatedly, is the paradoxical double-bind flavor that goes with ADD. Motivation is the keystone to compensating for lack of reflection, yet reflection plays a role in the cultivation of motivation. In the absence of powerful external structures (which best take the form of mentoring, approving relationships), it is difficult, if not impossible, to enhance motivation without first reflecting enough to clarify one's goals and strategies. It is a circular relationship, one that can cycle positively or negatively.

So, not to beat the horse to death, for me, a pitfall in the current debates surrounding ADD is the failure to acknowledge the potentially compensating role of motivation, leading to the undercounting of neurophysiologically, attentionally challenged people. Appreciating the interaction between underreflectiveness and motivation that is present in people with ADD is essential in formulating an effective treatment approach.

DEFINITIONS AND BEYOND

We started with a purely behavioral definition of ADD: the classic triad of distractibility, impulsivity, and hyperactivity. We then looked underneath, at the underactivity of inhibitory centers in the brain, at the preference for action over reflection, at the development of executive functioning, and at the compensatory powers of motivation and training of the brain.

Still, over and over, we have to remark how variable the picture of ADD can be. There is a wide range of levels of functioning, deficits and strengths all over the map, all sorts of different hyperactivities, and many complicated interactions with other psychiatric conditions. How can we make it clear just how common ADD is? How can we knit together the essential underlying features?

What I have discovered over the years is that if we are to "get" ADD, if we are to truly and fully appreciate it in all its glory, then, in addition to improving our definitions, we must also look at the typical ways in which its traits play themselves out in developing individuals. To that end, I would like to offer the list of issues that I have repeatedly observed in my years of treating people with ADD. I would say that . . . .

- ADD is about the structure of time.
- ADD is about the disparity between conceptual abilities and performance abilities.
- ADD is about difficulty getting comfortable.
- ADD is about controlling levels of stimulation.
- ADD is about trouble compensating for other deficits.
- ADD is about insecurity and self-doubt.
- ADD is about the struggle for intimacy.
- ADD is a conflict amplifier.
- ADD is about difficulty with authority.
- ADD is about solving the puzzle of life.

ADD Is about the Structure of Time

In *ADHD and the Nature of Self-Control* Dr. Barkley says that "time is the ultimate yet nearly invisible disability afflicting those with ADD." We might add that since our time is the only truly valuable thing we possess, and since we have already agreed that executive functioning (self-regulation in the service of maximized outcome) is affected in ADD, it certainly makes sense that ADD would influence how effectively we "spend" our valuable time.

What this means in practice is that people with raw, uncompensated ADD appear to be wasteful, heedless, inconsiderate, malicious, and even mean-spirited to others, as they seem to ignore both implicit social/temporal conventions and practical temporal/logistical considerations. People who haven't developed a reliable time sense — a reliable sense of the way their time is structured — are doomed to be inefficient in their own behalf, and offensive to those around them. All too often they will also be viewed as childish and immature.

Detailed descriptions of behavioral observations associated with ADD have traditionally noted difficulty with rule-bound behavior. "Kids with ADD don't listen" is a standard comment. It's not too much of a stretch to see that most rules are about time in one way or another: when to do something, when not to do something, how long to do or not do something, to keep quiet while standing in a line, to watch the ball during a game, say "excuse me" when you cough, and on and on and on.

All children begin their lives right-brained, purely experiential, with no notion of rules or time. We use the overarching term "socialization" to describe the process by which children learn temporal expectations and realities, a process which is generally accepted to involve the formation of a left-brained, verbal, planning self. Children with ADD, due to their decreased reflection, lag behind in acquiring rule-bound behavior and in becoming socialized, but they improve with age along with everyone else. Sometimes they catch up sufficiently to function adequately, at least temporarily. Sometimes they don't. Whether or not they appear to catch up, the development of the interior relationship between their left-brain planners and their right-brain doer/feelers, a relationship that is fundamental to effective socialization, is profoundly affected.

Once again, however, I would like to make an important distinction by saying that the relative difficulty in acquiring a reliable sense of the structure of time says nothing about whether or not such a sense can ultimately, in fact, be acquired or about how well such a sense might be utilized once it is acquired. By this, I mean to say that inadequate mastery of time is not, in itself, the primary deficit in ADD. Rather, it is a secondary result of excessive action and inadequate reflection, mediated, at least partly, by the ineffective left brain-right brain relationship, a secondary result that may or may not be present in an adult or adolescent with ADD. What one actually sees in the field is three different situations: (1) people who haven't mastered time and are plagued by chaos and various levels of misery, (2) people who have mastered time and are extremely aware and careful about it, sometimes excessively so, and (3) people whose mastery has been sufficient for one group of situations, but isn't sufficiently conscious or flexible to accommodate new or different ones.

No matter how comfortable with time people with ADD become, time and its mastery is always a central concern to them, a concern that sends ramifications rippling through every sphere of their lives.

ADD Is about the Disparity between Conceptual Abilities and Performance Abilities

Few things contribute to the sense of impotence and frustration in people with ADD more than the gap that can exist between their understanding of things and their ability to consistently act upon that understanding. They know what they have to do, but the knowledge is not always present when they need it. They study for a test and they understand what they're studying, but the next day the knowledge is gone. They tell themselves to be quiet, but before they know it, they're shooting off their mouths again.

They promise to do something and they mean it, but they just don't carry through. They feel that they are smart, but their grades don't show it. They mean to be good-hearted, but people seem to get mad at them anyway. Teachers or parents or bosses or friends lecture them, and they know the spiel so well that they become bored and tune out, yet later, they still perform as if they never heard the lecture. And they won't, not until they learn how to set up systems to remind themselves, not until they learn to master their time and themselves.

These kinds of things make people with ADD crazy and create oceans of self-doubt. As we shall see over and over, it's another paradox: People with ADD need to trust themselves, to look inside, in order to find the very individualized ways that they can learn to use their understandings, to make the knowledge be present when it's needed, and yet they do not trust themselves. How could they, as they flounder and sputter in those cold, doubt-filled waters they know so well?

ADD Is about Difficulty Getting Comfortable

Compare how it feels to drive a car unhindered on a highway to how it feels to drive the same car in stop-and-go traffic. When we drive without interference, we settle into a focused, relaxed state in which it is quite possible to think and daydream comfortably while still driving. In stop-and-go traffic, we are tense, jangled, herky-jerky, and uncomfortable, and soon we become very unhappy.

A universal truth is that absorbed focus is a relatively comfortable state, one that's not only comfortable but also relaxing, refreshing, and restorative. Focus is comfortable, and discomfort interferes with focus. It's circular. Comfort lets you focus, and focus makes you comfortable, which lets you focus-and round and round and round. Equally truthful is the reverse, because people with ADD are often hyperactive in a sensory way and can be made uncomfortable relatively easily. Such discomfort immediately disrupts the fragile motivation-attention equilibrium, and the rhyme can easily be sent around in the opposite direction: less comfort, less focus, less comfort, and so on.

We've already said several times that ADD involves increased motor and verbal activity. People with ADD are restless. They don't sit still. They are more easily made physically uncomfortable, more easily distracted by that discomfort, and more likely to react impulsively to the discomfort.

This difficulty with comfort exists both privately and publicly. When people with ADD are alone, they often are bored. They have trouble settling down, trouble being productive. When they are with others, they may be happier, but they are still often out of sync. Their higher levels of activity and intensity can disrupt the concentration and peace of mind of those around them. They make those around them uncomfortable, too. They talk too fast for other people; other people talk too slow for them. People with ADD want to go out most nights; other people would rather be home. People with ADD want more variety; other people may prefer routine. It's subtle but it's constant. People with ADD usually want more or they want to do it faster. This grates on other people. The disharmony grates.

Throughout their lives, people deficient in behavioral inhibition will find themselves in one of two situations: They will be in a situation, such as school or work, where they are pressured, in a more or less friendly manner but pressured nevertheless, to decrease their rate of behaving, to sit down and shut up, and this will be uncomfortable for them; or they will be in a situation where they will feel free to move, speak, and behave at their own rhythms, but if they are not alone, they may wind up grating on the people around them. They will receive more or less overt negative feedback, and this, too, will become uncomfortable and distracting.

I have been saying over and over that ADD does not, in fact, mean that attention cannot be paid or that it cannot be paid effectively. What it does mean is that in order to function effectively, people with ADD must pay attention to the dynamics of attention. The only way for people to combat ADD is to become connoisseurs of their own focus, and this inevitably entails appreciating the cyclical interaction of focus and comfort.

ADD Is about Controlling the Level of Stimulation

We were talking about focus and comfort. One of the things that makes a person with ADD comfortable and therefore able to focus is the right level and the right mix of stimulation — that is, the right mix of stimulation to turn on the inhibitory systems of the prefrontal cortex. I use the term "stimulation" in the broadest possible sense, including physical, intellectual, emotional, spiritual, and sexual. By "level," I refer to both rhythm and intensity.

For years, I have been using Figure 1 to illustrate the relationship between comfort and stimulation. In Figure 3.1, "B" stands for "boredom" and "O" stands for "overstimulation." The curve for average people has a broad plateau of comfort that is relatively independent of stimulation levels. The other curve is that for people with ADD. Notice the narrow plateau of comfort and the sharp cliffs of boredom and overstimulation.

Figure 1: Stimulation and Comfort Graph

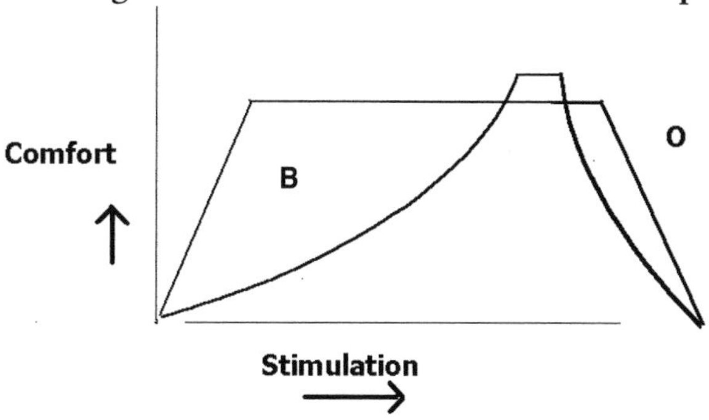

The management of comfort and stimulation, the balancing of the need to be safe and the need to be excited, to grow, is an essential task for anyone who would like to live a full life. It is even more important in the person with ADD, because control of comfort and stimulation is the doorway to motivation.

Earlier in this chapter, we discussed how people with ADD needed increased motivation to activate and then sustain an adequate state of attention. Motivation — technically, the desire to move — comes in only two or three varieties. I remember reading once that every possible human action can be seen either a moving toward, a moving away, or an explaining. When we consider the relationship between comfort and focus, we are also talking about a moving away, about the motivation to avoid discomfort. What should become clear is that if people with ADD are going to liberate their energies, if they are going to master time and focus and attention, they must first legitimize and perfect the pursuit of their own comfort. In other words, comfort is essential to get past the motivation to move away, to find the more productive motivation to move towards or to explain.

Once again, we can get a sense of the paradox that people with ADD face when they try to meet the demands that society places on them for effective, timely focus. On the one hand, they need to have input into and control over the nature and timing of the stimulation to which they are exposed if they are to be comfortable enough to focus, if they are to find out enough about their own focus and motivation to avoid chastisement, blame, or further negative overstimulation. Yet they are constantly being told to do things in ways that are not appropriate for them, by people who do not understand them. At the same time that they are learning about their own comfort and how it can enhance or interfere with their focus and attention, they are having their natural rhythms invalidated. They are constantly running up against rules they've missed, expectations they didn't notice, things they are doing on a rhythm and in a way that is different from 90 percent of the people around them.

It takes considerable wisdom or guidance or both for a person to become a dedicated explorer of the self when the self is constantly being found unacceptable. But without that exploration, comfort, focus, and effective living will be elusive indeed.

ADD Is about Compensating for Other Deficits and Difficulties

Everyone is born with a range of abilities. Everyone is gifted in some things and delayed in others, be it math or reading or music or coordination or public speaking or whatever. In a person of average attentional abilities, the natural tendency is to try to work harder on the relative deficit, to persevere.

es and intentions if they are to liberate their focus, and yet focus is required for that very process. It is vital that the wishes of others be weighed against what is useful for the self, and yet people with ADD are constantly being coerced into the more standard rhythms, are constantly being called selfish and lazy, are constantly told that, once again, they are simply not paying careful enough attention to the wishes of those around them. The struggle is about valuing the self enough to master it in the face of a demanding and often devaluing world.

ADD Is about Difficulty with Authority

We all make accommodations to the power relationships around us — to the police, our parents, our siblings, our bosses, our co-workers, our elders, the government, the motor vehicle department, the Internal Revenue Service. There are times to speak up and defend our rights, and there are times to go along quietly, to watch. Nor are the rules ever just what they seem at first. There are always several levels of rules, unspoken rules, or rules discussed only obliquely.

People with ADD, as we've noted already, aren't as easily rule-bound as other people, which can be good (more creativity) or not so good (defiance or heedlessness), but which, in any case, makes relating to authority a particular challenge. How much control do we need over the circumstances of our work in order to be comfortable? What happens if we don't have it? Can we accommodate to the prevailing rhythms and expectations around us? How do we feel about doing so? How do we go about resolving conflicts with authority when we have them? These are knotty issues for everyone, knottier for people with ADD. Knottier because they've almost certainly had many, many negative interactions with authority, because they've been criticized, yelled at, coerced, misunderstood.

Nevertheless, people with ADD must overcome these obstacles because the price of failure to reach an accommodation with authority and structure is high: anger, alienation, aimlessness, lack of meaningful work, lack of human contact. Conversely, if they can learn to distinguish and to embrace the good, healthy sorts of par-

Not so for people with ADD. The tendency of people with ADD is to impulsively avoid painful experiences, which makes it much less likely for them to maintain focus on an area in which they have no natural gift. Therefore, these deficits are likely to be amplified instead of corrected.

In people with ADD, other kinds of problems that are likely to require focus to master are also readily amplified. Situational problems such as divorce, troubled family members, or moving can have extra negative effects, as can physical, mental, and emotional problems, such as Obsessive-Compulsive Disorder (OCD) or Tourette's syndrome.

Whatever is wrong or difficult or different in children with ADD tends to be harder for them to focus on and to resolve.

ADD Is about Insecurity and Self-Doubt

No matter how confident, breezy, or extroverted people with ADD may seem, they have a deep core of self-doubt that exists inside and that can rear its head in a whole range of situations. Even well-functioning people with ADD often feel tremendously indecisive about taking new directions or making life changes. They have had so much difficulty in following through on decisions made in the past that they often become unable to trust themselves enough to move ahead at all. They also often have great difficulty saying no appropriately. They are so starved for approval, so raw interpersonally, that even when they know on some level that they are unlikely to be able to follow through on the request being made, they may say yes anyway, setting the stage for the next round of failure and insecurity.

ADD Is about the Struggle for Intimacy

Few things in life are more stimulating than the company of people we find appealing. Few things in life are more motivating or more focusing than the approval of those we admire, enjoy, respect, desire, and love. Most often, for people with ADD, and for everyone else as well, personal growth arrives in the form of relationships.

Not so for people with ADD. The tendency of people with ADD is to impulsively avoid painful experiences, which makes it much less likely for them to maintain focus on an area in which they have no natural gift. Therefore, these deficits are likely to be amplified instead of corrected.

In people with ADD, other kinds of problems that are likely to require focus to master are also readily amplified. Situational problems such as divorce, troubled family members, or moving can have extra negative effects, as can physical, mental, and emotional problems, such as Obsessive-Compulsive Disorder (OCD) or Tourette's syndrome.

Whatever is wrong or difficult or different in children with ADD tends to be harder for them to focus on and to resolve.

ADD Is about Insecurity and Self-Doubt

No matter how confident, breezy, or extroverted people with ADD may seem, they have a deep core of self-doubt that exists inside and that can rear its head in a whole range of situations. Even well-functioning people with ADD often feel tremendously indecisive about taking new directions or making life changes. They have had so much difficulty in following through on decisions made in the past that they often become unable to trust themselves enough to move ahead at all. They also often have great difficulty saying no appropriately. They are so starved for approval, so raw interpersonally, that even when they know on some level that they are unlikely to be able to follow through on the request being made, they may say yes anyway, setting the stage for the next round of failure and insecurity.

ADD Is about the Struggle for Intimacy

Few things in life are more stimulating than the company of people we find appealing. Few things in life are more motivating or more focusing than the approval of those we admire, enjoy, respect, desire, and love. Most often, for people with ADD, and for everyone else as well, personal growth arrives in the form of relationships.

People with ADD need other people more intensely than people without ADD do for several reasons. Because they have trouble reflecting, they often need to talk things out in order to think. ("How do I know what I think until I see what I say?") Because they have trouble structuring their time productively or enjoyably by themselves, they are prone to relying on others for help.

Unfortunately, they have a tendency to use people up. At first, a person without ADD may enjoy the high energy and creativity of a person with ADD, but often, at some point they become tired. On the one hand, people with ADD can be so focused on what they are saying and doing that they will often miss the subtle cues that they are wearing out their welcome. On the other hand, their impulsiveness will often lead them to make their wishes known in a repetitive way that seems demanding.

Some people with ADD are socially gifted, clever, funny, or empathic enough that they can draw enough people to them so that they don't become a drag on any one of them. Conversely, I have met more than a few people with ADD who have failed so consistently to make meaningful connections that they have long since given up, entirely sure that they will never be loved. Probably one of the more interesting and consistent phenomena I have observed in the hundreds of people with ADD I have known is an almost reverential attitude toward genuine friendship. People with ADD are among the most loyal and dedicated friends imaginable. Perhaps because they so often feel misunderstood and rejected, when they do feel accepted by someone they respect, it means an enormous amount indeed.

Even if a person with ADD solves the riddle of friendship — and many do — love and sex are other challenges entirely. Friendship takes place in public. It can be observed and studied. Romance, on the other hand, takes place in private and is, therefore, much harder to learn. Some people with ADD are shy, paralyzed by desire and uncertainty when it comes to the opposite sex. Even if they are able to learn how to make the initial romantic or sexual connections, they are often fickle, just as easily bored in romance as in other things, as easily distracted by the next attractive person.

Not only do people with ADD have difficulty setting up stable intimate relationships, but they also run into a whole set of other problems that go along with maintaining them. Even the most lovingly begun relationship will flounder if poor management of time and task are not identified and dealt with. Marriages in which one or both partners have ADD — -and this includes marriages that have a solid base of love — can be plagued by issues surrounding reliability, finances, child-rearing (especially when the children also have ADD), sexuality, and so on.

ADD Is a Conflict Amplifier

When people with ADD are distracted by divergent wishes, when they are not at one with themselves about their priorities and goals, their relatively limited powers of behavioral inhibition are tested and are more likely to fail.

I am sitting at my computer writing this book. I've taken my medicine, which helps me to stay on task. But the only reason I can actually stay on task and write this book is because my desk is clear, I've returned all my phone calls, I've called all the pharmacies for my patients, I've filed all my treatment reports, and I've sent out all my bills. All three of my children are occupied, my wife is satisfied with my errand production for the weekend, I'm not angry with anyone, and no one is especially angry with me. My business is thriving, I have enough money, and no one I care about needs me. I don't have to answer the phone for the next two hours if I don't want to. Nothing is troubling me. I'm in control of my environment, and I can focus.

Distraction and attentiveness are not numerical constants. They occur in a context. We have, and we need to have, many different sorts of alarm systems to remind us to take care of things that need to be taken care of. If a lot of stuff is messed up, if things are unclear and confusing, if conflict is raging inside us or around us, these alarms go off and distract us.

Conflict and lack of clarity create discomfort, which interferes with reflection and therefore creates more conflict and sets off more danger signals. Once again, a paradox: It is vital that people be aware of, reflect upon, and resolve conflicts about their wishes and intentions if they are to liberate their focus, and yet focus is required for that very process. It is vital that the wishes of others be weighed against what is useful for the self, and yet people with ADD are constantly being coerced into the more standard rhythms, are constantly being called selfish and lazy, are constantly told that, once again, they are simply not paying careful enough attention to the wishes of those around them. The struggle is about valuing the self enough to master it in the face of a demanding and often devaluing world.

ADD Is about Difficulty with Authority

We all make accommodations to the power relationships around us — to the police, our parents, our siblings, our bosses, our co-workers, our elders, the government, the motor vehicle department, the Internal Revenue Service. There are times to speak up and defend our rights, and there are times to go along quietly, to watch. Nor are the rules ever just what they seem at first. There are always several levels of rules, unspoken rules, or rules discussed only obliquely.

People with ADD, as we've noted already, aren't as easily rule-bound as other people, which can be good (more creativity) or not so good (defiance or heedlessness), but which, in any case, makes relating to authority a particular challenge. How much control do we need over the circumstances of our work in order to be comfortable? What happens if we don't have it? Can we accommodate to the prevailing rhythms and expectations around us? How do we feel about doing so? How do we go about resolving conflicts with authority when we have them? These are knotty issues for everyone, knottier for people with ADD. Knottier because they've almost certainly had many, many negative interactions with authority, because they've been criticized, yelled at, coerced, misunderstood.

Nevertheless, people with ADD must overcome these obstacles because the price of failure to reach an accommodation with authority and structure is high: anger, alienation, aimlessness, lack of meaningful work, lack of human contact. Conversely, if they can learn to distinguish and to embrace the good, healthy sorts of parenting and mentoring that exist out in the world, they can find people to guide them, to show them the path to inner peace and successful self-control.

Some people with ADD work alone. Some must be the boss. Some have had, at least intermittently, horrendous relations with supervisors, and some have forged mentorships of the highest caliber. No matter to what degree people with ADD have resolved these issues, they will find them resurfacing again and again, forming a central set of concerns throughout their adult lives.

ADD Is about Solving the Puzzle of Life

The puzzle of life? Can we say instead navigating the economic-occupational-and-interpersonal maze? What can we find to do that will support us adequately, not bother us excessively, and offer us at least some opportunity for growth and meaning? In other words, how do we structure our time so that we are balanced and healthy, self-reliant and yet connected, so that we have a chance to be fully human?

We must find meaningful work that we can bear — we all must — but to do that in our modern world requires foresight and planning. It requires structure. It requires understanding and obeying the rules. It requires sustained reflection, cultivated motivation, and adequate self-control.

This universal puzzle turns out to be several degrees of difficulty more complex for young adults with ADD, whether they are aware of their ADD or not. People with ADD are sensitive creatures. They need things just right — the right stimulation, the right rhythms, just enough comfort. The puzzle is complicated for everyone, but for people with ADD, it is more complicated, has more constraints, tighter parameters, and less wiggle room. It can still be solved, but it often has to be re-solved and then re-solved again.

—◆◆◆◆—

When all is said and done, the experience of growing up with ADD — especially when in the dark about it, as most people with

ADD are or were — is about feeling different, feeling confused, feeling inferior, feeling behind. It is about out-of-sync and often sad children, about rebellious and angry teenagers, about floundering and confused young adults, about puzzled and stuck middle-agers. It can be about people finding their own way, often without much help, about struggling for awareness, about defining the self and mastering it. Finally, it can also be about incredibly energetic, productive, empowered people who have stared their limitations in the face and emerged confident and triumphant.

I am hopeful that this discussion of ADD and its ramifications will be helpful to stuck individuals who want to know if this condition is a factor in their situation. In my office practice, I use the Brown ADD scales, three forty-item checklists for children, adolescents, and adults. These questionnaires are much broader than the DSM criteria. They have been well-validated, and patients find them informative.

We will defer for now talking in detail about how people at the lower end of the range of inhibitory abilities can select for more positive, less dysfunctional outcomes. There is, indeed, much to say on this topic — about proper conditions in the formative years, about medications, about trance — and we are moving there as directly as possible.

First, let's recall that the premise of this book is that being stuck (defined as having trouble with procrastination, impulsiveness, disorganization, motivation, and time management) is quite a common syndrome, and that it is, in fact, a complex weave of three separate factors: ADD, depression, and dissociation.

One down, two to go.

CHAPTER 4

DEPRESSION

Depression-Based Stuckness

You experience clear changes in your patterns and rhythms of sleep, appetite, energy, anxiety, irritability, and concentration.

You have a family history of depression, substance abuse, or suicide.

You're unable to experience pleasure.

You engage in obsessive, pointless, or unproductive thinking.

You display pervasive, unjustified negativity.

Your emotional reactions are out of proportion to the situations.

You experience loss of motivation and apathy.

You have an acute sense of not being yourself.

Bottom line: You know what to do, but you're too ill to do it.

A wise clinician, when presented with an adult who is functioning poorly or inconsistently, does well to wonder whether the patient might have ADD. This makes sense, because in our ever-more-complex world, poor use of certain types of attention and poor functioning become more and more synonymous, more and more intertwined.

If, however, we look at stuck folks in general, we see that depression, which is also called affective disorder, accounts for many more problems with focus and concentration than does ADD. Depression, in all its myriad disguises, is a thread that runs through any informed treatment for the chronically stuck.

Consider the following four examples:

- *Eighteen-year-old high school student.* Insomnia and no appetite for one month, panic attacks, and general anxiety for two weeks, now totally dysfunctional, all following the discovery that she needs to repeat her senior year of high school. Complains that she can't pay attention to anything she has to do.

    Diagnosis: Norepinephrine/stress depression (type I)
    Treatment: Nortriptyline
    Result: No symptoms within four weeks

- *Thirty-year-old doctor.* Five years of increasing fatigue, indecisiveness, weight gain, and no pleasure. Worse in the winter. Multiple family members positive for depression. Drags himself around doing the bare minimum. Very disturbed about procrastination in arranging the ophthalmology residency he has always wanted.

    Diagnosis: Serotonin/hereditary/seasonal depression (type II)
    Treatment: Prozac
    Result: Strong response at four weeks

- *Fifty-eight-year-old not-successful-enough-for-his-wife businessman.* Sleeps okay, eats okay, but more withdrawn lately, less interested in things, even running, which he did religiously for thirty years. Both he and his wife complaining that he avoids doing things at work and at home that he knows he should be doing.

Diagnosis: Dopamine/pleasure depression (type III)
Treatment: Wellbutrin
Result: Improvement in six weeks; enjoys running again

• *Thirty-five-year-old commercial director.* Diagnosed with ADD in childhood. Great marriage, great career, but frequently moody in odd, unpredictable patterns. From time to time, cannot work because of incapacitating depression that can last for days and then suddenly clears. When feeling well, always high energy. Unclear, difficult-to-isolate hypomanic episodes. Feels tortured by unpredictable moodiness.

Diagnosis: GABA/bipolar depression without clear mania (type IV)
Treatment: Lamictal
Result: Complete absence of depressive periods in one week

All four of these people experienced difficulty with focus and attention, with organization and follow-through, with time management and reliability, with mood and motivation. None of them were getting it done as they or others thought they should. Two of them (the doctor and the director) had ADD, and all of them suffered from various forms of depression.

Over the past fifteen years of treating depressed patients, I have come to the conclusion that there are four types of depression, each correlating with a distinct biochemical system. These systems/syndromes of depression correspond roughly to four different neurotransmitter systems: Type I-norepinephrine, Type II-serotonin, Type III-dopamine, and Type IV-gamma alpha butyric acid (GABA).

The chart on page 61 provides the identifying factors of each type, as well as the medications to which they respond best. Type IV is less clearly linked to its neurotransmitter than are the other three types, related to what we will call the bipolar-spectrum disorders. Type II (serotonin depression) and type IV (bipolar depression) are primarily inherited, and they are usually lifelong unless treated with medication. Type I (norepinephrine depression) and type III (dopamine depression) are what I call acquired — that is, based somewhat on situation and lifestyle, they sometimes can be fully cured and medication ultimately discontinued. An individual can be affected by just one or a combination of these four basic systems. The abilities to focus and organize, and the abilities to properly plan and function efficiently are affected by an imbalance in any of these four systems, and unless all the affected systems are adequately addressed, comfortable functioning will not be achieved or restored.

These four systems have revealed themselves indirectly over the past decade in response to the increasingly specific medication treatments that have been developed. Using this four-type system, I have been able to offer an overwhelming majority of my patients marked to full improvement in targeted symptoms. Of course, the catch phrase here is "targeted symptoms." Pills do not make people happy. They don't organize anyone. They don't find anyone intimacy. They don't solve developmental crises. And that's just a few of the many things they don't do.

What they in fact do is address a number of specific, more or less clearly defined syndromes (clusters of symptoms) that interfere with necessary growth, development, or problem solving. Sometimes, just getting rid of irritating symptoms such as poor sleep, no energy, anxiety, crankiness, and no motivation, combined with some counseling, is enough to get things going.

MOOD VERSUS ILLNESS

It is important at the outset to make the distinction between depression the mood and depression the illness. The illness is distinguished from the mood by the presence of what are called vegetative signs, most commonly alterations in the patterns of sleep and appetite, but also changes in energy level, nervous reactivity and the ability to concentrate. Everyone has experienced a depressed mood, feeling like everything sucks and always will, but this bummed-out feeling is usually temporary and clearly related to specific circumstances. Not everyone, however, finds himself waking up like a shot in the middle of the night, unable to fall back to sleep, mind filled with pointless nonsense. Conversely, not everyone is unable to get out of bed even after fourteen hours of sleep. It is particularly meaningful when either of these changes is a clear departure from years of more-regular sleeping patterns.

Depressed mood may not even be the most prominent symptom or emotion in depression the illness. Very often, panic, irritability, chronic pain, listlessness, or any of a range of other symptoms is more prominent than pure sadness, hopelessness, or despair.

It would perhaps be better if we called depression the illness neurotransmitter imbalance. Neurotransmitters are small molecules that are released into the synapse, the tiny space between the end of one nerve and the beginning of the next. When we talk about the presence of vegetative signs, we are really talking about the observable physical indicators of neurotransmitter imbalance, which are the kinds of symptoms that will be alleviated by medications that affect the amount of neurotransmitter available in the synapse.

As we've said, depression the mood is not necessarily synonymous with depression the illness. It is quite possible to be unhappy, even chronically so, and not be ill in a way that can be helped by medicine. On the other hand, chronic unhappiness, or chronic anxiousness or anger for that matter, are absolutely and definitely stressors that can lead, in time, to depression the illness.

The rapid and effective treatment of depression involves several steps. First, we have to accurately identify all the subtypes of depression that are present at any given time and match the antidepressants to the systems involved. Second, we need to identify the complicating factors (such as ADD, dissociation, homelessness, joblessness, lovelessness) that helped to create the depression and now are helping to sustain it. It is very important to temporally sequence the onset of the various moods and symptoms to determine which ones are likely to respond to medicine. Once medication-sensitive symptoms have been identified and removed, we can determine which symptoms remain and choose what combination of psychoeducation, lifestyle change, and psychotherapy is required. (For a complete discussion of this, see Chapter 10.)

Some people resist the idea of medication. Nobody likes the idea of taking drugs. Everyone wants to know how long they will need to take them. The good news is that people with Type I depressions often can go off their medications entirely. Type II depressions are tougher to handle without medication. For patients with inherited depressions, it often helps to think of the medication as a vitamin. If your general practitioner said, "You're anemic. You have to take iron," you would. It's not all that different.

THE FOUR DEPRESSIVE SYSTEMS

Before we move on to reviewing the four depressive systems in greater detail, let me state for the record my unequivocal bias: If any of the four systems is affected in the ways I will describe, medication will be necessary. Type I and III can sometimes be treated without medication, although the longer and more firmly entrenched the symptoms have been the less likely that relief can be provided in a reasonable time frame without them. Types II and IV are virtually impossible to treat without medication.

Four separate systems are involved in depression, each of them quite capable of impairing attention, of creating stuckness. It is possible, even common, for one person to have more than one type of depression, either simultaneously or in sequence. I cannot stress enough that all four patterns must be looked for separately and treated if present. Many patients mistakenly hop from one medicine to another, believing that nothing works, when

Figure 2: The Four Depressive Systems

Type	I	II	III	IV
Name	Stress depression (acquired)	Serotonin depressions (hereditary)	Pleasure depression (acquired/post addictive)	Bipolar depression (heriditary)
Neuro-transmitter	Norepinephrine	Serotonin	Dopamine	GABA
Symptoms	Middle awakening decreased appetite Panic attacks General anxiety	Hypersomnia Hyperphagia Irritability Perfomance anxiety	Decreases in Pleasure Interest Energy Motivation	Sudden shifts Mimics all others Obsessive Explosive Racing thoughts
Subtypes	Panic disorder Generalized Anxiety Disorder Post Tramatic Stress Disorder	Obsessive Seasonal Female hormonal Socially phobic	Situational/ Maturational Post Addictive	With or without mania or hypomania
Meds	Tricyclics Effexor Remeron Wellbutrin? Cymbalta SSRI's slower to work	SSRI's Wellbutrin Serzone Effexor Cymbalta	Wellbutrin	Trileptal Lamictal Depakote Neurontin Lithium

what they need is the layering of several drugs to target multiple systems.

Depression is a condition of epidemic proportions, one that will affect between 20 and 25 percent of the population (60 to 75 million Americans). Only a very small percentage of sufferers receive sophisticated medication treatment. Three out of five are never treated. Four out of five of those who are treated are treated by general practitioners, who are usually leery of prescribing more than one antidepressant at a time.

On balance, it seems fair to say that a great many people remain stuck, at least partially, because they have not had knowledgeable enough psychopharmacological treatment for their neurotransmitter imbalances. I think it is vital that people who aren't "getting it done" ask themselves whether they fit into one or more of the following four categories, and whether they have been medicated in a manner that addresses each of those patterns.

Type I Norepinephrine/Stress Depressions
Type I depressions, which can be thought of as stress depressions, involve the neurotransmitter norepinephrine and are known to be related to running oneself in a hyperaroused, or hyperadrenalized, state. This type of depression is most commonly characterized by insomnia. The insomnia includes both difficulty falling asleep and even more importantly, since it's the cardinal sign of this type of depression — difficulty staying asleep. It is marked by awakening to full alertness at typical times in the middle of the night, then being unable to fall back asleep for hours, if at all. People with this type of depression additionally tend to lose their appetite and sometimes lose weight as well. They are also frequently plagued by panic attacks, generalized anxiety, and waking up early with an anxious dread.

People have been writing about this type of depression for centuries, from the early Greeks description of "melancholia," to Van Morrison's song of the same name, and we have always recognized it as an illness. It can come in disparate garb, with any of its many associated symptoms, physical and mental, prominent in different people. What ties them together are the underlying features of a period of chronic hyperarousal followed after a time by poor sleep, poor appetite, agitation alternating with exhaustion, and, importantly, poor concentration.

Arousal in human beings, regardless of its cause, is always physiologically the same. When psychophysiological variables such as heart rate, blood pressure, skin conductivity, and resting muscle tension are measured, we see that fear looks the same as anger, which looks the same as sexual excitement, which looks the same as happiness after pulling consecutive all-nighters to meet an impending deadline.

Arousal is nonspecific, and chronic hyperarousal leads to decreasingly effective modulation of the arousal system, with this ineffective modulation being synonymous with norepinephrine depression. This family of depressions is almost always the direct result of chronic hyperarousal, no matter what the cause of that arousal may be.

Type I depressions are best treated with either tricyclic antidepressants, an older family of drugs that includes Elavil (amitriptyline), Pamelor (nortriptyline), Tofranil (imipramine), and Norpramin (desipramine), or with newer drugs that affect more than one system, such as Wellbutrin, which affects both the norepinephrine and the dopamine systems, and Effexor, Serzone, Cymbalta, and Remeron, which affect both the norepinephrine and the serotonin systems.

Type II Serotonin/Hereditary Depressions

Type II depressions, on the other hand, are associated with the neurotransmitter serotonin and tend to be characterized by fatigue, hypersomnia (sleeping too much), and binge eating. They also seem to be associated with irritability, obsessive thinking, interpersonal hypersensitivity, and social anxiety. Some subsets of Type II depression tend to be worse in winter. In some women, they cycle with the menses. Only in the past few decades has this type of depression been recognized and treated. This makes a certain sense. If you can't sleep and you can't eat, it's obvious you're sick. If you sleep too much and eat too much, and you're cranky about it to boot, you're just a slob with a bad attitude; get with the program.

Type II depressions are treated with any of a number of drugs that affect just serotonin, including Prozac, Paxil, Zoloft, Luvox, and Lexapro, as well as others that affect both serotonin and norepinephrine, such as Effexor, Serzone, Cymbalta, and Remeron. Some seasonally variable Type II depressions respond to therapy with full-spectrum light.

If you think of Oblomov, the great Russian layabout, for serotonin depressions and sleepless pacing for norepinephrine depressions, you will begin to get the distinction.

We are much clearer about both the causes and the remedies for stress-related norepinephrine depressions than we are about those for the often-chronic serotonin depressions. Anyone can develop the stress-depression picture if their stress is severe and persistent enough. Serotonin depressions have a much more hereditary feel about them, since they often breed true within families and can occur and recur seemingly unrelated to life events. Stress-related hyperarousal norepinephrine depressions can be resolved and prevented in any number of tried-and-true methods if the patient is willing to learn new skills and wiser attitudes and make lifestyle changes. For a good example, see the University of Massachusetts Stress Reduction Program, which is detailed by Jon Kabat-Zinn, Ph.D., in *Full Catastrophe Living* (New York: Delta, 1990). However, in my experience, there is a much smaller likelihood that anything other than the right medicines will keep away a majority of the Type II serotonin depressions.

Although Type I depressions, especially panic depressions, can settle in for the long haul, they are much more likely to be transitory. A frequent pattern is to see a lifelong, seasonally worsening Type II depression with an intermittent superimposition of a Type I stress depression; the stress in this case is the stress of living with a Type II depression that can prevent getting anything done.

Type III Dopamine/Pleasure Depressions
Type III depressions involve a third neurotransmitter, dopamine.

Dopamine has a lot of different functions in a lot of different places in the brain. Parkinson's disease, the movement disorder, and schizophrenia both involve dopamine neurons. Dopamine is also affected in people who are addicted to pleasurable substances such as nicotine, marijuana, or cocaine. People with Type III depression have trouble enjoying themselves. Nothing seems worth the effort. They are listless and lack energy and motivation, but often retain normal rhythms of sleep and appetite. Only one drug currently available is known to have an antidepressant affect on this system, and that drug is Wellbutrin, also marketed as Zyban for smoking cessation.

One of the interesting things about Type III depressions is that they sometimes arise as a complication of another depression and are revealed only after a more dramatic Type I or Type II depression has already been treated. I have heard a number of people complain that their Prozac or other serotonin drug doesn't work anymore. They've raised the dose and it's working a little better, but still not like when they first started taking it. Very often, this is because Prozac has some effect on dopamine at first, but what is really needed is to address this third pleasure system directly. Sometimes after Wellbutrin is added, a great improve-

---

ANXIETY DISORDERS

Most of the medically treatable anxiety disorders currently in the DSM-IV also fit easily into our conception of depression as the overt symptom of neurotransmitter imbalance. Types I and II depression both involve anxiety, but they are different sorts of anxiety. Type I is danger anxiety. It's about panic, heart-pounding for no apparent reason, shortness of breath, a sense of dizziness, or passing out. There's a feeling that something terrible is about to happen, or there's a nameless dread, a sense of impending nonspecific doom, often with a sense of physical unwellness that may be hard to pin down. Type II anxiety is stranger anxiety. It's more likely to be social, about people or about performing adequately in front of people. It can also be very physical, with nausea, sweating, and stammering, or it can be brooding and obsessive.

To be helpful and clear for individuals currently in treatment, I would say that people with panic disorder and a lot of people with generalized anxiety disorder or post-traumatic stress disorder would fit into our model of Type I depression.

ment is seen.

Type III depressions can be subtle. They can sneak up slowly and seem logical, and they can include some smattering of either Type I or Type II symptoms. Type III depressions also account for some of the symptoms in people who are diagnosed as dysthymic. In addition, when drug withdrawal, especially of marijuana or nicotine, is involved, even if Type I symptoms are also present, a full recovery can be elusive unless the stressed dopamine neurons are supported with Wellbutrin.

Type IV Bipolar Spectrum Depressions

Type IV is the depression that goes along with manic-depressive disorder, also called bipolar disorder. Rapid advances are being made in this area, with a number of new medicines becoming available in recent years. These medicines include Depakote, Lamictal, Trileptal, Topamax, and Gabatril.

Traditionally, experts have said that one in ten depressives are, in fact, bipolar-manic or hypomanic (which is the same but less), with periods of high energy, little sleep, elevated or irritable mood, distractibility, and pressured speech. Mania may also be accompanied by flat-out craziness, delusions, and bizarre behavior. Hypomania is much less obvious and also much more com-

---

Similarly, many people currently diagnosed with social phobia or obsessive-compulsive disorder would fit into our model of Type II depression.

It is important to recognize anxiety disorder as a subset of depression and to treat it with the appropriately matched antidepressant. One of the more common misfortunes for people with these types of depression is to be treated with and become addicted to a minor tranquilizer such as Klonopin, Xanax, or Ativan. These drugs should be used in an acute crisis and only rarely more than occasionally. They do not treat the underlying imbalance. In fact, in norepinephrine-based panic disorders, they worsen it, and they may prolong the condition indefinitely, long after the initial stressors have been forgotten.

Type II depressions have a number of documented subtypes (seasonal affective disorder, female hormonal depression, social phobia, obsessive depression, and obsessive-compulsive disorder) in which anxiety is more or less of a factor, and different drugs may be a little better for the different types. For more detailed information on these subtypes and their treatment, see Chapter 10.

mon than previously recognized. Racing, difficult-to-control thoughts that don't make sense can be due to hypomania, particularly if they are sudden in onset and somewhat distinct from previous patterns of thought. Anyone who has cared for or known a manic-depressive understands that people with this disorder can become depressed in a wide range of ways, in different ways at different times, some of which can make the depression look, at least temporarily, like one of the other three types. It appears that people with a Type IV depression can sometimes anyway get better without antidepressants if a mood stabilizer is used instead..

Recently, I've seen a number of my patients with complex, unresponsive depressions with varied symptom pictures respond to a mood-stabilizing drug even when they had no clear history of mania. Certainly, when the family history includes what we sometimes call manic equivalents (for example, alcoholism, suicides, or unstable work or marital histories), the likelihood that the person will benefit from a mood stabilizer, all of which were first antiepileptic drugs, is very high. Bipolar disorder, with or without mania, can be a very, irregular illness, and when an individual doesn't quite fit into any of the other categories, Type IV is often the answer.

The questions about whether and how antidepressants should be used in bipolar patients remain unresolved. Some authorities believe that antidepressants should be used sparingly, if at all, in people who respond to mood stabilizers. They feel that over time, antidepressants inevitably destabilize bipolar disorder. On the other hand, some patients at least seem to have both a Type IV bipolar depression as well as one of the other three depressions, and a mixture of antidepressants and mood stabilizers may be required. In general, I would say that I make every effort to minimize antidepressant use in patients who I have identified as having a condition responsive to mood stabilizers. However, I have also seen patients who seem to require and tolerate taking a ceiling medication (the mood stabilizer) and a floor medication (the antidepressant).

DEPRESSION AND ADD

Let's start by doing some math.

Let's assume that at some time in their lives, 25 percent of the population will have a neurotransmitter abnormality. That's roughly 75 million American people. These neurotransmitter abnormalities include both acquired (Types I and III) and inherited (Ttypes II and IV) depressions as we have described, and both depressive and anxiety disorders as described in the DSM-IV.

We have already said that the estimates for ADD in the population range from 5 percent to 10 percent. I feel that if ADD were understood as we presented it in the last chapter, as a relative reflection deficit, this number could easily slide higher, perhaps to as much as 15 percent of the population. But for argument's sake, we'll use 7.5 percent as our figure, which would mean that roughly 22.5 million Americans had ADD.

Suicide and Bipolar Disorder in Children and Adolescents

There has recently been some public health debate about the use of antidepressants in children and adolescents that is really about the ability of antidepressants and stimulants to create or to reveal, depending on your view, bipolar illness. We have known for decades that any antidepressant and any stimulant can bring on manic or hypomanic episodes. The children who killed themselves after taking a serotonin drug most likely had a bipolar element to their depressive illnesses, and their thoughts became "racily" manic while they were still otherwise depressed. This mixed state, manic while still depressed, is a dangerous one indeed. Thankfully, it is also a state that usually develops gradually over a few days to a few weeks such that an adequate therapeutic relationship should allow for its early detection.

I address the nature of and the therapy for the bipolar-spectrum disorders a bit further in Chapter 10, and I discuss the issue of bipolar reactions to stimulants in Chapter 9. For now, I will say that bipolar disorder is the most volatile and variable of the depressions, and that it can often escape accurate detection for many years, especially if it is partially responsive to antidepressants. I see bipolar disorder as electrical in nature, largely because it responds well to antiepileptic drugs. I also see it as somehow being at a deeper level than the other three biochemical types of depression. It is therefore able to mimic any of them, and it is considerably more variable and volatile. Its proper treatment requires the persistent, careful, individualized use of medication. If this is done, a full cure can be achieved.

If ADD and depression varied independently — that is, if they had no interaction with each other — we would multiply the 75 million people with depression by 7.5 percent for the percentage of people who have ADD and get 5.6 million. That's the minimum number of Americans, about 1.8 percent of the population, who suffer from both ADD (read inherited underreflectiveness) and depression (read neurotransmitter abnormality).

This minimum 1.8 percent of the population represents about twice the number of people who suffer from schizophrenia, an inherited disease that uniformly affects 1 percent of the population. Think about the long academic and intellectual history that accompanies this latter disease, and compare the disease with a condition that is at least twice as prevalent and hasn't yet, to my knowledge, had one single work (prior to this one) devoted to its study.

And of course, ADD and depression do, in fact, interact, in a powerful and consistent way, so the numbers start to get huge. The fact is that ADD, through a series of mechanisms, selects very strongly to the Type I stress depressions and the panic disorders that are related to them and to the Type III pleasure depressions. Rather than 25 percent of people with ADD suffering from neurotransmitter abnormalities, it's more like 50 percent or even 65 percent, which means that about 15 million Americans have both ADD and depression. That's 5 percent of us, or one in every twenty, walking around with depression and ADD. If we choose to redefine ADD as the bottom 15 percent of reflectiveness then one in every 10 Americans, 30 million of us, end up with both neurophysiological underreflectiveness and neurotransmitter imbalances and abnormalities. Astounding, eh?

Several clear pathways exist by which underreflectiveness (ADD) leads to chronic hyperarousal and substance abuse, and from there to neurotransmitter imbalance. Natural mechanisms of compensation lead to chronic hyperarousal, and chronic hyperarousal leads to a norepinephrine/stress depression. One of the primary mechanisms by which we modulate arousal is the release of adrenaline, the stress hormone, from the adrenal glands. When our body releases adrenaline, we are ready for danger. We are in what is called the fight-or-flight response. Heart rate and blood pressure go up, as does muscle tension. In addition, focus is improved.

This is very important in the interplay we are describing. The first line of defense, the most natural way for hyperactive, distractible people to improve their focus, is to intensify and heighten their arousal, to release adrenaline. The more intelligent, better compensated, and higher functioning people with ADD become, the more they need to learn to modulate the level of stimulation in order to be focused and comfortable.

Unfortunately, as we have said, even pleasant sorts of hyperarousal, let alone the fear or the anger that is often present for the underreflective, can eventually lead to Type I neurotransmitter abnormalities, to depression and anxiety. Think about a person whose attentional and reflective abilities are already taxed by the ever-more-complex world in which we live. Then add on the decreased concentration, poor sleep, and chronic anxiety that accompany this form of imbalance, and you can see a person who just can't maintain his or her previously high level of functioning.

The underreflective are also at risk for substance abuse and the depressions that go with it. One of the facts of life for many of the underreflective is their frequent chastisement by authority figures. Sometimes this leads to an outright rejection of authority, accompanied by chronic anger and resentment (which can itself lead to a Type I depression). Sometimes the authority figures and their voices are internalized, leading to the development of what might be called a harsh superego, a critical and demanding stance toward oneself. This stance can be useful in overcoming the tendency toward unreliability that can develop in the underreflective. However, many people often find it difficult to let go of that critical stance when it's time to relax and have fun.

The point here is that for both the resentful and the self-critical, the challenge of mind- and mood-altering recreational substances is a difficult one because these substances temporarily quiet the uncomfortable tension-producing voices in their heads. Marijuana seems to be the self-medication of choice for the underreflective, but cocaine, alcohol, nicotine, and even opiates are also used. Substance-abuse professionals I know have informally told me that more than half of the patients they treat can be seen as meeting the criteria for ADD or learning disabilities when they are examined carefully. There is no question that mind-altering substances, although perhaps helpful and pleasurable at first, can eventually lead to both Type I and Type III depressions when chronically used.

ADD, when accompanied by being stuck as we have described it (having problems with procrastination, disorganization, impulsiveness, lack of motivation, and time management), leads to very real life stress. Executive functioning as a set of skills is learned less easily by the underreflective, and the very lack of these skills tends to create a life of chaotic underfunctioning, constant crises, and frequent, if not constant, stress. Loneliness, poverty, and poor work and family relationships are real life issues that, in and of themselves, tend to create hyperarousal and/or substance abuse and therefore Type I and III depressions.

Dissociation is often another important mediating factor in neurotransmitter abnormalities. In the next chapter, we will discuss dissociation in considerable detail. This complex but common phenomenon has to do with the flow of information from one "self" to another, with the relationship of the left-brain planners and the right-brain feeler-seer-doers. What this means in more practical terms is that we get stuck in a state in which we're hyperaroused and in which we don't have the resources to soothe ourselves. Very often, these dissociated aspects of the self are found to be the ultimate cause of the tension and the behaviors that can lead to the acquired types of depression we have been discussing.

CHAPTER 5

Dissociation

Dissociation-Based Stuckness

You don't start things, or you put them off and then forget about them.

You're always late.

You make promises you don't keep.

You get trapped in anxious or depressed moods.

You don't see and accept responsibility for the larger patterns of behavior. You're "in denial."

You're prone to addictions — food, drugs, sex, gambling, exercise, even work — at the expense of a balanced, healthy life.

There's no coherence between your intentions and your actions.

You have a history of childhood trauma (induced by, for example, ADD, learning disabilities, atypical

73

> sexuality, substance-abusing parents, or divorced
> parents).
>
> *Bottom line: You know what to do, but your left
> and right brains disagree about doing it.*

THE EFFECTS OF TRAUMA

One of the unanticipated results of the terrorist attack on the World Trade Center has been, no doubt, an uptick of interest in traumatology. Traumatology is the study and treatment of individuals who have been subjected to a broad gamut of negative events, from the horrific, unimaginable excesses of torture to the more mundane, chronic tension of living with alcoholic parents. In adults, we know that acute, intense trauma such as the World Trade Center attack leads to post-traumatic stress disorder (PTSD), and that chronic stress leads to the norepinephrine depressions we described in Chapter 4. These two conditions are, in fact, quite similar, having in common disturbed sleep, loss of appetite, hyperarousal, anxiety, and panic attacks. Both of these adult stress reactions are mediated by neurotransmitter imbalances, and they are best treated with a combination of medication and a rather structured sort of therapy (see Chapter 10).

In children, however, stress and trauma are more likely to have lasting effects through their influence on dissociation, on the way in which the brain manages the performance of two or more (often many more) separate functions simultaneously. If you look up "dissociate" in a dictionary, you'll find that it's defined as "to break the connection between; disunite." The DSM-IV says that "the essential feature of the Dissociative Disorders is a disruption in the usually integrated functions of consciousness, memory, identity, or perception of the environment."

Put these two together, and we get the idea that a dissociative disorder involves the disruption, the disuniting, the disintegration of complex aspects of mental functioning that were previously connected. A dissociation is a split, a separation. In the context of this work, "dissociation" is a broad term for a constant, dynamic mental process in which different aspects of brain function, different bundles of data are shuffled about, connected, disconnected, and reconnected again, associated with each other and then dissociated (dis-associated), moving in and out of conscious awareness. The impact of dissociation on mental health is grossly underappreciated because of the tremendous variation in the range and types of mental functions that may be joined or split, integrated or dissociated.

Acute, intense trauma in early childhood leads to what used to be called multiple personality disorder (MPD) and what is now more technically and exactly referred to as dissociative identity disorder (DID). This is a fascinating condition with an unusual history, written about extensively in the eighteenth century and then lost for fifty years or so in the haze of confusion surrounding Eugen Bleuler's description of schizophrenia. Schizophrenia and multiple personality disorder share the symptom of hearing voices. In schizophrenia, the cause is biological, a problem of brain metabolism and brain structure, and medication can often eliminate it. In multiple personality disorder, the cause is entirely psychological and experiential, and medicines have only adjunctive utility in its treatment. The underlying idea behind multiple personality disorder is that several distinct and independent personalities exist within the same body, and that apparently these various selves may or may not know very much about each other's existence or behavior. Sometimes, the suppression, or dissociation, of some of the personalities is incomplete, hence the experience of voices. Most people know about multiple personality disorder, if at all, from the movies, starting with the infamous *Sybil*, the movie in which Sally Field portrayed a woman with seventeen personalities, right through *Primal Instinct*, the Richard Gere legal thriller in which Ed Norton plays a fellow who fakes MPD to get away with murder.

Although it has generated skepticism in some quarters along the way, MPD/DID is no longer regarded as controversial in academic psychiatry. Instead, it is regarded as a genuine disorder that almost always occurs in the presence of overwhelming trauma in early childhood. The intense trauma creates a situation in which the child needs to keep various powerfully negative feelings and thoughts out of consciousness in order to continue developing in a normal manner. To accomplish this purpose, a "self" is created to "hold" the particular destructive content and then that self is "walled off." Once this mechanism, this creation of separate "selves," is learned in childhood, it can be used more and more often to hold stressful, indigestible material, creating complex webs of personalities, each of which has its own history, its own fund of information, and its own relationships with all the other selves. For example, the patient who first opened my eyes to this fascinating condition was molested and raped at the age of five, and by the time I met her, when she was thirty-six years old, she had created fourteen separate personalities.

This complex illness is one end of a continuum of dissociative phenomena that demonstrates the remarkable ability of the human brain to protect itself by controlling the flow of information storage and retrieval. It is, however, decidedly only one end of the spectrum. At the other end are milder but more chronic forms of trauma that cause problems in adulthood not through the creation of networks of personalities but by interfering with the developing relationship between the left-brain labeling and planning aspects of the self and the right-brain feeling and doing aspects of the self. This particular sort of dissociation sets the stage for the very kind of ineffective, stuck, attentionally — impaired lives we have been talking in this book. In between these poles lies a whole range of conditions in which other types of splits can occur, such as anxiety, depression, eating disorders, sexual dysfunction, and substance abuse.

We began this discussion by comparing the effects of traumatic experience on adults and children. The point here is that dissociation, the effects of childhood trauma upon information flow that we have been referring to and will be describing in further detail below, unlike adult post-traumatic conditions, does not respond to medication. It can, however, respond to a range of

Figure 3: The Effects of Trauma in Adults and Children

	Adults	Children
Acute	PTSD (Post-traumatic Stress Disorder)	MPD/DID (Multiple Personality Disorder/Dissociative Identity Disorder)
Chronic	Panic Disorder/Agitated-Stress Depression	Right/Left Brain Dissociation

"inner" techniques specifically designed to tap into a person's naturally occurring abilities to direct information flow, abilities that can be amazingly easy to use.

These techniques, which are guided imaginings, primarily visual but using other senses as well, are also a part of the everyday global culture. What literate individual hasn't heard of vision quests or of the inner child? These images resonate because they address some fundamental truths about the nature of the mind. What all the techniques have in common is that they seek to integrate the dissociated, to reunite that which has been split.

THE HISTORY OF THE SELVES

We are continually, on a moment-to-moment basis, bringing mental content in and out of our awareness, and we tend to do this automatically. When we are driving a familiar route and we are thinking about what we are going to say to our spouse or boss or friend, we often "wake up" to find ourselves at our destination without really remembering getting there. Our body drove us there, but the watching part of us didn't even notice it. If something had jumped into the road, however, we'd still have slammed on the brakes. When we go to the movies, we can easily forget about the toothache we've had, only to rediscover the ache when the film is over. Long before we can talk in any meaningful way about it, we are attaching and splitting, associating and dissociating, to further our aims. We are managing our information flow in complex and subtle ways.

To understand dissociation, how it can go awry, and how we can fix it, we need to start at the very beginning and talk about the way the mind is first set up, about the way it starts the lifelong task of classifying and storing information.

From the moment we are born, we deal with information, sorting and storing, learning to recognize repetitive neural patterns. One of the earliest mental milestones is called object constancy, the ability to mentally represent something in its absence, to hold on to the memory of a constellation of stimuli after the stimuli have been removed. We know that infants have achieved object constancy when they continue to look for the ball when we move it behind the pillow, when they look for a particular person to hold their bottle instead of just looking for the bottle itself.

Once we can reliably represent and then recall a constellation of stimuli, we use that ability to begin the arduous and detailed job of sorting out the "me" from the "not me," creating ourselves (our - "selves") from scratch. This is a prodigious feat of information processing, as any modeler of computer intelligences can tell you. It means breaking down literally billions of neural impulses into recognizable patterns, and it takes a baby about eighteen months, going at it full time, to do the job. When babies can point to their chests and say their names, we know that they have arrived at their first, primordial, indivisible self.

Very quickly, this initial unitary self begins to break down into parts, parts that correspond, initially at least, to important people, repetitive activities, and sensory modalities. Many is the child who acts "like a different person" with each parent. An example is the bilingual child who always seems to speak the right language to the right parent. As the activities and behaviors required of a child multiply, the self becomes further and further differentiated into definable patterns of experience and behavior.

It is this breaking down into parts, into what might be called the sub-selves, that underlies the phenomenon we call dissociation. All human beings have their own unique branching trees of sub-selves based on their personal life experiences, and it is by influencing the development of and the relationships between the various sub-selves that trauma has its very variable effects. An academic literature exists in which these sub-selves are also called ego states, and these sub-selves, these ego states, are widely understood to be containers that humans create to hold all sorts of complex information. "Ego State" is a term that is currently most identified with John and Helen Watkins, academic hypnotists from the University of Montana and the authors of *Ego States Theory and Therapy* (New York: Norton, 1997), and their disciples Maggie Phillips and Claire Frederick, authors of *Healing the Divided Self* (New York: Norton, 1995). "Ego state therapy" is an overview term for a therapy that has been devised to counteract the disintegrating and dissociating effects of various sorts of trauma on the developing network of sub-selves. The Watkins summarize it as a "family therapy for the self" during which aspects of the self are personified and asked to relate more positively with each other.

The Watkins define an ego state as "an organized system of behavior and experience whose elements are bound together by some common principle, and which is separated from other such states by a boundary that is more or less permeable." At the most basic level, what differentiates one self, one ego state, from another is a particular pattern of electrical activities within the brain. Once we have formed the initial self in infancy, we make selves all the time, creating patterns of electrical brain activity for different purposes. It is useful to think of these selves as the containers, the holders, the foundations of human meaning. We have selves for the things we do, for the people we love, for all sorts of complex functions. We have a self for every kind of input and every kind of output, and for most possible combinations.

LEFT-BRAIN SELVES AND RIGHT-BRAIN SELVES

When we first mentioned dissociation in Chapter 1, we introduced the idea that there are two contrasting ways of processing and storing information, which we called left-brained and right-brained. In the early stages of childhood, the selves that are created are all essentially right-brained. What do we mean by this?

The original distinctions won the Nobel Prize for Roger Sperry, Ph.D., and his associates. These researchers examined split-brain patients, patients in whom the corpus callosum, the main connection between the left and the right cerebral hemispheres, was severed in order to control intractable seizures. What these examinations revealed was that the verbal abilities in these patients were primarily contained in the left hemisphere and the visual and spatial abilities were contained in the right hemisphere. The examinations also revealed that in the split-brain patients, these hemispheres could function independently, that each could contain knowledge not available to the other. The right brain could point to an object it had seen, and the left brain could remain unable to name that object because it (through visual-field manipulation) had not seen it. They were dissociated — in these cases, anatomically so.

For the purposes of this discussion, when we say "left-brained" and "right-brained," we are talking about two complementary modes of thinking that are at first primarily located as electrical activity in their respective hemispheres. They do not always stay so tightly localized. In people who develop in a healthy manner and remain relatively untraumatized, the selves become increasingly complex and increasingly able to hold both thinking styles in mind at once.

We can begin to distinguish these two mental modes by saying that the right brain is primarily nonverbal, closer to reality, closer to the direct experience of the sensory transducers. It is visual, spatial, musical, emotional, social, and sexual. It's about the body and its movement and position. The left brain is one step removed. It's symbolic; it's representational. The right brain "sees" a whole picture, and, more important, it can infer the whole even when it sees only some of the disconnected parts. The left brain takes things one bit of information at a time. It is literal, much less skilled at inference. The right brain is there first, both developmentally and probably evolutionarily or anthropologically as well, cataloging experience in patterns, knowing things without necessarily being able to describe them. Then the left brain comes along to label and catalogue the experience in language, in symbols. The left brain judges. The right brain experiences. The left brain analyzes. The right brain accepts. The left brain plans. The right brain acts. The left brain is about goals. The right brain is about process. The left brain sees details and facts, but the right brain sees the ineffable, which cannot be described in words, which is too complex for words. The left brain is about interacting with the outer world. The right brain is about contact with the inner world.

The right brain is visual, experiential, holistic, and pattern-seeing. This is why it is able to make inferences from incomplete data, to fill in gaps. It is able to understand things that cannot be justified. It is able to go beyond the facts and details. The left brain is verbal, judging, comparing, digital, and goal-directed. It is responsible for naming and planning, for following the rules, for being good. These are two complementary modes, each essential to full humanity.

Perhaps the most immediate way to make it clear is to say that the left-brained verbal self is what we think of as our "everyday" self. It's the voice we use when we talk to ourselves; it's the one we "think" is making all the decisions, our verbal conscious awareness. Buddhists, when they talk about the "chattering" of our "monkey mind" during meditation, are talking about the endless stream of "judging" thoughts that emanate from this part of ourselves, the endless stream that can interfere with a deeper awareness of our right-brain, experiencing selves.

Although we are talking about left and right brains, we need to remember that this refers only to the cerebral cortex, the topmost part of the brain. Humans, in fact, possess what is called a triune (three-part) brain. The bottommost part, which leads into the spinal cord, is about movement. The middle part is about feelings, both emotional and bodily/visceral. It's only the top part, the thinking brain, that is divided in half. What's important is that in the first, formative years of life, only the right brain — the experiential, pattern-seeing part — is online, therefore, all body and emotional knowledge is stored and accessed, at least initially, only in the right-brained, visual manner. This results in a right brain (half of the top third of the brain plus both bottom thirds) that is five times as large as the left brain (the other half of the top third of the brain).

We said a while back that to understand how the development of dissociation creates dysfunction, we had to go back to the beginning. Think for a moment of small children of two or three and about the delightful combination of unselfconsciousness and rapid learning they possess, of the joyfulness with which they meet the world when they are safe and well-tended. They are the prototype of pure right-brain functioning. It may or may not be in the conscious awareness, but it is unselfconscious. It does not judge. It just is. Its learning consists of an increasingly varied set of states (or selves) that are combinations of moving, sensing, and feeling. All of this learning is organized and stored in the kind of right-brained patterns we have been describing, patterns that resemble pictures or maps, visually, spatially, or bodily, patterns of knowledge and experience that eventually become sub-selves or ego states. These selves can know some rather complex things, but, at least at first, they can't talk very well about what they know. Children know not to put their fingers in sockets long before they can talk about it.

Pure right-brainedness has an idyllic, timeless quality, but there is more to life than that. Such a child knows nothing about time, about cause and effect, about arbitrary rules. Knowing the rules is important. ("Don't put your finger in a socket.") We need a labeling system, a language, to deal with the complex world. Painstakingly, over several years, we begin to decipher the system our parents are using and, as we have already been doing, as we always do, we create a self to hold that complex information. That self helps us to avoid pitfalls, allows us to plan, gets us what we want, helps us to be good. This part of ourselves, the left brain, is developed to assist us in coping with the ever-more-complicated demands of human development. It is slow and exacting by nature. It labels everything carefully, and it compares relative value to avoid danger. It superimposes itself upon an already existing system of knowing that is entirely different in nature, that is, by definition, ineffable, that is beyond (or at least not easily translatable into) words.

Therefore, prior to age five or so, our selves become more complex, but they remain essentially unselfconscious, process-oriented, timeless. Then, the left brain, long germinating in its task of mastering language, asserts itself. In contrast to the already-much-divided right brain, the left brain is relatively unified. The left brain creates an ongoing, uninterrupted, labeled, and named archive of experience, an archive that eventually becomes the everyday sense of self, the voice in our head with which we are so familiar by adulthood.

As the left brain develops, it creates a whole new spectrum of selves — or, rather, it alters all the existing selves, intertwining itself with all the different combinations of the moving, feeling, and sensing selves that were already being integrated through the right brain. It adds self-consciousness. It adds planning. It adds goals.

At this early point, relations between the two realms are good. The logical, time-oriented, goal-directed, keeping-track self is now present in all the other selves, and it adds to the ease of keeping all the selves apprised of each other's capabilities. This can be called generalizing, the ability to use skills learned in one context in a second, similar context. The left brain assists in sorting experience in a way that makes it more accessible to planned remembering, to switching fluidly from one self to another, from one set of subroutines to another, as is needed by the situation at hand. The left brain, in turn, is open to the insightful pattern-seeing, intuitive knowing of all the right-brain selves and can be logical in their service.

TRAUMA AND THE INTEGRATION OF THE LEFT AND RIGHT BRAINS

Let us suppose that into this new alliance comes an overwhelmingly traumatic moment — a war, a rape, a beating, or the death of a parent, for example. The conscious self is horrified, endangered, and overwhelmed. In defense, it sends out a wave of revulsion and rejection, a wave of judgment, at the self that is holding this awful emotional state. The Watkins say that when children are presented with an overwhelming, unendurable trauma, a trauma that threatens to destroy the growing left-brain sense of self, they have only three possible responses: suicide, madness, or dissociation. Dissociation: The making of a new, cut-off self, to hold the deadly, disorganizing pain away from the ongoing growth of the logical, goal-directed watching self, the one we need to help us master the world, the one that keeps us safe, the one that knows danger. We have to preserve that left-brain self, so we encode the very strong negative memory with an equally strong barrier.

The right-brain emotional self responds to this wave of rejection by dissociating, by splitting off, by creating that barrier to the normal flow of information between selves. The primary effect of this is that any associations that come from the cut-off right-brain part are censored and not allowed into the left-brain consciousness, where they are too disturbing for adequate functioning to continue. In addition, a blockade is erected to prevent the flow of new information and experience into the cut-off part, thereby effectively freezing its maturation (and creating the much-vaunted inner child).

If the trauma is powerful enough, we develop multiple personality disorder, in which whole identities are split from each other. If the disorder is less severe, we get three other sorts of splits: (1) between left-brain reasoning and the control of emotions, (2) between left-brain reasoning and the control of behavior, and (3) between left-brain reasoning and the control of sensation. These three sorts of dissociations, which we will describe in more detail below, are extremely common. They are mediating factors in the genesis of an enormously wide range of psychopathological conditions, from anxiety and depression to substance abuse and other compulsive behaviors, to eating disorders and sexual dysfunction.

Even in the absence of any obvious dramatic trauma, an unavoidable consequence of childhood, of the process of understanding and adapting to the complex demands of reality, is that we judge certain aspects of ourselves to be unacceptable, to be "bad," and we tend to dissociate those aspects of ourselves. This may happen acutely, but much more commonly, it happens chronically. It is easy to see how we lose contact with some of our right-brain potentialities simply because our judging left-brain self finds them unsatisfactory. For instance, if our parents find our early expressions of a sexual self — rubbing our genitals or even, perhaps, becoming aroused while being physical with them — to be too unsettling, it is quite natural for our left-brain self to acquire that same attitude and to build barriers to prevent sexual thoughts, the sexual self, from emerging and developing. If our parents are very concerned about our weight and our eating, and we feel bad about them, it is natural for us to cut ourselves off from our eating selves and to develop anorexia, bulimia, or binge eating. If we have ADD and we are constantly upbraided about our organizational selves, about our ability to keep track of what we are doing, we will naturally cut ourselves off from painful contact with our timekeeping selves, and we will become chronic procrastinators.

Our left-brain, planning self, the one that develops around labeling and naming, has been called many things: the superego, the conscience, the parental introject. The essential task of the left brain is to keep us out of trouble, to keep track of what we're supposed to do and make sure we do it, to keep us safe so that we may return to our more comfortable, more unselfconscious, flowing right brain. It must also create and sustain more complex left-right brain selves, the selves from which truly directed creativity can arise.

Obviously, we need a balance between planning and acting. When the left brain dominates unleavened, we experience chronic tension and joylessness. When the right brain dominates unleavened, we live with chaos and shortsightedness.

One of the functions of our left brain is to constantly explain things to all the other selves that are listening. It turns out that our left-brain verbal self tends to talk to our right-brain inner selves in the same manner that our parents and the world talked to us as children. This can be good or bad. If our folks were encouraging, empathic, and understanding, we'll have a strong inner voice helping us to pull our (selves) together and to integrate us in the face of challenges. If, on the other hand, our folks were scornful and devaluing, that is how we will address our inner selves, which will, like any normal person, withdraw — dissociate — from that kind of treatment.

BRAIN INTEGRATION AND HUMAN POTENTIAL

Everyone is rejected or coerced at some time during the socialization of childhood. This results in two types of people: those whose left-right brain relationship is impaired enough by this process to develop overtly pathological behaviors and feelings (i.e. psychiatric illness); and just about everyone else who struggles to a greater or lesser degree to make and benefit from a more collaborative sort of contact with their nonverbal, intuitive, experiencing, exploring, process-oriented, creative, spiritual, sexual, right-brained selves.

Once we begin to appreciate the left-right brain dichotomy, we notice that it is represented everywhere in human culture and history. It appears as far back as the time of the ancient Hindus, who spoke of the outer, everyday Atman and the inner, spiritual Brahman. Freud used the terms "superego' and "id"; Jung referred to the "persona" and the "shadow." Looking back at a central human myth, it is not a stretch at all, it seems to me, to see the judging, labeling, goal-directed left brain as the apple that Adam ate, giving him the knowledge of right and wrong (good and bad), and expelling him from the "garden" of right-brained, experiential unselfconsciousness. And just as Adam was expelled from the Garden of Eden, so, too, all children, as they begin to label and value and judge, lose contact, at least somewhat, with their unselfconscious body-mind, with the ineffable, nonverbal garden within.

Everyone loses some contact with their inner selves, and great wide swaths of religion and culture from all over the world can be seen as part of the never-ending human struggle to reclaim that contact, to become more fully ourselves. In my view, meditation, Buddhism, Taoism, yoga, Guirdjieff, Joseph Campbell's hero journey, the many different types of psychotherapy — the whole pursuit of "enlightenment" in general — can all be seen as addressing the central issue of the integration of left-right-brain functioning.

A favorite hypnotic text of mine, *Hypnotherapy Scripts* by Ronald A. Havens and Catherine Walters (New York: Brunner-Routledge, 2002), uses the metaphor of a captain and his crew to describe the interaction of functions between the left and the right brains. The left brain is the captain, charting the course, deploying resources, arranging for the training of his men. The crew executes the captain's commands, often performing functions that the captain himself cannot perform. There are many ways in which such an arrangement can work. Ideally, the captain consults the crew, gets their invaluable front-line input, and makes decisions and commands only after he judges both the ability and the willingness of his crew to follow them. But what if the captain is harsh and closed-minded? His crew may be overtly defiant — or, worse, covertly so. What if the captain is anxious and overcontrolling, and doesn't trust his crew? He may try to do everything himself, at the price of tremendous inefficiency. What if the captain has poor charts and inaccurate information? And so on.

THE DISSOCIATION SUBTYPES

When we begin to think in terms of left-right brain integration, we find a wide variety of human phenomena becoming much more understandable. Anyone familiar with the literature on adult children of alcoholics knows that these patients, injured in childhood by unempathic parenting, are seen to fall into one of two categories: the hyperresponsible and the hyperirresponsible. It's not much of a jump to see that these are other names for being stuck in the left brain (overly goal-directed) or in the right brain (under goal-directed). The children of alcoholics learn very quickly that their feelings of rage, shame, abandonment, and fear need to be suppressed, that they are not nearly as important as the feelings of their barely functioning parents. Soon the spontaneous right-brain self becomes a dormant, suppressed vestige, and the child becomes parentified, prematurely and excessively left-brained. What happens later, of course, is that half remain that way. In the other half, the total right-brain suppression is broken through, and the self that emerges is primitive, selfish, heedless, a hyperirresponsible right brain totally unleavened by a history of left-right brain co-consciousness.

I referred earlier to three different subtypes of post-traumatic dissociative splits: reason and emotion, reason and behavior, and reason and sensation. A closer look at all three may give the abstract idea of dissociation a more recognizable feel.

The Split Between Reason and Emotion
In the split between reason and emotion, a particular feeling, frequently fear or sadness but often shame or guilt or anger, occurs in an exaggerated way in inappropriate contexts and cannot seem to be reasoned away. The person often knows full well that the intensity and duration of the emotional response is out of proportion to the apparent stimulus but feels unable to control it. The ego state or self that holds the feeling was created and dissociated in childhood and does not contain the more mature mood-stabilization mechanisms that were learned afterwards.

K. is a perfect example of this type of difficulty. K. was a fiftyish redhead, still quite attractive, who had been the office manager of a small investment firm, made about $80,000 a year, and took a buyout when the firm was swallowed by a much bigger fish. Shortly after leaving her job, she went to school to be an aesthetician, learning about skin care, wraps, facials, and so forth. She came to me after graduation because she had experienced two "panic attacks," as she called them, when she made two separate attempts to return to work, first as an aesthetician in a salon and then back in an office setting.

These panic attacks were not the biologically-mediated neurotransmitter abnormalities we discussed in Chapter 4. They were, in fact, the result of the emergence of a dissociated ego state, a personality fragment from childhood that was frightened of failure and had no resources for managing, modulating, or eliminating those fears. Although K. was indeed panicked those two times and feared the return of these symptoms, she generally continued to sleep and eat normally.

K. had a rather harsh mother who was a perfectionist and was never satisfied. When K. did the inner-child exercises, she found a frightened six-year-old who felt inadequate and was afraid of displeasing her mommy. Although K. had no children, she was a devoted aunt, and she had plenty of experience to draw on when I asked her to nurture and soothe the child she found. She discovered that she was quite capable of calming the child and herself, and soon she mastered these feelings and returned to work.

This is an example of someone in whom the adult mood-modulating skills were dissociated from a particular type of emotion. This can occur in a variety of ways. When K. began to talk about her romantic history, we discovered that she had repeated the same pattern over and over. As soon as she would become intimate enough with someone to contemplate a commitment, she would begin to feel trapped, she would find fault with the person, and she would push him away.

When we had K. imagine this trapped feeling and go to the meadow where one meets the children, she met an older child, a fourteen-year-old, whose mother had made her abandon her first love, a Hispanic boy, out of prejudice. This ego state re-experienced the disappointment of losing this boy and acted on it over and over, rejecting her lovers before she could lose them. The grown-up K. felt like a helpless observer of her own irrational responses in these romantic situations. Once again, after visualizing a series of meetings with the adolescent part of herself, she was able to respond to romantic situations from a broader emotional palette.

Dissociation from intensely negative unresolved issues in a childhood self is an astoundingly common modern human experience. Witness the enormous cultural resonance of the image of the inner child.

The Split Between Reason and Behavior

The split between reason and behavior is also around us everywhere. It takes many different forms. The essential underlying ingredient is an experiential right-brained self that feels talked down to and misunderstood by the left-brain planner. Ego-state techniques treat each of these selves as separate individuals. Individuals who feel misunderstood tend to turn off and tune out whatever advice or instruction the offending authority figure might be offering. The techniques that aid in reintegrating a split between reason and behavior are all about inner guides, about learning a different way of speaking to and relating with the part of you that is actually making the behavioral decisions.

Splits between reason and behavior can involve addictions (drugs, alcohol, sex, or gambling) or unreliability (procrastination or disorganization). In the case of addictions, the left-brain planner keeps wanting to stop, and keeps promising to stop, but the beleaguered, underfed, isolated, and disapproved-of experiential self has long ago learned that this bossy, judging voice does not understand and, even worse, speaks in an unpleasant way. The experiential self is not very likely to listen to this hectoring killjoy.

In unreliable folks, the right-brain doing self long ago learned to dismiss the left brain as an alarmist drill sergeant who'll work them both until they drop if allowed. The planner and the doer don't get along, and the inner self feels no obligation to heed carelessly worded instructions about which it has not even been consulted.

Of course, to a certain extent, talking about different types of splits is not exactly true to life. Splits due to emotions and splits due to addictions or responsibilities often coexist in one person.

J., age thirty-eight, came to see me a few weeks after he'd lost yet another high-pressure accounting job because of a cocaine binge. He couldn't understand why he kept sabotaging himself, why he wouldn't even call in sick instead of just not showing up. J. was a rather bright kid with ADD. He was smart enough never to be recognized as having ADD, but he got a lot of negative feedback from his parents and teachers for his inconsistencies. He was a competitive person and, in order to perform well, he developed a rather harsh attitude with himself: He learned to suppress or ignore his discomforts and his anger and to work very hard to please all the authority figures around him. As an adult, J. kept finding himself in situations where his competence would bring him more and more work, and he would keep accepting the work, further and further dissociating from his own growing discomfort. When he could no longer stand the pace he was imposing on himself, his suppressed right brain would revolt in a heedless, regressed manner, and he would once again shoot himself in the foot.

The Split Between Reason and Sensation

The split between reason and sensation underlies eating disorders, sexual problems, and a wide range of physical and psychophysiological health problems. There are many types of sensation, and the sensations we suppress may be pleasurable or painful. However, indiscriminate suppression of sensation robs us of information that we sorely need if we are to live as well as we can.

T. was an actress and dancer who was, unfortunately, molested periodically between the ages of six and eight. As might be expected, she was somewhat mistrustful, and she became my patient only in slow stages. At first, she came only for medication. After a year or so, she started wanting to talk to me about the effects of her traumatic experiences on her sexuality and on her work. Although she was quite attractive, she had very little interest in sex and did not enjoy it much. If she became aroused, she often became anxious. Although she craved attention when performing, felt an ecstatic, almost erotic wholeness when on stage, she found the attention that her looks and her obvious sexual energy drew toward her in real life to be very disturbing. She expended an enormous amount of energy vigilantly defending herself against connecting with men.

T. is a perfect example of the complex ways in which sensation can be dissociated in the face of trauma. Because she was at least partly aroused during the experiences, and because she knew that she had been enjoying the flirtatiousness that preceded the experiences, she felt guilty about the molestation, and she had been labeling sexual feelings as bad and shutting them off behind a warning system of anxiety. But T. was a libidinous person (in fact — surprise, surprise — T. also has ADD) and very bright, so she found an outlet in performing, where her sexuality was acceptable.

T. was a complex person of tremendous energy and talent, and her sexuality was largely restored, her vigilant defensiveness abandoned, and her ambivalence about her career resolved, all using variations on basic ego-state techniques. Some of T's treatment is discussed in Chapter 7, but for our purposes here, the point to be made is that the repression or dissociation of sexual feelings and ideas can distort many aspects of emotional and occupational functioning, with predictably negative results.

Dissociation of digestive sensations is at the crux of eating disorders. Binge eaters are dissociated from feelings of fullness and from the discomfort caused by overeating. Anorectics are dissociated from feelings of hunger. Bulimics alternate between the two. The most profound dissociation in eating-disorder patients is a separation from a stable, approving voice that allows them to view themselves as good.

This part of ourselves is usually provided by our experiences with our parents. It's called the parental introject, the image of our parents that we hold inside when they are not present. In the eating-disorder patient, that stable, approving voice is absent for some reason, a more negative voice is usually present, and self-regard becomes dependent upon atypical eating behaviors and the sensory dissociations that allow them.

Some of the more common and insidious forms of sensory dissociation are the ones that allow the continuation of unhealthy habits and lifestyles that also feel bad, from drinking and smoking to inactivity and excessive agitation. Our body constantly sends us signals — hangovers, coughing, joint pain, headaches, ulcers, fatigue, you name it — but we are able to keep these signals out of mind, out of awareness, if not all the time, at least at the moments we are once again about to act against our own best health.

———•◦◆◦•———

I hope it is clear that dissociation, the splitting and disintegrating of brain functions that would better work together, is the mechanism by which childhood traumatic experiences are stored and express themselves. The range of functions that can be separated is legion, and the effects of that separation can be varied, but the underlying cause is always the same: the labeling of parts of the self as bad and unacceptable, first by the outside world and then by judging parts of the self.

Dissociation can be easy to correct. In Chapter 7, we will discuss its treatment in full. Before we can do that, we need to talk a little bit about trance, because trance, hypnosis, and self-hypnosis are the keys to any effective treatment of dissociative disorders.

CHAPTER 6

Hypnosis and Self-Hypnosis

What is hypnosis? That's an easy one. Hypnosis is guided trance, a trance that is entered into intentionally in the presence of another person.

But what is a trance?

First and foremost, a trance is not an exotic or unknown state of mind. It is a state that occurs naturally in almost everyone, although it is not usually recognized as such. We all drift in and out of trance all day, whether we know it or not. Every time we get absorbed enough to become unselfconscious, every time we quiet the inner, judging monologue and put more of our circuits on experiencing, we're in a trance. Most often these everyday trances occur when we are alone, although we can also be entranced by another person, while listening to a vivid speaker, for instance, or watching an exotic dancer. We do much of our best work, if we are lucky, in a trance, in that timeless state of engaged well-being that psychologist Abraham Maslow calls "peak experience" and researcher Mihaly Csikszentmihalyi (pronounced Chicks-a-ME-hi) calls "flow."

Trances vary enormously in depth and intensity, from the very light trance of, say, driving or reading the newspaper to very deep states in which even surgery can be performed, and from which the subject awakens after a considerable period of time with no memory of the trance whatsoever. By and large the trances I will present in this volume are rather light trances, expressly intended to be remembered and mulled over in between times.

The single defining characteristic of trance is focused awareness, a narrowing of attention, and there are about as many different types of trance as there are aspects of experience we can narrow our focus upon. In the final analysis, trance can be divided into two subcategories: (1) trance in which we are focused internally, narrowing inward through a vivid process of imagining, and (2) trance in which we are focused externally, upon some event or activity occurring in our environment.

Some writers attempt to define trance by listing its well-known varieties, such as prayer, meditation, singing, dancing, reading, playing an instrument, a sport, making love, listening to music, and watching a movie, all of which can, but do not necessarily, lead to trance. One of my favorite writers on the subject, Stephen Gilligan, Ph.D., focuses on the properties of trance, such as time and space distortion, suggestibility, lack of awareness of surroundings, suspension of critical faculties, and effortless, uninhibited expression. One can also note the physical changes that often accompany trance, particularly the internally-focused type, in which the breathing deepens, the body is immobile, the facial folds lose prominence as they relax, and the eyes move rapidly beneath the lids.

A BRIEF EXAMPLE OF A TRANCE

Does that make it real? Of course not. Trance is an experience, not a description. So try this:

> Close your eyes.
> Focus on your breathing.
> All your awareness
> On the sensation of the air
> Moving in and out of your body.
> If a thought comes into your mind,
> Let it just float away

Like clouds passing before the sun
Or raindrops sliding down a windowpane.

Come back to your breath.
Become one with your breath.
Observe what is occurring
As the breath moves in and out of your body,
To your chest,
To your abdomen,
To your neck and cheeks and face,
Until,
Eventually,
You feel as if you are
Being breathed.
That's right,
Stay that way,
Focusing on your breath.
So peaceful, so safe.
Then slowly come back.

Now, that's a trance.

TRANCE: USES AND PROPERTIES

Trance is about absorption, the types of absorption, the properties of absorption. Central to the relationship between trance and
absorption is the notion that trance is not aware of itself. This
underscores that in trance, we alter the level of activity of our left
brain, the part of us that self-consciously keeps track of what and
how we are doing. It tells us that to whatever degree we are
absorbed in our experience, the moment we become aware of our
absorption, that absorption lessens. Trance is our natural way of
accessing and amplifying our right-brained nonverbal abilities,
the abilities that handle all the more complex learning and performing we do. Hypnosis, or self-hypnosis, is the process by

which we learn to access these abilities in a more conscious and reliable manner.

The importance of trance is immediately apparent when we look at a fundamental comparison drawn from cognitive testing research. Our left-brain consciousness can hold three items in mind at once and can process about nine bits of information per second. Our right brain can hold an infinite number of visually represented items in mind at once (a picture is worth a thousand words) and can process thirty bits of information per second. When we recruit our nonverbal trance abilities, we magnify the complexity and depth of our understanding immeasurably.

The first and foremost use of trance is simply to clear the mind of needless verbal worrying and to allow the body to heal and relax. The body knows very well how to do this if its circuits aren't being excessively aroused by an overdeveloped judging voice. We just aren't used to shutting that voice off, certainly not in today's dot-com, cell-phone, get-it-done-yesterday world. At its very essence, trance induction is instruction in occupying the goal-directed self long enough for awareness to center on various libraries of underappreciated, nonverbal knowings.

The second important use of trance is to rearrange the relationships among the various parts of the self, to get the planner talking to the doers and the feelers, to make an integrated, efficient system for choosing and executing behaviors.

TRANCE AND STUCKNESS

Trance is a wonderful tool for treating stuckness because it can be used so effectively to address all three strands of causation. When your stuckness is about ADD, trance can work to create powerful, nonverbal, right-brained systems for enhancing executive functioning, systems that can more than compensate for the underlying neurophysiological deficit. In a depressed stuckness, the question of medication is primary. However, trance can be enormously helpful in the treatment and prophylaxis of stress-related panic depressions and also substance abuse-related depressions (and for substance abuse in general, by the way), which so depend on a reintegration of the cut-off parts of the self.

Where trance is the indisputable mainstay of treatment, however, is in the dissociative disorders. Disorganization, procrastination, and the avoidance of mental work are not, in adults, only manifestations of ADD as a neurophysiological problem but also the consequences of a dissociative condition, a disjunction of left-brain planning functions from right-brain feeling and doing functions. Although I am not the first to claim that dissociation is fundamentally about the left-right brain relationship (a vast literature exists on dissociation, and some define it more narrowly), I am convinced that dissociation has been vastly underappreciated as an operative factor in the genesis of a wide range of conditions. It follows, then, that trance is likewise a tremendously underutilized treatment technique. Safe, efficient, and cost-effective, trance training is the therapeutic wave of the future.

HYPNOSIS OR SELF-HYPNOSIS: WHICH IS FOR YOU?

If trance is about discovering sources of hidden wisdom within yourself and tapping them to achieve better self-control and healthier functioning, how does one go about this process? Do you need a hypnotist, or can you do it yourself? Is it hard? How long does it take? What do you actually do?

You may want to begin your trance work with a good hypnotherapist. A hypnotherapist is a trance technician, someone who knows how to help you discover your own preferred method of arriving at an intentional trance, someone who can use trance to show you all the things you know that you didn't know you knew, all the abilities you have that you didn't know you had. On the other hand, you may do even better alone, using ideas about trance as a guide to a more private meditation. Some people find it difficult to become absorbed when there is another person in the room. It can take so very little to bring us out of trance, to amplify our left-brained self-consciousness and disrupt our right-brained state of focused attention. We are so trained to be aware of the wishes of others that sometimes, the mere presence of another person may be enough to inhibit or interrupt our trance.

That said, there is no such thing as a person who cannot be hypnotized, and there is no such thing as a person who cannot benefit from trance training if the proper trance entry is found. The goal of both the hypnotist and the self-hypnotist is to discover the trance patterns that already exist and to make them available for use and further development. If you want to try doing that on your own, the rest of this chapter will give you a start. But first, a few words about trance and safety.

All trances are, at the deepest level, voluntary, and your unconscious guards you much as a watchdog might guard your mansion. The dog may be sleeping by the gate, but if anyone unexpected comes along, he'll be up and barking in an instant. Your unconscious, or your inner self, is the same. It won't let you do anything in trance that is truly bad for you or that you wouldn't want to do at least on some level. Still, it's possible that you'll become frightened or uneasy when attempting to explore trance on your own. If that happens, or if you run into any other unusual or confusing experiences, just stop doing trance by yourself and seek a qualified practitioner versed in techniques of hypnosis or meditation.

SELF-HYPNOSIS

To undertake self-hypnosis, you'll have to make time for it, a commitment of a certain number of minutes several times a day, preferably at the same time of day. Ten minutes three times a day is great. Even three to five minutes as little as twice a day can be very helpful. Twenty minutes three times a day is an ideal rarely achieved. Upon awakening and before bed are good times. So are when arriving at a new place, starting a new task, or at any time of crisis or indecision. It's a good idea to mix trances of pure, empty-minded rest and recreation with trances of more active exploratory growth, so try to make time for both.

Whenever you can, take this time for yourself in a quiet, safe setting where you are unlikely to be interrupted. Close the door, turn off the phone. The more regularity you can achieve in timing and setting, the easier the process will be, but any time, any place can work. Sometimes, I pull over in my car. Some patients actually find the subway, with all its white noise, quite conducive. But don't miss your stop! Just do something, as often and as regularly as possible.

Recordings are not necessary for self-hypnosis. Thousands of wonderful hypnosis, meditation, and guided imagery audio files are available, and a Google search can prove overwhelming. Recording your own voice is the simplest method. It can also be helpful in choosing and refining trance-entry techniques and later in developing growth and integration exercises.

THE GREAT DIVIDE: THOSE WHO SEE VERSUS THOSE WHO FEEL

The difficulty in trance induction, if there is one, usually lies in the use of the wrong imaginative modality. By "imaginative modality," I mean the sort of inner experience — visual, kinesthetic, auditory, gustatory, what have you — that most easily absorbs and narrows the attention of a particular person. As you begin to create your own routine for structured self-absorption, your first task is to discover your own most natural entry into trance.

Try this. Close your eyes and see your mother's face. Now see a room in your home, and look around. If you can see these images easily, if you can manipulate them easily in time and space, you're what we'll call a Type A, a visualizer.

Now try this. Hold out your hands, palms up, and think about a pulsating wave of feeling moving rhythmically from one hand to the other. Feel it moving back and forth, and then elongate and accentuate it. If you can feel it strongly, you're a Type B, a feeler.

A lot of people are Type A and a lot are Type B with a strong secondary A (Type AB), and all of these folks will have an easy time using the first induction sequence described below. For people who are only Type B, people who can't see the image of their mother or home in a sustainable way (I'm like that myself), the second sequence will probably be more effective. The essential thing to grasp is that if you are not someone who can easily imagine things visually, persisting in the attempt will only serve to arouse your self-conscious left-brain judging systems and ultimately defeat the purpose. This does not mean that trance is not possible for you, only that you'll most likely have more success with nonvisual paths of access.

THE FOUR-STEP PROCESS

In trance, we have two objectives. The first is cultivating entry into a relaxed yet alert state of inner absorption. The second is to use this state in a basic and then more complex, exploratory manner.

Below is a typical four-step trance pathway for Type A and Type AB. Most people find it easier to follow the steps if they close their eyes, but others feel it works just as well to keep their eyes open and focus their gaze on a particular spot.

1. Focus on your breath. Feel it going in and out, and observe its effects on your body, as described earlier in this chapter. Do this for about one to two minutes.

2. While part of your mind remains aware of your breathing, imagine a staircase, in as much detail as possible, and see, feel, and hear yourself descending that staircase. The farther down you go, the more relaxed you become, the less aware you are of your surroundings. Take your time fully imagining the descent, for about one to three minutes.

3. At the bottom of the stairs is an archway leading into a cavern, and off to one side in the cavern is a pulsing life force. With a part of your mind still aware of your breathing, imagine this pulsing force fully. It is the pulse of life. See it, feel it, hear it. Slow it down, slower, and slower, finding a rhythm that is soothing and comfortable for you. Do this for as long as you like, imagining the pulse in a variety of ways until you find one that suits you.

4. Leaving a part of yourself behind to focus on the pulse,
even as you have been leaving a part of yourself behind
attending to your breath, you can then find yourself outside the cavern in one of your favorite spots, such as a
beach or a mountain lake. Imagine it fully. See the sky and
the water, smell the air, feel the breeze, and the warmth of
the sun. Scan your body, relaxing each part. Then, still in
that place, focus on your breathing, and go through the
whole process once more.

Repeat these steps again and again, as many times as necessary
to clear your mind of worry and intent and to fill it with the experience of your body in the moment, its breath, its pulse, its life.

The whole sequence should take about ten minutes at first,
and then it can be condensed more and more as your trance skills
grow. With a little practice, you should find it easy to arrive at and
recognize the state you're looking for, often described as a restful
feeling of floating. This state is a platform from which many journeys can be launched. For the fourth step, the beach and body
scan is only one possibility, a possibility that lends itself to a repetitive, deepening loop. Other locations, such as a meadow or a
conference room, lend themselves to exploring interactions with
other parts of the self.

If you're a Type B feeler, you'll probably have more success
with the following four-step trance pathway. Notice that these
instructions are devoid of requests to see things, because such
requests would only interfere with the process in a purely Type B
person.

1. Focus on your breath. Focus all of your awareness on the
sensation of the air moving in and out of your nostrils.
Elongate your breath and slow it down. Imagine a balloon
between your belly button and your spine. Fill up that
balloon with your breath, and then slowly let the air out
of the balloon. This is called diaphragmatic breathing, and

it turns on all the relaxational systems in the body. Spend a minute or two on this

2. While part of your mind remains aware of your breathing, rest your hands on your thighs, palms up, and imagine and feel a rhythmic pulsation in your hands. When I first started doing this, I would focus all my attention on one index finger, and I would feel and then amplify a wave of tingling pulse in that finger. I've found in recent years that an alternating pulse, moving back and forth from one hand to the other, is even more effective for me. Choose whatever works for you. This sort of pulsation or wave of feeling can be localized in almost any body part, although the hands, the feet, the fingers, the toes, the lips, and the nose seem the easiest for most folks.

3. Remaining aware of your breathing and of the pulsing sensation, imagine a band of light across your toes, not seeing it, but feeling it. Imagine the area under the band becoming warm, comfortable, and relaxed, then allow the band to slowly move up your body.

4. Now imagine that you are lying, with your eyes closed, in a safe and comfortable place, perhaps on a mountainside or beach. Feel what it's like to be there. Feel the breeze and the sunshine on your face, the emotions of contentment and safety.

The same as with the first sequence, repeat this sequence as necessary so that it absorbs you fully in your experience of the moment.

When using these sequences, or any of the literally thousands of possible variations, you may find yourself becoming distracted. This is not at all uncommon. At first, thoughts and worries will intrude frequently. When thoughts come into your mind, let them float away like clouds passing before the sun or raindrops sliding down a windowpane. The key is not to hold on to them, not to chase them, but to return to your breath — the breath is always there — and to your other steps (layers, you might say). Be sure to set some specific period of time (five, ten, or fifteen minutes) during which you will continue to make this effort, even if it is difficult or frustrating.

The fact that the above trance sequences each contain four steps is key. The left brain can process only three items at a time. What we are essentially doing in these exercises is occupying the left brain with three tasks (breathing, descending the stairs, and sensing the life force in the first example) so that when we add the fourth step, we automatically default into a right-brain state. That's really the secret.

There are many different things that can be focused on in steps 2 and 3 of both sequences. Some people find it best to listen to something, such as music or waves or a metronome. Some respond better to smells or tastes. Bodily sensations, including movement, position, touch, and temperature, can also be the objects of internal focus. Spatial, schematic sorts of imagining are similar but not identical to the visual, and they are often strong in people who cannot visualize easily. For people who are visual, the range of images, and the emotional content that can accompany them, is vast.

THE FELT SENSE

As you become more adept at designing trance sequences, do not forget about the felt sense. A felt sense is a complex yet clear sort of intuition that combines physical and emotional feelings with conceptual knowledge. Our universal ability to read emotion in each other's faces is one example. The ability to hear the tonal meaning that lies beyond the words we speak or to feel the atmosphere in a room are other felt senses. Perhaps the best example of a felt sense is what it feels like when we imagine ourselves talking to, or even just in the presence of, a particular person. For instance, imagine that your head is lying in your mother's lap. Then, imagine that it is lying in your lover's lap. See the difference? Felt senses like this can be powerful foci of absorption, and often, a useful step 2 or 3 involves becoming absorbed in the face, voice, manner, or tone of an important "other."

The most powerful sorts of steps 2 and 3 are often those that combine multiple modalities. Descending a staircase is a perfect example, as is lying on a beach. A good beginning trance step is scattershot, hitting as many types of inner foci as possible in the hope that one will stick. Your job is to determine what sticks for you. Test your imagination and see what absorbs you the easiest. Step 1 is always breathing. Experiment with various steps 2 and 3 until you find the routines that work best for you. Then stick with those routines. Once you have a reliable trance-induction routine, you will find a whole range of experiences opening up for you. In the above sequences, we used a peaceful physical location as step 4, vividly imagined to allow for a clear mind and a resting body, but there is a virtually endless spectrum of possibilities, including body trances, wisdom or vision trances, and trances involving meetings with inner selves (inner guides, inner children, or inner parents). Each type of trance represents a range of trance foci for step 4, from the very simple and general to the quite detailed, and each can be pitched toward Type A visualizers or Type B feelers. Step 4 is where you can really customize your routine according to your intent at the moment. Once you've mastered entering the trance state, you will find no end to the creativity you can use while inventing new, growth-enhancing inner experiences.

———◆◈◆———

In the chapters that follow, I will describe different varieties of step 4 as they apply to the different strands of stuckness. There are also many good books that offer dozens and dozens of hypnotic metaphors that you can use to create a step 4 for every purpose. You will find some of these books listed in the Reference List at the back of the book.

CHAPTER 7

The Treatment of Dissociation

Our purpose overall in this volume is to demonstrate the complicated ways in which depression, dissociation, and ADD interact to cause ineffective living. It is also to illustrate how these interwoven strands of causation can be addressed.

Dissociation is common, variable in its presentation, and sometimes surprisingly easy to fix. The trick to its treatment is recognizing the disorder's presence. Once its presence has been acknowledged, its treatment is as deceptively simple as it is remarkably powerful. What its treatment really amounts to is the personification of the parts of the self. When we personify a part, a function, a behavior that doesn't make sense, we treat it as if it were a person of its own — a whole person who needs to be understood properly and negotiated with skillfully.

As it turns out, inner selves come in three main types — inner children, inner parents, and inner guides/alter egos. The techniques for dealing with these three main types all work best with the visually inclined, but they also can be adapted somewhat for individuals with other primary sense modalities, such as spatial, tactile, or kinesthetic.

Once I have determined which conditions exist in a given patient, I think about therapy in terms of three levels of intervention: (1) information, or what is often called psycho-education, (2) medication, and (3) integration, by which I mean psychotherapy that is grounded in, but not limited to, training in the balanced access and utilization of the left and the right brains. Some of the psychoeducational material that I usually present has already been discussed in Chapters 3 through 5. Very often, I give my patients psychoeducational material in conjunction with teaching them trance-utilization techniques, such as when I instruct people with ADD in time management. A lot of the psychoeducation is about medication and what it can and can't do. The three levels of intervention are woven together just as much as the three conditions.

In my practice, psychoeducation is a combination of direct instruction from me and assigned reading (sometimes called bibliotherapy). Although some direct self-help literature is available for patients with the more profound sorts of dissociation, such as multiple personality disorder, very little can be found on the middling, less dramatic or severe forms of dissociation we are talking about here. At the end of this chapter, I will discuss some of the more general, indirectly applicable reading material that I often recommend for people struggling with dissociation.

In Chapter 5, I attempted to explain the nature and causes of dissociation, and when I present that same material to patients, I find that they usually understand the left brain-right brain material fairly readily. The idea of multiple parts of the self that may or may not be working well with one another also seems to be pretty easy to swallow. I usually employ the metaphor of a small town with a fire at one end and a reservoir filled with water at the other end, explaining that what we're doing here is laying down some pipe, making some connections, so that we can get what is needed where it's needed when it's needed. People preparing themselves for these exercises need to understand that all the parts necessary to make the desired changes are available inside of them. It's just a question of arranging the pieces to make a new and better shape. This is usually all the psychoeducation required to prepare dissociated patients to participate with me in the exercises described below.

INNER-CHILD EXERCISES

We've already talked about two inner-child exercises. Chapter 2 presented an inner-child technique that I used with Cathy, the dot-commer with the unreliable boyfriend, and Chapter 5 contains the same sort of exercise in the discussion of K., the fiftyish commitment-phobe.

Inner-child exercises are about nurturance. Whatever the situation that caused the personality fragment to form, and whatever the emotion trapped in that childlike fragment, the underlying task is to mobilize the part of the person that loves or has ever loved a child and to bring that part into contact with the part that is needlessly suffering.

In American culture, it's not uncommon for adults who gaze upon a troubled three- or four-year-old in the company of an adult to sympathize easily with the child, to wonder what's going on and want to help. When I get my patients to "see" themselves at the age at which they first suffered any particular untoward emotion, they almost universally find that they see themselves quite differently now than they did then. They realize that they are far more capable of accepting, approving of, and loving their brave, vulnerable, struggling little selves now than they were at the time.

The first time I encountered these techniques, they were called "interactive imagery re-parenting exercises," and I think that the name really cuts to the essence. What we are attempting to do is offer the trapped child the nurturing behavior it required at the time but did not receive from the parents. The fact is that you, the patient, are the only one capable of reaching that cut-off fragment of your self and doing this essential re-parenting. Your parents are no longer the people they were when you were injured, if they are even still alive, so they can't really do it. Nor is anyone else very likely to be able to bring out that part of you unless they are trained to do so.

I first encountered re-parenting exercises in a seminar handout written by Dr. Richard Landis, a neo-Ericksonian therapist from Southern California. Dr. Landis recommends imagining a meadow in a vivid, multi-sensory way, focusing on unresolved issues and feelings from the past and then looking over to the side of the meadow to see a child with the same issues and feelings sitting on a bench or a fallen tree. Of course, the child we see is us, at the initial moments in which we felt the emotions that continue to trouble us. Dr. Landis suggests imagining the child's hair and clothing in detail, and then making contact with the child. He instructs us to tell the child that we are "him, all grown up." Dr. Landis warns that, at first, the child may not believe us, but we know so much about him or her that after a little while, the child can't help but accept that we are who we say we are.

Once we have made contact and are speaking with this part of the self, we are to provide the child with information he or she did not have at the time. Usually, this information concerns the true strengths and weakness, the foibles, the failures, and the circumstances of our parents or other caretakers. We are to specifically tell the child (1) that it's not all his or her fault, (2) that he or she did the best that was possible under the circumstances, and (3) that we will visit regularly as long as he or she needs us.

This can be a very powerful technique, and anyone who wishes to use it for growth and integration would do well to seek the knowledge and guidance of a skilled professional. If you try an inner-child exercise on your own, you may feel some powerful and unpleasant emotions, such as sadness, fear, or shame, upon making contact with an inner child. You do not need to be frightened by these feelings. Rather, stop for the time being, and then continue your exploration once you have sought appropriate guidance.

If you are reading the chapters of this book in order, you will have already read Chapter 6, which gives step-by-step instructions for creating your own relaxing trance. Before you begin an inner-child exercise, you should make sure that you have practiced relaxation often enough so that, at the very least, you can fairly easily slip into a centered state of breath focus and imagine yourself in a safe, beautiful place. As long as you are confident in your basic trance ability to clear your mind and relax your body at any moment, you can always say good-bye and leave the scene if you encounter something difficult and return again later if you like.

Some individuals may need to use a structured trance/relaxation induction, a four-step plan as described in Chapter 6, if they are to visualize anything or to become absorbed in anything that they might visualize. For others, it will be as simple as closing their eyes and looking in the meadow for the child. Still others will never "see" anything, no matter how much preparatory trance they get into, but they may well "feel" the presence of the child on their lap or "hear" the child's voice.

What we are actually doing here is creating a situation in which the right and the left brains are being used at the same time. When I guide a patient into connecting with different parts of the self in this way, I always use the phrase "and when you meet the child, you will feel that you are both him and you at the same time." This duality, the "both-and" instead of "either-or," is an essential feature of right-brain thinking. At the same time that you feel a surge of the right-brain feelings from which you've been hiding, another part of you will be with the child reassuring him. The child self gets both distance and compassion from the "older, outer" self. It is this very combination of distance and compassion that the child originally lacked and that repeated contact with the "outer," everyday grown-up will provide.

Whether you see a therapist or not, it's a good idea to use the interactive trances regularly and meet with the inner child. Do it on your own more often than you do with the therapist. A therapist is better for meeting new parts of the self and for setting up and reinforcing the parameters of the meetings you will have with these newly contacted parts. You must, however, spend sufficient time with the child on your own for the techniques to be as effective as possible. The point is to stay with the strong feelings you may encounter instead of running away from them. You want to feel these feelings, to tolerate and focus on them. An overwhelming majority of the time, if you can tolerate the feelings for even a few minutes, two things will become clear. First, the feelings weren't all that terrible, horrible, awful, intolerable anyway. That is, you've probably been through a lot worse since then, much bigger disappointments, and you've handled them. It's just that you were so little then, and you knew so little. Second, it's actually pretty easy to cheer up four- or five-year-olds. You don't have to talk to them a lot. It's not really about logic. It's about stroking and murmuring. It's about telling them they're good, and giving them Chunky bars (remember those?), and playing catch, and pushing them on a swing (because, after all, the meadow has swings, doesn't it?). I like to tell folks that a little babbling brook runs through the meadow, and it has a sandy bottom and a lot of overhanging trees that make the light a lovely, cool green. You and the child can take off your shoes, and the two of you can walk upstream, talking about things, the child telling you about the way things were, you telling the child about all that's happened since. After a while, you'll come to a waterfall with a pool at the bottom, and alongside the pool you'll find a checkered cloth with a picnic basket and some fluffy white towels that have been warming in the sun, and you just jump into the water, splashing around together.

Well, you get the idea. You have to be creative, use your imagination, and remember that the meadow is a magic place. The only boundaries are the ones you put there. Take the child to the circus, to the zoo, to the ballpark. Take the child anywhere you've ever had a good time or anywhere you think you would have liked to have had a good time.

You don't really have to solve the problem for the child. You just have to make the child feel differently. You have to help the child let go of the tension. You have to be there regularly, as long as you're needed, sharing the wisdom and the experience that were never previously available to this shamed, sad, angry, or frightened child.

Doing this exercise once is not going to fix whatever problem you wish to solve. When a person first attains sobriety in Alcoholics Anonymous (AA) or another twelve-step program, they are told "ninety days, ninety meetings" — that is, make a meeting every day for ninety days. I say the same thing. Once you make the initial contact, you must meet with the child inside — or the children inside, as the case may be — on a regular basis. Twice a day for five minutes is ideal, but five minutes three times a week will do as a minimum. It doesn't really matter what you imagine as long as it's loving and positive. It's the accumulated time spent with the left and the right brains turned on at the same time that creates the new connections and allows for different feelings and better self control.

What will happen if you do this — and I have seen it happen a hundred times — is that after a few weeks, the sense of separateness will begin to diminish. The child will essentially disappear as a separate entity except when you specifically call him or her. In situations that previously would have upset you or made you uncomfortable, you will now be aware of your previous feelings, but more as a part of a lot of other attitudes. You will not be overwhelmed by them. Instead, you will shortly be able to use all of your life's experiences and accumulated self-soothing and self-care abilities to find a more comfortable attitude, one that reflects your current reality instead of your painful past. By meeting with the child, you've changed the child, added to the child, made the child a whole self with a particular emphasis instead of a fragmented self with a narrow, exclusive focus and inadequate resources.

The Case of R.
R. was a tall, bearish fellow with dirty-blond hair who first came to me when he was beginning school to become a physician's assistant after more than a decade of riding an ambulance as an emergency medical technician. R. felt pretty bad about himself. He was overweight, and he had a habit of seducing and dating four or five heavy and heavily dependent maternal women at one time, none of whom he ultimately wanted to be with. He doubted he could do the schoolwork for which he'd signed on, he felt trapped by his relationships, and he was starting to feel depressed

in a way he recognized from a previous episode during which he had taken Prozac.

R., it turned out, had addictive, chaotic parents. His mother was addicted to intramuscular opiates, and his alcoholic, angry father had abandoned the household when R. was nine or so, only to return in R.'s late adolescence. While his dad was gone, R. was molested by a "kindly" neighbor who his addled mom was only too happy to have "looking after" him.

The reason I mention R. is that we found three separate suffering fragments in him, one from age eight, who was sent to the pharmacy to get his increasingly frantic mother her "medicine"; another from age twelve, who was being molested by the scoutmaster across the street; and a third from age sixteen, a geeky, graceless, ostracized junior in high school. We discovered each of these guys as we looked at behaviors and attitudes that clearly did not fit into R.'s current reality. When we tried to find out why he doubted his academic abilities, we found the eight-year-old who felt less-than because he knew his mother was a junkie. When we looked for the reason R. felt attached to overweight, maternal women, we found the child who had been molested and who felt it was at least partly his fault, who doubted his heterosexuality. When we looked at his inability to enjoy his accomplishments, to take vacations, to pursue the things he enjoyed, we found the sixteen-year-old who mistrusted himself so completely that he had stopped using his own pleasure as a guide in making decisions about his behavior.

What we wound up doing after a while was having campfires with all the kids, roasting marshmallows and having a group hug, and making the different boys nurture each other, too.

As I usually do in these situations, I asked R. to imagine his love as a radiant energy that emanated from his body and that he could see as an aura of colored light surrounding himself and the children. He imagined himself and the children with that aura of love, that radiant energy, and then I asked him to turn up the heat, to turn up the volume, until the children could feel the heat, the intensity, of the enveloping love.

Next, I asked R. to pick up each child before he left, to reassure him that he would soon return, and to be specific about when. As he picked up a child, I instructed him to look the child right in the eye and say, together with the child, "Now . . . now . . . now, we're in this together, now we're in this together" He was to repeat this solemnly several times while maintaining firm eye contact with the child.

In general, if you successfully perform this exercise for a month, if you create a warm bond with the child so that it is pleasurable for you to be together, you will find a whole range of positive emotions becoming available, emotions that were trapped behind a blockade that kept out sadness, fear, and shame. Just remember that your imaginings in the meadow (or whatever place you choose to use) do not have to be limited by what actually happened, but rather should reflect your most idealized romantic yearnings, the best that might have been. When the inner child is accepted and fed positive imaginings, all of the innocence, wonder, curiosity, and excitement of childhood can return.

Variations for the Less Visual

As we have said, a substantial minority of individuals lack adequate visual abilities to perform the exercises as described. For these folks, a further discussion and some recommended reading are called for.

First, the reading. The book is called *The Courage to Love* (New York: W.W. Norton and Company, 1997), and it's by another neo-Ericksonian, Stephen Gilligan, Ph.D. Dr. Gilligan studied personally with Dr. Erickson, and his volume on hypnotherapy, *Therapeutic Trances* (New York: Brunner/Mazel, 1987), has perhaps influenced my thinking and the direction of my career more profoundly than anything else I can think of. *The Courage to Love* describes self-relations therapy. It is explicitly about reconnecting the left and the right brains, and it uses language that is friendly and accessible to the less visually inclined.

Dr. Gilligan opens by comparing the "outer everyday, cognitive" self and the "inner bodily somatic" self, contrasting these two selves using the two German words "essen" and "fressen." "Essen" means "to eat," as in to dine, as in to sit down and eat with attendant manners. "Fressen" means "to feed," as in to devour, to eat in a more animalistic, id-like sense. Dr. Gilligan uses this contrast elegantly to bring into relief some of the distinctions and differences between left- and right-brain functioning. In *Therapeutic Trances*, he lists more than thirty word pairs that have been used at different times to make this contrast clearer.

Once he makes the distinction between the outer, essen-like, left-brained self and the inner, fressen-like, right-brained self, Gilligan talks about the idea that in every life, in every childhood, in every development, the inner self is either blessed or cursed by those responsible for it. Blessings are like water to the soil of life; curses are like salt. To the extent that we are unwittingly the victims of the curses of those who care for us, and later the victims of our own curses, we need to make contact with our inner self and, with courage, we need to reject the curses, accept love, and bless the deeper self.

In Dr. Gilligan's view, once we are aware of the inner-outer construction, we can simply close our eyes and seek contact with the inner self. Dr. Gilligan assumes that contact can and will come in any possible sort of internal sensory experience, including the visual, but also auditory (as a dialogue with a voice), visceral (as gut feelings), kinesthetic (as a movement or position), spatial (like a map or a Venn diagram), sexual, spiritual, musical, or any other nonverbal experience.

The Case of W.

W. was a lawyer, married, with no kids but with two alcoholic parents. She came to see me six or seven years ago with a mild serotonin depression and a lifelong, intermittent drinking problem, at that time active. W. was taking, and still is taking, a small dose of Paxil, which kept away a certain kind of sluggish darkness and obsessiveness that plagued her when she was stressed. However, it didn't stop her from drinking.

What stopped her (and she's been sober for more than ten years now in spite of a major loss or two) was a Gilliganesque inner-child exercise. W. was decidedly not visual, but she had been in AA several times before and had found that she liked meditation and Buddhism. There had been times in her life when she had attended meditation sessions regularly, and we found that we were able to develop a nonvisual relaxation technique for her using one-pointed breathing, chi energy alternating between her hands, yoga chakra energy moving up her spine, and a warm feeling of contentment created by resting comfortably in a safe place. This four-step process could take her to a place of comfort that previously had been much more difficult for her to reach.

Once in this state, W. thought about how she felt just before she decided she was going to get a drink, and she thought about making contact with the inner part responsible for that decision. The frustrated, tired, sad part that answered when she called said she was seven years old. I already knew that W., the eldest of three siblings, was a parentified child who, classically, felt as a child that if only she could behave well enough, if only she could be good enough, that Mom and Dad wouldn't drink, argue, and pass out. Although W. could not see the child, and any instructions to do so would make her lose whatever sense of contact she did have, W. could decidedly feel the seven-year-old in her lap. She was able to have a sense of stroking the child's hair and of cradling the child's head on her shoulder. She was able to ask questions and get answers, even if the answers weren't always in words but more like waves of feelings and fleeting images. Maybe the term "felt sense" is again the more appropriate. What happened is hard to describe, but it was very real and quite compelling.

W. was able to nurture and soothe this part of herself because she was relaxed enough not to question the ways in which the contact was made. About a year into therapy, within a few weeks of learning these techniques (and just after she had a several-month relapse of drinking), she was able to make contact reliably by herself — to soothe the child when needed, to carry a sense of the girl around with her whenever she was enjoying herself as well. Slowly, they began to merge.

W. remains sober. She was able to use what I call a sense of place, a sense that is very physical and also spatial, a sense with a huge range, one that encompasses the feeling you have just knowing that other particular people are or aren't in the house, to the sense you might get when feeling the stillness and isolation of some remote scenic vista.

INNER-PARENT EXERCISES

If inner-child exercises are about nurturance, then inner-parent exercises are about assertiveness and the shedding of inhibitions. It turns out that there is a man, an elderly Kashmiri Indian, who lives in a suburb of New York City and who has devoted his life to developing inner-parent visualization exercises. His name is Dr. Akhtar Ahsen, and he is one of the most learned and impressive professionals I have ever met, and I have passed through some very fine institutions of higher learning in my time. Dr. Ahsen writes continually and has produced over twenty volumes on the uses of image and myth in understanding and transforming human behavior.

Dr. Ahsen's seminal work is the Eidetic Parents Test. The test is a two-hour, completely standardized set of visual prompts and accompanying questions. In its purest form, as currently administered by Dr. Ahsen, the prompts are read by one of Dr. Ahsen's nonprofessional assistants, who records every verbal response to the prompts verbatim. Dr. Ahsen then reads the transcript and prepares an individualized set of visualizations.

The first prompt in the series (which includes twenty-six prompts) asks you to see your parents standing next to each other in front of the house in which you lived with them, and then to see each of them inside the house in their typical locations. The related questions ask how your parents stand when they are next to each other. Do they seem attached? What moods are they in? How do you feel when you see them together? What are they doing in their separate places inside the house? How do you feel when you are alone with each of them?

The prompts are very systematic and lead you through a thorough examination of your nervous system to look for parentally related inhibitions. You see each parent give and take, each parent run. You look into each of their gazes, and you listen to each of their voices. You watch them breathe, you look at their hearts and circulatory systems. In its most complete form, it has you look at their skin, their brains, and their genitals.

I met Dr. Ahsen about ten years ago, when he was already well into his late seventies but still as robust and alert as a much younger man. I had heard his name mentioned repeatedly over the years in different places as a particular expert on visualization. Dr. Ahsen's techniques can be very powerful, but I do not think they will ever be very widely used. The complete test is cumbersome, formal, and perhaps off-putting to most potential patients, and unfortunately, Dr. Ahsen has not been successful enough in packaging his material in such a manner as to catch the sustained interest of either therapists or patients. I find Dr. Ahsen to be a majestic figure, but if I say that he is an old-school intellectual who seems to have walked out of an 1890 European drawing room, I may begin to give you the flavor of the man. He has collected thousands of detailed case studies illustrating his techniques and has written many, many volumes, but unfortunately, few of his books are easy reads even for seasoned professionals.

I was very fortunate to be able to visit with Dr. Ahsen twice, for several hours each time, and because my contact with him and his methods so altered my thinking about and practice of parental visualizations, I will attempt to summarize briefly the crux of what I took away from those contacts. Of course, it is impossible for me to do justice to the depth of Dr. Ahsen's work in just a few pages. If you are intrigued or puzzled, there is a vast body of Dr. Ahsen's writing that will reward the persistent.

Basically, what I learned from Dr. Ahsen is that you have to see yourself resolving your problems with your parents, and you have to see your parents resolving their problems with themselves and with each other, even if these resolutions never occurred or never could have occurred in real life. You need to do this in order to free your nervous system from the effects of these problems.

Dr. Ahsen taught me not to be too literal about the word "see." Dr. Ahsen asks you to answer his structured questions as best you can, even if the visual images are neither clear nor stable. The first time I took the test, I discovered that, even though I had my usual not-very-clear, random, uncontrolled, heat photo-like kaleidoscopic glimpses type of visualization, I could nevertheless quite easily answer all sorts of questions about the content of those images. I had been visualizing all along; I was just quibbling with the cinematography. If I accepted the images as they came, they brought me a lot of information, as they will for you, too.

Dr. Ahsen says that images are our most natural way of recording information, and that all images are recorded along with the complex emotions that go with them. He talks about a natural sequence of impulse, tension, and relaxation, and says that images of situations in which the tension created by an impulse was unresolved are the ones that retain excess power over us and deter us from self-actualization. He believes that the majority of our inhibitions and psychosomatic illnesses come from just such unresolved tension and its continued recurrence in the present, as we are reminded of and relive our frustrations and disappointments.

The inner-parent exercises are designed to release the tension that is held in these images. The exercise that I adapted for myself after my experiences with Dr. Ahsen begins with seeing your parents in the house where you spent the bulk of your childhood, in the places where they usually spent their time. You sit with each parent in turn, just looking at him or her. For example, you sit with your father in his characteristic location in the house and examine how you feel being with him. If you feel ignored or criticized or unloved or anything similar, you need to get in his face and confront him, demanding what you need.

Dr. Ahsen's instructions in his original transcript are quite graphic at this juncture. He says to "jump up and down, to pound on your parent's chest, to slam the cabinet doors and smash the pots and pans if necessary." He tells you to expect to have to fight hard to get your parent's attention and understanding, for your parent will defend his or her point of view. He says that you will have to endure and fight through waves of guilt, despair, disappointment, fear, and rage, and you will want to give up but you must not. If you persevere, eventually your parent will pay attention. Even as your parent argues with you, you may notice that he or she is sort of smiling, glad to see you fighting for yourself so energetically.

Often, your parents will have issues and difficulties of their own that prevented them from giving you what you needed. In the second phase of this exercise, using the same force and perseverance, you need to confront your parents with their own problems — for example, drinking, rage, shyness, coldness, distance, or an unfulfilling marriage or career. As in the first part of the exercise, they will defend themselves, and you will experience discouragement and despair. But you can prevail, and they can begin to act on their problems in your visualization and you can see them solve their problems.

The third section involves seeing both parents together and again banging the cabinets and jumping up and down, doing whatever it takes to make them deal with the reality of each other as they never did but should have.

Of terrific importance here is that you need to imagine these scenarios even though your parents may have never done these things and probably never would have. Remember that you are not really dealing with your parents. You are dealing with the powerful models of them that you constructed in your mind over the years.

Even though these experiences with parents are imagined, they can have very powerful effects. Dr. Ahsen once asked me the following question, and I ask it of you: "What is the difference between the effect upon an individual of an experienced and then remembered event and the effect upon that individual of a vividly imagined and then remembered event?" The answer, of course, is that there may be no difference, so consequently, the effect of creative imaginings may be profound indeed. In these dialogues with your parents, you will need to see your parents as they might have been under the best of circumstances. The crux of the exercise is for you to assert and make known the perceptions that you had at the time, and to insist that your parents act upon them in order to become the parents you required but did not get.

Of course, the inner-child and inner-parent exercises are not as distinct from each other as I have drawn them. They are two sides of the same coin. Almost inevitably, when you interact with your parents in this way, you will feel yourself to be a child, as you did then. In the inner-child exercises, an everyday grown-up self interacts in a nurturing manner with an upset child who is also him or her. In the inner-parent exercises, an inner child demands nurturance from a resistant parent who is also him or her.

One of the ways in which I have modified Dr. Ahsen's work for myself is that I often combine these exercises, essentially making a triad of an inner child, an inner parent, and an observing inner guide (the same one who went looking for the inner child to begin with). The parent can be brought into the same meadow where we met the child, and the same caveats about imagination and creativity apply.

Three Parental Journeys

Y. is a woman I have seen intermittently over many years. She is uneducated but street smart, and she has suffered from a range of anxious symptoms over the period I have known her. The interesting thing about Y. is that she is an extremely gifted trance subject, and over the years, she has repeatedly gotten herself into what Dr. Gilligan calls bad trances. In the same way that the deep focus of trance can be used to train a person to associate certain ideas with relaxation, many patients use a similar kind of focus to create negative associations with anxiety and fearfulness.

In the particular interaction I want to describe, Y. was complaining that she had, and had always had, a problem with sex. It seems that every time she started to become intimate, she would imagine her mother looking at her, and she would freeze up. I used a very simple visualization exercise in which I asked Y. to imagine herself in bed and then to see her mother standing across the room. I asked Y. to imagine a force field around her, a glowing blue aura that looked like the invisible fields they used to show on *Star Trek* when someone was locked in the brig. I told her that whenever something touched the field, it would make a buzz-zap sound, like a bug zapper, and bounce the intruder back into the distance. I asked Y. to see her mother shrinking, shrinking, shrinking, until she was about the size of a bee or a wasp, then to give her wings as if she were an insect. Y. saw her now-tiny mother being bounced back by the force field again and again. Of course, by this time, Y. was laughing and laughing at the image of her mother buzzing about helplessly, looking like Jeff Goldblum in *The Fly*, a little head on a wasp's body, attacking the force field over and over again, like a miniature kamikaze. That was really all it took. Y. never saw or felt mom in the bedroom again.

E. was quite a bit more complex. When I met him, he was in his early fifties, a lawyer in private practice, and had been suffering from a poorly treated stress depression for almost a decade. He was one of those unfortunate souls who were not treated with antidepressants that matched their symptoms. (In E.'s case, the symptom was awakening at 4:30 A.M. with a nameless but intense feeling of dread that lasted well into midmorning, no matter the circumstances of the day.) Instead, E. had been given the flavor of the month, in his case Prozac. He'd been on Prozac for five years with minimal, if any, improvement. I quickly switched him to nortriptyline, after which he improved dramatically.

Of course, as is often the case, once the most prominent and debilitating symptom was removed, other issues came to light. E. was an intelligent man, renowned for the quality of his appeals, but he was a terrible procrastinator and pretty much always had been. Although he had performed well in college and law school, he left each and every assignment to the last minute, and he continued this habit in his legal practice. He was chronically tense and chronically berating himself, which played a significant part in the development of the stress depression that he'd been suffering with for almost a decade before we met.

As you may have guessed, E. also had ADD (as did both his children). This explained a lot both about his work habits and about what had been going on in his family all these years (another great source of tension). Mrs. E., who did not have ADD, struggled to deal with and understand her bright but not very organized or reliable brood. I prescribed Ritalin for E., and although he became somewhat better able to concentrate when he finally got down to work, he still procrastinated terribly.

So, yes, E. is one of our paradigmatic cases, depressed, battling ADD, and dissociated when he continued to procrastinate despite medication for both the ADD and the depression. We began to try inner-child exercises. It so happened that E. had had an interesting relationship with his father, by then deceased. E.'s mom was the one who probably had the ADD. His dad was a strong, physical man, not very verbal, but the kind of man who said what he would do and did what he said. E., on the other hand, was an intellectual kid, quite talkative and not very athletic. E. loved his father very much, missed him terribly, but also felt like he had always been a disappointment to him, not enough like him. It clearly continued to pained him.

What was interesting about all this, and why I bring it up at this juncture, is that the guided visualization began to work only when we included E.'s father in the exercises. E. himself was unable to influence his discouraged, distracted inner child very much until we started having meetings with his father as well. His father had been a loving man, who did, in fact, approve of E. Like many ADD kids E. needed feedback and intensity and was ashamed underneath already anyway. E. felt disapproved of and inadequate in front of his father.

Over the months that I worked with E., he was able to realize that he simply didn't like the unstructured yet heavy workload that went along with private practice law. Fortunately, he was able to arrange a job for himself within the judiciary system, and the task that he simply could not get himself to do was wrapping up the work of his old practice as he approached the date to begin his new employment.

Once we realized that E.'s father needed to actively approve of E.'s efforts, the exercises went very smoothly. It was easy to get the three of them (dad, little E., and E.) together and to ask dad for love and help, which dad willingly gave. E. was then able to wrap up his practice. E. has now retired from the court job, he takes Ritalin occasionally, and he is no longer depressed. When he feels himself having difficulty getting down to something he must do, he calls a meeting with little E. and dad, and soon he's on his way.

One more example: D., a highly intelligent, chronically depressed woman of fifty with a nasty case of chronic fatigue syndrome and a difficult marriage. When I first met her, she was virtually housebound with panic disorder and agoraphobia, and she was dissociated almost all of the time. D. had been badly traumatized as a child by a mother who apparently suffered from some sort of chronic viral infection, although, at the time, she was thought to have, I believe, neurasthenia, which is very similar to chronic fatigue syndrome. (Interestingly, D.'s sister, who lived 2,500 miles away, seemed to have the same neurasthenic syndrome, showing, I believe the hereditary nature of chronic fatigue syndrome.)

When I met D., she had been out of the hospital for about a year after detoxification from a minor tranquilizer addiction. In D.'s case, the addiction had been entirely iatrogenic — that is, caused by doctors. She had been given Ativan — a medicine that I tell people is like three beers in a pill — for her panic attacks. When her panic kept re-emerging, the doctor kept raising the dose. This is a very bad thing to do to someone, and I think the fact that it is a common practice is one of the failures of the modern psychiatric-training system. Although I will freely give out stimulants to anyone I believe has an attentional problem, I am extremely tight to the vest with minor tranquilizers, including Valium, the prototype, and its descendants Klonopin, Ativan, and Xanax, by far the most toxic of the group. The side effects from trying to get off them feel exactly like the symptoms that caused you to go on them, often only worse, as was the case for D. When I met D., she was firmly against drugs (and still is).

D.'s depression and panic disorder weren't typical at all. She may have had a type I stress depression years back, but now she was dissociated most of the time. She didn't have an actual multiple personality disorder, but it was very close, the only difference being that the main personality had a full memory of all that transpired. D. remembered everything that happened to her, but there were large portions of each day that were spent trapped in various dysphoric childhood ego states. These trapped, resourceless ego states were what her previous doctor had been calling panic disorder, and because she was genuinely intolerant of all antidepressant medication, she had been medicated with minor tranquilizers.

My work with D. could form an entire book in itself, and in no way, shape, or form am I prepared to write that book here. By and large, D. was not the sort of person who was able to do the required re-associative work without considerable professional guidance. In brief, D.'s mother had handled her own chronic fatigue syndrome and Type II depression (the serotonin-obsessive-tired-cranky kind) poorly. She had abused little D. in a number of ways, from beating her to screaming at her, by neglecting her for many hours, and, ultimately, after suffering a more complete breakdown, by sending her away to kindly relatives for a period of time. When I met D., she was truly a family of selves, with about eight or so important ones. As I said, the only thing that prevented D. from being a case of multiple personality disorder is that she remembered everything and could tell you what was going on at all times and what had happened at all times. She just felt as if she had absolutely no control over the way she felt at any given time, whether she thought those feelings were justified and logical or not.

After several years of hypnotic work, D. was able to essentially merge all the parts into a greater whole. She now goes anywhere and everywhere, to the extent that her stamina allows, and she has realized her lifelong dream of becoming a truly accomplished painter, working in a variety of media. She continues to suffer from a nasty case of what seems like an unusual viral syndrome with chronic fatigue and migrating joint pain, as well as from the Type II serotonin depression she inherited from her mother. She treats herself with a range of herbs and supplements.

I mention D. here because one of the turning points, and there were many, came when we started bringing a mother entity into the round-table discussions we had been having.

Think for a minute what it would be like to observe two people in a room for an hour, during which time one of the people keeps addressing the other by different names. Every time the first person calls the second person by a different name, the second person responds in a different voice. Imagine that the first person is acting as a moderator, attempting to help all the different inhabitants of the second person to come to a consensus on a course of action, and you'd have a pretty good idea of what my sessions with D. were like for quite a while.

They were really quite a fascinating crew, the pieces of D. One of the main pieces was called the Watcher, and the Watcher was the reason D. wasn't a case of multiple personality disorder, in which a person tends to lose bunches of time and doesn't remember a lot of the things they do. The Watcher kept track of everything and was my guide in finding the various pieces as they came to light. Exactly as John and Helen Watkins describe (although I hadn't read the Watkins at the time), D. had ego states for important people, important events, and important activities. We tended to name them by what they were wearing or what they did: There was the pinafore girl and the red-scarf lady (the red scarf was a sexual piece). There was a child cringing in a cabinet in the dark, there was a confused child for the time spent with the kindly relatives, and there were twins who seemed to be about eighteen months old, one happy, one sad (they seemed to correspond to aspects of D.'s mother).

It seemed that D.'s panic symptoms were mostly related to a range of young girls, six or seven of them, who were trapped in the tension states that had created them. D.'s work here was to reabsorb these girls into a larger, integrated whole, and the way she accomplished this was by creating alliances between the different ego states during our "group therapy" meetings. For example, we would take girls of six or eight and ask them to look after the eighteen-month-old twins, also identifying for them more-grown-up selves to call if needed.

Often, we would ask for and "create" new selves simply by "naming" them and asking them to help us. I might ask the Watcher to find me a part of the self that loved children and had cared for them, and when that part appeared, I would assign her certain tasks.

We were making these teams, but we were not making as much progress as we should have been. We discovered there was a "mother" part that was harshly critical and judgmental, who frightened a lot of the girls and made them feel bad. Here's where we did a few things I especially want you to notice, things that should be done often.

First, we asked to see the mother part, and when we did, we asked D. to see her mother with compassion by using the nurturing parts we'd been calling on to help the children. We asked D. to notice the hurt little girl living inside her mom. Sometimes, I went so far as to suggest that a little door open up in the mother's chest and reveal a sad little girl sitting inside.

When D. could see her mother's weakness, her physical limitations, her tantrums, her chronic unhappiness, we asked her whether her mother might not be tired and deserve a rest. We said to the mother part that we knew she had been working hard and doing her best against considerable obstacles all this time, and maybe she was tired and had done enough. The mother part agreed that of course she was tired and wanted rest, of course she'd worked long and hard enough.

Everyone agreed, so we then went about constructing a safe place for the mother part. It was a beautiful, light, airy room with lots of plants and big picture windows where she could rest and let down her burden. D. escorted her mom to the room, laid her down to sleep, and closed the door behind her.

This proved to be a significant internal mental event, and a critical self-doubting aspect seemed to disappear. It did not return.

A Basic Inner-Parent Exercise

You may or may not need to use your basic trance induction as preparation for these exercises. Most often, people do not need much preparation. The images we have of our parents are very strong and close to the surface. Always be sure that you can return to a centered, safe place should you encounter strong feelings from which you need distance. That is, do not do these exercises without guidance unless you have read Chapter 6 and have worked on creating a basic relaxational trance. Be prepared to consult a hypnotherapeutic professional should the need arise.

If you are a good visualizer, just see your parents together before you in front of the house you lived in with them. If you cannot visualize easily, simply close your eyes and sense that they are standing in front of you. You'll be amazed at the things you may "know" and can answer about your parents even with a different sort of "sight."

Notice how you feel when you are with them together. Ask yourself what part of you is present with them like this. In particular, ask yourself the age of the part. (The chance is good that your age will match the age at which you are seeing your parents.) The part of you that is meeting with your parents is a combination of your inner child for that age and your everyday, grown-up left-brain self. You can and should go back and forth somewhat between those two perspectives, feeling and speaking as the child but observing and advising as the adult. Later, you will split the child and the adult so that they can meet together with either or both parents, if need be.

Ask yourself what the child sees about the parents that the adult can now analyze and interpret. How did they relate? Communicate? Did they love each other? Were they getting what they needed from each other? Keep these ideas in mind as you proceed.

The next step is to meet with each parent separately in their favorite place in the house, to note how you feel in their presence, and then to assertively demand attention, understanding, and behavioral change. As we said, you must persevere and imagine yourself doing whatever is necessary to break through whatever walls of defensiveness or complacency your parents used to avoid dealing with your unhappiness. You must make your needs and wishes clear, and express your energy and emotion in doing so. Remember, we said that this can be painful, and yet you must also approach your parent with an underlying, nurturing compassion, setting aside your anger and disappointment at their previous failings as soon you are able to imagine them responding in a more appropriate manner.

You must see your parents step up and meet your need for engagement, and see them problem-solve with you. They must address (1) their relationship with you, (2) their satisfaction with their own lives, and (3) their relations with other members of the family. See them solve or make substantial progress on these issues. Get them to agree to treat you with respect and acceptance and to negotiate with you in good faith.

You should not expect to accomplish everything in one sitting. This step may take quite a while, depending on how much time you can devote to it on a regular basis and how draining it is for you to do this work. Remember that you must imagine your parents as the best selves that they might have been if they had been able to surmount the legacies they brought with them from their families. You must not be limited in your imagination by actual events. The parents you are changing are the ones that live in your head, so the limitations of your flesh-and-blood parents are irrelevant.

After meeting with one parent, meet separately with your other parent and go through this same process. Then meet with both parents together, making them be assertive with and responsive to each other. Watch them come to a better arrangement between themselves, one that lets you off the hook of satisfying their unmet needs. Again, do not be stopped by what really did or did not transpire.

As a variant, instead of negotiating with your parents directly in the form of a child with a splash of adult, you may find it easier to undertake a visit in which your adult, left-brain self, the one that goes to the meadow to begin with, meets with the parents and child and acts as a mediator.

Whenever you end a visit with your parents, tell them that you know they are trying hard to be good parents and thank them for their efforts. Keep visiting with them until you feel comfortable and safe in their presence.

If these exercises work properly, you'll find it easier to speak up assertively and to negotiate effectively. You may find that a critical, carping voice in your head is a lot quieter or even gone, and this makes you less inhibited. You may find yourself trying new things, talking to strangers more easily, and generally being less self-conscious and more spontaneous.

INNER-GUIDE EXERCISES

Alberto, the graduate student from Chapter 2 who needed to finish a paper to get his master's degree and keep his job, was introduced to his inner self, or, as I intoned at the time, "your visual self, your body self, your movement self, your spatial self, your musical self, your sexual self, your spiritual self, your emotional self, your social self, the part of you that reads peoples faces, and knows what they're feeling." The reasons to get in touch with your inner, nonverbal selves are many, not the least of which is the old saw that "a picture is worth a thousand words." When we are trying to make a complex decision, the ability to "see" a virtually infinite number of elements in a visual field is a considerable advantage.

We have already said, but it bears repeating, that the outer, left-brain, judging self is largely unitary, It may have some dichotomy between male (father) and female (mother) voices, or between a praising, blessing voice and a critical, cursing voice, but in general, the everyday self is pretty consistent in its content. The right-brain, on the other hand, is multiple, sometimes very much so, and it is not at all consistent.

When we go inward, searching for a nonverbal self (perhaps we really should call it a less verbal self, since these selves can talk, sometimes a lot; but they are essentially more metaphorical than

literal, more analog rather than digital), what we find is extremely variable and depends on the situation and the immediately preceding stimuli. What does seem to be clear is the existence of a
sum-function inner self, one that consists of, represents, and can
call upon, all its constituent parts (selves); and that further, it is
possible to have reliable access to this "right-brain librarian."

The idea of naming and then summoning parts of the self is a
powerful one indeed, and one of the roles of the sum-function
inner self is to mediate the summoning of other parts. I have seen
this sum-function inner self called by many names. Dr. Landis calls
it "the interface" between the conscious and the unconscious. Dr.
Havens calls it "the librarian of the selves." D., as we saw, called it
"the Watcher." An expert on multiple personality disorder to whom
I once referred a patient called it "the one who knows everything."
The name of the inner self can also be linked to the animal or natural world, as it is in many Native American vision-quest rituals.

My first goal in discussing the inner self with patients is to
describe it and the way it functions as best I can. Then, I try to
determine how to find it. One of my favorite metaphors for con-
veying my sense of what we are up to here is an orchestra. It's a
vast, limitless orchestra, stretching as far as the eye can see, divided into sections. Although many of the orchestra members belong
to more than one section and wear three or four hats, they somehow are grouped so that they can rise by section and convey the
shape of that section if necessary.

At the front of the orchestra is the conductor (the sum-function inner self). To the side of the conductor away from the
orchestra is the visiting soloist (the outer self). Between the
orchestra (the many right-brained selves) and the conductor is a
considerable space, a slot, into which various members and combinations of members of the orchestra can come forward as sum-
moned by the conductor.

I like this image because it gives a sense of the vast array of
resources and the number of combinations that are at the dispos-
al of the "conductor," and because the idea of "playing together
harmoniously" resonates beyond music into the core of what we

are trying to accomplish for the parts of the self.

So, to begin this exercise, your first job is simply to find a quiet place where you won't be disturbed, think about the right-brained inner aspects of yourself that you are seeking, and go down some stairs into your customized conference room with the intention of meeting yourself and seeing who you find.

The Case of Q.

Q. was nineteen when I met him. It was springtime, and he was home going to a local college, having flunked out from a college away from home the preceding fall semester. He had spiky, partially dyed red hair and a pierced tongue. Despite his appearance, he was basically a nice, Irish Catholic school kid from Long Island. His big thing was playing the guitar — he was apparently quite good at it — and now he was going to a music school part-time.

Q. had a history of ADD. He was really smart and had done reasonably well in high school, doing it his own way, studying very little but quite efficiently. Now he seemed to be flunking out of college for the second time, and his parents felt he might be depressed. He certainly seemed so. He'd been lying in bed doing nothing for about two weeks, not wanting to go to class or his job and often missing both. When I asked him what was going on, he told me he'd given up, he just could not get himself to do what he knew he needed to and even wanted to. It came down to two unpleasant things: a boring job and a boring class. All the good things he was doing at school, including taking interesting classes, depended on doing the boring stuff. When he saw that, once again, he wasn't able to get himself to do the boring stuff, he stopped doing almost everything.

Q. and I started talking about his inner self, and I asked him about playing the guitar. The reason I'm bringing up Q. here is that his guitar-playing self was an immediately effective doorway to his right brain. I just asked him to imagine himself sitting down opposite the part of himself that played guitar, and I asked him if he knew this guy he was seeing.

Well, hell yeah, they knew each other. They knew each other damn well. Q. loved and respected this part of himself. I suggested that this part of him — this unselfconsciously physical, body-movement = self — was at least somewhat involved in his difficulty with tolerating certain things, and should be asked for help. When I added that he ought to explain things clearly and negotiate constructively with this part of him — well, Q. was off to the races. In fact, I saw Q. only that one time. He never needed to return. Once he started conversing and negotiating with "inner Q.," once he and inner Q. agreed that efficiently performing the unpleasant chores would allow them both to enjoy more "guitar time," Q. started taking care of business, and that was that.

A couple of points about this story. Q. was very typical in that almost anyone who is committed to the study and performance of an artful body discipline such as painting, dance, crafts, music, athletics, or martial arts will find that art to be a useful doorway to trance and their right-brained selves and capabilities. You may have observed that the behavioral message Q. ultimately got out of his one session with me was not very complex. Q. knew what he had to do. He had heard it, and could hear it again any time he wanted, from his parents. When, however, he was able to personify his resistance and see that it was linked to other positive parts of himself, he was able to stop hating that part of himself and to reintegrate himself enough to make the changes he needed to make.

General Considerations

For Q., finding his inner self was easy. It's not always so. When you first search for an inner self, you may find it to be confusing because that self can be a lightning-quick chameleon. The inner self has its own agenda, an agenda to which it clings tenaciously. The priorities of the inner self, in rigid order, are self-preservation, avoidance of pain/seeking of pleasure, and — then and only then — development and growth. If your outer self has seemed dangerous or painful to your inner self, if your inner self is sufficiently mistrustful of your motives and actions, it may well have concluded that avoiding you is the safest tactic.

To overcome such resistance, you must carry the proper attitude into your search for the inner self. To begin with, you must be accepting and forgiving. You must be humble. You must be respectful, because in the end, this part of you is really much stronger than your everyday self. You cannot be autocratic or dictatorial. You must seek your deeper self in a spirit of inquiry in which you see any initial contact, no matter what it be, as a success. You must reassure your inner self that you are not here to harangue it or to blame it, but to understand it. You want to form a new partnership in which you both will thrive and prosper. You must assume that everything your inner self has ever done, whatever the result of those actions may have been, has been, at the base, to protect you both from pain or injury of some kind. It's your job to discover just what that pain or injury is or was, and then to use a two-winner philosophy to find a solution that meets both your needs.

Very often, the initial thing I do when I am creating such a meeting with a patient for the first time is to ask the patient to imagine apologizing to the inner self for his or her poor understanding of their relationship. Remember that we tend to talk to our inner selves the way we were spoken to as a child. If we were demeaned, despised, or disrespected, that is generally how we speak to ourselves. We must tell our inner self that we are sorry if we have spoken harshly, if we've been mean or cruel, and we must ask this part of us to meet with us regularly to improve our relationship. I'll often ask that the patient imagine getting up from the table and giving the inner self a warm, welcoming, and accepting embrace.

Even if you have the right attitude, you may still run into some roadblocks if your inner self is alienated enough. There are some situations in which an inner self simply will not come out and work with you. One of my patients was a very bright but particularly out-of-control guy, the type with an office that hadn't been touched, let alone cleaned, in fifteen years. He was a hermit with a few odd, solitary, but absorbing businesses, an aged mother, and no social life or friends. When he went inside, he found a feral child, a child raised by animals. In an amazing series of trances, this guy became part of a vivid drama unfolding between this animalistic child, who did not speak but who would grab scraps of food, and a silent older man with a beard who seemed to be watching over the child somehow. It all took place in a rural setting that included some farmland and some forest, like a fairy tale, and the patient was only slightly able to effect what happened there. We spent weeks getting the child to accept food and a bed in an empty cottage, but he never spoke. It was all fascinating to me, and to the patient as well, but after three or four months at twice a month, it wasn't going anywhere and it wasn't influencing the patient's life very much at all. His life was still total chaos, so we stopped.

This kind of thing is pretty unusual, and again, if anything especially surprising or disconcerting happens while you're doing an inner-child, inner-parent, or inner-guide exercise, it's back to the league of neo-Ericksonian hypnotherapists for you. The fact is that the overwhelming majority of people find this very easy to do. Their nonverbal selves are often right below the surface, and have always been there just waiting to come out. We often use these parts of ourselves to great good, whether we think of it in those terms or not. They are, after all, often the best, most creative parts of ourselves.

One common response upon meeting the inner self, similar to Q.'s, is, "Yeah, I know that self. We've done a lot of stuff together over the years." This usually means that negotiations will be smooth and comfortable, and that an increase in efficiency and self-control are just around the corner. It is also common to discover an inner self that is angry and not very willing to communicate, or that is sad and has given up. If you encounter any of these attitudes, just remember that you can usually break through them if you can convey to the inner self the right sense of humility and a commitment to future respectful communication.

The cardinal feature of the inner self, as opposed to the inner child or the inner parent, is that it is more or less an age-appropriate adult. Often, this inner self will be somewhat younger than you are now. The older you are, the more likely there will be a disparity in ages. My seventy-eight-year-old dad says he's still really nineteen inside. Whatever you see in terms of clothing, age, weight, and facial expression when you first make contact will tell you something about what you are dealing with and how to address it. Most often, once your inner self appears, you will find that you are able to make contact with it and converse in some way.

As we've mentioned, a majority of people "see" the inner self. Many find that sensing it in some other way is easier. I find that I can converse quite well with myself even with only the barest of visual glimpses now and then. Sometimes, the conversation is hardly verbal at all. The responses to your questions may be images or sensations or just a sense of knowing. Keep in the front of your mind that communication with the inner self happens rather automatically, much less formally, for most people most of the time. Simply stopping to get centered and to ask yourself what your real purpose is or to consult your intuition is the most basic method. In other words, we need to be flexible concerning the manner in which we make contact.

That being said, once we have made contact, we want to ask the name and age of the inner self right away, and we want to make sure we are in touch with the genuine sum function self, with the interface, with the wisest, broadest-visioned inner self, not with an unrepresentative fragment, such as inner child or a parent or an addict or what have you.

Where you proceed from here depends, of course, entirely on the purpose of your visit. The most common reasons that I undertake such journeys with my patients are problems with procrastination, disorganization, and time management. Other reasons include our attempt to stop self-destructive behaviors, to seek direction in complex situations, and to stimulate and enhance creativity. For the latter two purposes, very little personification of the inner self is required. Simply entering your relaxed trance with the intention of addressing a particular situation — artistic, interpersonal, or occupational — and asking your inner self to work on it, both in and out of your awareness, will suffice to generate new approaches, some of which will intuitively "fit."

Getting down to difficult tasks and ceasing self-destructive behaviors are more complex negotiations, but ones that are not all that different from any other successful negotiation. A successful negotiation requires you to understand the nuances of the other's position. Of course, on a certain level, you know your own conflicting positions quite well, but remember that you have been in conflict about this, that your judging self and your experiential self have been going to considerable lengths to avoid being present simultaneously. What you will be doing in this meeting is looking carefully at the subtle nature of the objections your inner self has to whatever it is you wish it would do, and then altering your requests so that they are more palatable. You will also need to explain to the inner self exactly why you need to move in a certain direction and how not doing so is getting in the way for both of you.

Underneath this negotiation is the understanding that the left brain's most important task is to plan for the safe, regular, and varied emergence of the right-brained selves and for the development of increasingly complex, mixed left and right states. In the healthiest people, the deeper, intuitive understandings of the right brain are never far away. Long periods of time are spent in right-brained, timeless, peak or flow states.

Once the outer self comes to properly appreciate the inner self's objections (most of which are along the lines of "I can't — I already tried it and it didn't work;" "I'm too frightened;" "I'll fail again and I've had enough of that;" "I'll lose my temper"), the outer self needs to look at incentives and at cutting the task into manageable pieces (telling the inner self, for example, "We can spend this much time doing this if we spend just this little bit of time doing that.")

Sometimes, getting the inner self off the dime requires that new information be explained and put into context: "Look, we have this ADD stuff. We never knew we had it. It explains a lot of things. This is what it's like, and this medicine we are taking has made things easier, so we ought to try doing X again. But let's try it this way this time."

Making your requests as discreet and as specific as possible is quite important initially, as well as over the long haul. If your request is vague, you may get lip service but no results. The inner self is quite slippery, a master at indirection and distraction. You may get it to agree to do something later, but if you do not specify exactly when and for how long the something should be done, you may find it accomplishing very little.

Even if you have agreed on a course of action with your inner self, and you have specified the time and place, you aren't finished yet. At this point, you will find it helpful to ask if there is anything that might interfere with carrying out the agreement you have made and to then further agree how these obstacles might be handled.

At the end of any such negotiation, you will need to review what has been agreed upon, to make certain it is clear and specific enough, and to vigorously reaffirm the agreement. The farewell has a lot in common with those of other inner dialogues in that you should imagine a strong, loving embrace followed by a considerable period of direct eye contact during which I recommend you use a cheerleaderlike approach: "Are we ready? Are we sure? Are we sure we're sure? Are we? Yeah? Yeah!"

You may or may not need your basic trance induction to do this exercise. You most often will not need it. In summary, when you make contact with your inner self, ask its name and age, apologize for any poor relations and request to improve them, bring up the particular problem or situation concerning you, and ask your inner self for help. Find a two-winner solution by lowering your expectations and finding new incentives, nail your agreements down, and say good-bye with feeling, arranging future meetings at the same time.

PSYCHOEDUCATION AND INTEGRATION

The three types of exercises we discussed in this chapter, if applied in an ongoing manner, can go a long way in helping to reintegrate dissociated functions. Even when patients work with me regularly, they must also do the exercises on a regular basis on their own at home if they are to have the best possible effect.

I also like to use two important sources of psychoeducational material with individuals who seem to be stuck in some way that indicates a mild but persistent dissociation. The first is Zen Buddhism and the Tao Te Ching, and the second is the work of the comparative mythologist Joseph Campbell.

In my office at home, I have eight different translations of the *Tao Te Ching*. I am constantly giving one or another of them away to patients and buying replacements. I recommend the 1988 translation by Stephen Mitchell for the average western reader, since I continue to find it the most readily accessible. I prefer the 1997 translation by science fiction writer Ursula K. Le Guin for the literary. Also excellent is the 1986 R. L. Wing translation, which directly and extensively discusses the Tao in terms of left-and-right-brain integration.

The Tao is a book of eighty-one poems and reputedly is the most frequently translated text in the world, save the Christian Bible. The Tao is said to have been written in the fifth century by Lao Tzu, a name that can be roughly translated as "Old Boy." It is generally understood to have arisen in the context of the encounter between the Buddhism coming over the Himalayas from India and the Confucianism that existed in China at the time. Confucius, the revered Chinese sage, wrote about balance and harmony within oneself and between oneself and society. Buddhism can be said to be concerned with the underlying spiritual nature of the universe, and Zen Buddhism, of which the Tao Te Ching is a seminal text, can be said to be concerned with harmonizing and balancing the underlying nature of the universe with one's obligations to oneself and to one's society.

According to R. L. Wing, "the goal of Taoist philosophy is to combine these two (the 'worldly/left-brained' and the 'universal/right-brained') minds into a working perspective." The poems of the Tao form, in fact, a subtle and elegant guide to learning to turn on both sides of your brain at once, to being "fully present," to recapturing the inner intuitive selves that socialization and trauma distance from us. They can be read in an hour, and they can be reread ad infinitum as a resource and guide to the reintegration of dissociated selves.

In Chapter 5, I mentioned the idea that the story of Adam and Eve in the Garden of Eden can be seen as the story of the development of the left brain. I like to present Dr. Joseph Campbell's ubiquitous hero myth as the matching bookend to Adam and Eve, as the story that tells how we are to go about regaining our lost right-brained, unselfconscious inner selves.

Dr. Campbell, now deceased, was a professor of comparative mythology at Vassar, and was also the star of a 1988 PBS interview series with Bill Moyers called *Joseph Campbell and the Power of Myth*. Campbell steeped himself in every major mythological, cosmological, and religious tradition and then asked the questions: What is it we are trying to tell ourselves with our worldful stories? What information about living was important enough to commit to memory and transmit orally in a world in which the common people did not yet have a written language?

Of course, as many know from hearing or reading Dr. Campbell, what he found was that all stories essentially follow the same cycle (separation, initiation, return). They all involve a hero who receives a "call to adventure," perhaps just an awareness that something isn't right, and who then goes on a journey of initiation. The initiation always involves a challenge, and the challenge always requires that the hero "look within" (to find his right-brained self) and "seek his bliss" (accept his right-brained inner self). Basically, Campbell shows us that a huge chunk of human culture is really metaphorical instruction in the reclamation of the right-brained self from the ravages of ever-more-complex socialization.

What I draw from the combination of the *Tao Te Ching* and the work of Dr. Campbell is an awareness that the integration of the left and the right brains, the need to find the inner self and to be fully human, is inescapably a part of the human condition, something that we must all face. We find no end to the cultures and traditions that revolve around this inherently human challenge once we know how to look.

CHAPTER 8

The Treatment of ADD:
Executive Functioning and
the Management of Time and Task

Considering how many millions of individuals are affected by ADD, its psychotherapeutic and psycho-educational treatment is a much-neglected topic. Part of this neglect is due to an inexact definition of ADD, one that overemphasizes dysfunction. Part is due to a fragmented and undertrained psychotherapeutic workforce. And part of the neglect is due to a complex and variable clinical picture that overlaps and is complicated by other conditions. A great deal of work still needs to be done, work that is just beginning, to create therapies that are specifically targeted to the true nature and common clinical course of ADD.

To maximize psychotherapy for ADD, two different sorts of problems must be addressed: (1) the underlying developmental neurophysiological situation in ADD, and (2) the accumulated effects of living with ADD, whether they involve neurotransmitter abnormalities, fragmentation of ego states, executive functioning in particular or left/right brain integration in general.

The recognition and treatment of ADD is also complicated by the tremendous variability in level of functioning among affected individuals, and understanding this variability would seem a likely place to start looking for some clues to effective treatment. The key discriminating factor appears to me to be the quality and nature of the individual's relationship with time. Those who have mastered a way to keep track of and adjust the structure and rhythm of their activities, who have unleashed their energy, can be enormously successful. Those who have not fare much less well.

For this reason, I have, for several years now, been developing a number of mental tools and exercises designed to utilize right-brain pattern-seeing intelligence to structure time and activity. These exercises are routinely combined with visits with inner right-brained parts of the self for the purpose of unifying and integrating behind this time-structuring effort.

Our underlying intention here is to look at ways in which people with ADD can use their right-brain abilities to gain control over their lives, to master their patterns of activity, to become reliable, trustworthy individuals. Remember that the right-brain pattern-seeing, holistic intelligence is quite different from its slower, more stolid left-brain counterpart, and it can be quite useful. (A picture is worth a thousand words.) Remember also that people with ADD, because of their painful early lives, often dissociate their left- and right-brain abilities and therefore underutilize their right brain for goal-directed purposes. The process described herein is designed to merge and meld both ways of functioning, to reverse that dissociation, to use right-brain perceptions to achieve left-brain goals.

Our discussion of the psychotherapy of adolescents and adults with ADD will be divided between two separate chapters. In this chapter, we will discuss in detail the tools I have been using to improve executive functioning, to teach the management of time and tasks — time maps, pessimistically planned transitions, and request-handling algorithms. In Chapter 9, we will look more generally at ADD in the context of trance meditation and the training of the brain.

TIME MAPS

Imagine, if you will, a series of rectangles stretching out infinitely in one direction, like a never-ending piano keyboard (white keys only). Each rectangle is divided into three equal sections, as shown in Figure 4.

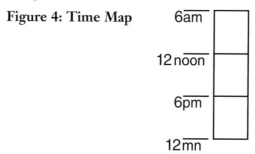

Figure 4: Time Map

Each piano key is a day, of course, and the three segments represent, running from top to bottom, morning, afternoon, and evening. Now think about a series of seven such rectangles, labeled as shown in Figure 5.

Figure 5: Time Map

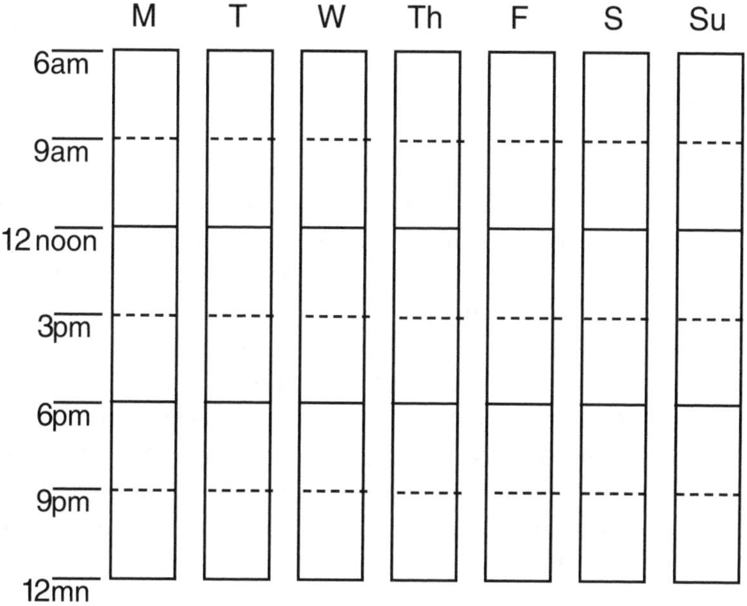

What we are looking at now is an empty visual and spatial template, or time map, for imagining and structuring time. Each of the three six-hour sections (6 A.M. to noon, noon to 6 P.M., and 6 P.M. to midnight) can be further divided in half, so we can think of a day as divided into six blocks of three hours each (early morning, late morning, early afternoon, late afternoon, early evening, and late evening). Six blocks per day times seven days equals forty-two segments per week.

I have been using time maps with my patients for years now, and it was only recently that I realized the true genesis of this spatial vision of time. I modeled it on the program cards I first received as a seventh grader at Junior High School 189 in Flushing, Queens. When I was in seventh grade, it was a transitional grade, the first year that the students moved from room to room and the teachers stayed put. In sixth grade, the children had stayed put and the teachers had moved about.

As any educator can tell you, this transitional year required a large-scale increase in organization. The program card handed out at the beginning of the year contained the location of your classes, the names of your teachers, and the start times of the periods. And more than anything else I might or might not have learned in seventh grade, I learned how to use that program card.

I'm still using it, more or less.

Time maps can be used to efficiently budget time, and just as when budgeting money, the first step is to get a handle on the fixed expenses. So too, to use this tool for the purpose it was designed, we have to fill in those activities to which we are already obligated or committed to see what time is left over for our personal use. We need to use the ability to see time as space, to look off in the distance and see a repeating series of weekdays and weekends, a series within which there are many other repeating rhythms. Although visual and spatial ways of "seeing" time are not identical, they both share the ability to zoom in and out, the ability to rapidly shift from the worm's-eye view to the eagle's-eye view, the ability to see a day, or to pull back and see a week, or to pull back even further and see a month. In just a few "snapshots" taken at various heights above the two-dimensional roadmap/ puzzle of time, we can encapsulate an immense amount of information, and we can then access it rapidly and reliably. Much has been written about the nature of so-called spatial abilities and their relationship to temporal parameters. For example, when you ask people to draw a map of their world, of the spatial relationships among the places they frequently go, what you find is that, although the direction from the center, from home, is accurate, the distance from home on that spatial map of any particular place actually reflects the time it takes to get there, not the physical distance in miles.

The spatial sense is maplike, and the essence of the knowledge contained in a map is about the relationships among elements. Some spatial maps have to do with body movement, some with limb or digit positioning (sports or music), some with geographic location, some with geographic movement. The level and range of information that can be contained in the human sense of "whereness" is truly astounding and virtually unlimited. I am reminded of the studies of the pygmies' sense of "whereness" within the jungle, their unerring navigation to useful animal and plant locations — literally thousands of them — or of the way that images of maps and of flight simulators zooming in and out have become so commonplace in our computerized world.

Memory expert Tony Buzan, in his wonderful book *Use Both Sides of Your Brain* (New York: Dutton, 1976), describes what he calls mind-mapping, a spatially oriented way of taking notes that involves diagramming in a remarkably simple and effective manner. Spatial intelligence is perhaps the paradigmatic pattern-seeing intelligence. Yet, I would say it is a relatively underappreciated sense compared to its more popular siblings, sound, sight, and touch. I can easily imagine myself flying high over a landscape of time, different rhythms of activity represented by different-colored strands, a woven river, a braided belt, flowing past me. My sense of this flowing tapestry is what keeps me centered and focused, what allows me to be the dependable, reliable person I need to be.

The very first step in using spatial abilities to regulate time and behavior is to look at the rhythms of activity that already exist and to "see" them laid out across the endless piano keys stretching out in front of us. We have to do that regularly, over and over, day after day, morning after morning and evening after evening, until we can see the patterns clearly, can feel ourselves moving through the week like we would move through a repetitively traveled, multistage journey, like salespeople on their routes, hitting the same stops at the same time each week, except when they don't.

Except when they don't.

This is crucial. Because when you see the patterns that repeat, you can also begin to see what's left over, what's not already committed (there's not likely to be all that much time not committed, mind you). You can begin to see where you have room to maneuver, where you can tinker, where you can insert new rhythms or alter old ones.

Once you've placed your current rhythms of activity in the snapshots of time as space taken at various heights (day, week, and month) but before you make any changes in the patterns, we need to discuss another feature of the time map: the pessimistically planned transition.

PESSIMISTICALLY PLANNED TRANSITIONS

The power of properly appreciating the features of a successful transition cannot be underestimated. As I have said before, ADD would more accurately be labeled attention modulation disorder. What this translates into practically is that transitions, from one location to another or even from one activity to another, are the logistical weak link, the point at which modulation of attention occurs appropriately or not, the point at which things can go awry, and consequently, a point we need to give special attention if we are to master ourselves.

First and foremost, transitions have to be appreciated spatially in our time maps as the rectangles, not the lines. They take up space on the template. That's why the spatio-temporal template is finite. There are only so many hours in the day, so many days in the week. If we view transitions as mere moments rather than as solid blocks of time, we will routinely overestimate the amount of time actually available for performing our tasks, frequently disappointing ourselves and those around us.

Transitions are better seen as complete — that is, having a beginning, a middle, and an end. The beginning of a transition is synonymous with the end of an activity. The end of a transition is synonymous with the beginning of the next activity. Think of the lines between the rectangles as activities. When we mark the opening and closing of each of our activities with their habitual chains of behavior, when we become aware of our little rituals for coming and going, for starting and ending, then time maps become truly useful. I've found it helpful to think of transitions as chords — single sounds made up of three distinct notes — and each of the three notes as moments in time. Each note (moment) has its own significance, its own purpose. The three notes (moments) are:

When do I want to get there?

When do I want to leave?

When do I want to get ready to leave?

The transitional space, the rectangle between activities on our time maps, is divided in two: (1) the time between when we begin to prepare to leave and when we actually leave, and (2) the time between when we leave and when we arrive.

I call this the Pessimistically Planned Transition (PPT) because it encourages selecting a departure time based on the worst-case travel scenario. (You can be either a timely pessimist or a late optimist.) Equally, I suggest being pessimistic about getting ready to leave by giving yourself extra time to wander around before leaving.

The first area within the rectangle of a transition — the time spent getting ready to leave — offers the possibility of radical improvement in reliability and efficiency. This area within the chord of transition itself breaks down into a chord, into another three notes, that we use in the process of getting ready to leave. This time, the three notes are:

What did I bring here?

What do I have to take with me?

Did I leave this place the way I found it?

Read and reread these three questions for a minute, turn them over in your mind, and you may be able to see that they require reflection, that they require what is technically referred to as sequencing. Since we know that the essential underlying issue in ADD is a tendency toward underreflectiveness, we need to be very aware of how we wish to use our reflective abilities at these critical transitional moments. Like a sniper with only a few precious bullets, we need to aim our reflection carefully. Think about the process of gathering your belongings to leave your house for the day. Think about all the places you want to go during the day and about what you need to have with you at each place. If you use the kind of spatial or temporal imagery we have been describing, it takes but a second to call up the time map of your day and to "see" where you'll be going. If you ponder it for a moment, you'll see how easy it is to naturally associate large amounts of specific information with the sense of "whereness" you use to navigate this mental map. If you think about reviewing your journey through the day the same way you would make sure you had all the directions and information you needed before departing on a complex vacation trip, you can begin to see the power of this structured sort of reflection.

The three questions that we ask when we plan each transition followed by the three questions we ask as we are preparing to leave can be very powerful indeed. If we answer the questions properly, we will arrive on time, having everything we need with us. We will prepare ourselves to return efficiently to what we were doing when we had to stop, and we won't have to leave a mess behind to annoy those with whom we live and work. When we respect and understand the role of the well-executed transition in effective living, we are ready to use our time maps in conjunction with our next tool.

likely to take. Deciding if we can handle a task now requires that we anticipate its effect on our day if we take a "detour" of a certain length, that we look at the pieces of the puzzle and understand the full effects of shifting them around.

In general, pessimistic predictions about time are better than optimistic predictions. The only pitfall in doing things now is in underestimating either the time required for the task or the consequent derangement of other pieces of the day's puzzle. It is always useful to remember that although people may be disappointed if you refuse to handle their tasks, they will be much more upset if you say yes and wind up meaning no.

THE WEEKLY TIME MAP

All along, we have been talking about using right-brain intelligences to organize our activities efficiently. Remembering to perform one-time events at a later moment is consistently difficult at home and at work for hyperactive people unless and until they learn that they must anchor every request to a specific time and place. In addition, they must devise an explicit system for all repetitive tasks.

When I introduce the idea of time maps to patients with ADD, I often ask them to make a list of all the different actions they might perform in an average week. Most people use 95 percent of their time on the same five to ten activities in fairly regular patterns. Part of the value of using time maps to see activity patterns is that we can then become aware of our habits or systems for dealing with tasks that are typically performed in given locations. To put it another way, once we become aware of how we govern our activities on a macro level — that is, where we are physically — we need to get a sense of how we organize our activities on a micro level — that is, what we do once we get there. If we are to remember to perform one-time events at a later date, we need to be aware of the routines, rhythms, and rituals we undertake as we move from place to place.

I am a person who works in three different locations. In order to function efficiently, I have developed a number of habits that

THE REQUEST-HANDLING ALGORITHM

In *Driven to Distraction* (New York: Touchstone, 1995), Edward M. Hallowell, M.D. and John J. Ratey, M.D., talk about a rule for paperwork, OHIO, which stands for "Only Handle It Once." It doesn't quite work that way for me. In fact, I handle paperwork twice, once as a request for attention and once when I take care of the task. Opening an envelope or handling a piece of paper is, to me, a subset of the much larger category of tasks in general, of the category that holds any and all requests for my time and attention.

Algorithms are another use of spatial intelligence. An algorithm is a decision tree, a spatial arrangement in which branches with different actions lead to different outcomes in a few rapid steps. We will now construct a compact request-handling algorithm, the purpose of which is to help us handle requests only once, with "handle" used in the sense of making a quick decision about whether the request will be granted and then ensuring that the approved request is actually performed.

An algorithm is a map, a diagram that allows us to choose easily among competing courses of action. Let's look at Figure 6 (p. 152), which presents a map for responding to requests.

If we are adequately familiar with our time maps, if we have really taken the trouble to flesh out the map for the day, week, and month, these few simple questions can help us to realize quickly and reliably whether we are likely to perform any given task. You may notice that the response algorithm ends in one of three questions, each of which is best answered by referring to a different variant of the time map.

When we ask ourselves whether or not we wish to handle a one-time event now, whether it is best for us to just move into action mode at once (which is, of course, just what the hyperactive person is prone to do), we need to consult our time map of the day. We need to ask, "What happens to the map of the day if we take X amount of time now to handle that request?"

If we decide to handle a one-time event at a later time, we need to look at our time map of the week, see when we have an uncommitted space, and anchor the task; that is, pin down when

Figure 6

and where we will handle it. If we don't, we will be considerably less likely to accomplish it.

Finally, if decide to take on a task that clearly requires multiple sittings, we will need to look at our time map for the month and see where in the puzzle of our weekly schedule we have time to insert a new repetitive activity.

Many people with ADD suffer from what I call narcissistic overcompensation. They react to past failures by saying yes to everyone and taking on all sorts of tasks that they have little chance of accomplishing. One of the underlying purposes of the "request algorithm/time map" combination is to function as a brake/reality check on that sort of thing, to use our reflective

powers efficiently to "see" the patterns of our activity, and t "watch" the "shape" of the pieces change as we consider variou temporal arrangements.

Using these maps well requires being willing to say no. If w look at our map and see that there is no space for an activity no and we can find no obvious space later, we must trust what we se We must also realize that this map, this puzzle in front of us, cor tains and implies and refers to so much information, to so mar kinds of information, that it is literally impossible, not to mentic an incredible waste of time, to convey even a fraction of it to an one else and then expect them to make a decision for us. We mu decide for ourselves. No one else has even remotely enoug information to do so. We must trust what we see, and we mu answer no as indicated.

Using the request-handling algorithm leads us to one of thr different time-map consultations: (1) we look at our day to ask we can do it now, (2) we look at our week to see if we can do later, or (3) we look at a series of weeks to see if we can add a ne repetitive activity, or rhythm. What follows is a little more det: on each of them.

THE DAILY TIME MAP

At the most basic level, performing small tasks now is almo always preferable to performing them later. If we do it now, wha ever it is, it is only one task. If we intend to do it later, it quick becomes two tasks: whatever the original task is plus the task remembering to do it later.

I have discovered over many years that I am not very good that second task, the remembering to do it later. The smaller th detail and the less important it is to me — especially if deep dow1 I think the whole thing is stupid and unnecessary to begin with — the less likely I am to remember it.

So, especially if it's something small and trivial — and even it's something middle-sized — now is usually preferable to later

Using a time map requires that we make generally accurat estimates of the amount of time given tasks and transitions ar

are keyed to the way I arrive at and leave from these locations. The habits are spatially based; that is, they do not depend on my logical, left-brained, list-based; verbal memory. Rather, I simply put something in the right place so that I see it when I'm packing up and I take it with me. All day long, as I see patients in my offices, I put things into piles on my desk or into my briefcase. No matter where I go, no matter which of my three offices I'm at, the first thing I do is take out the charts and pieces of paper I've been carrying in my briefcase and lay them out in front of me so that I can dealt with them. The last thing I do, no matter where I am, is look around at the piles I've created throughout the day and load up my briefcase for departure, taking with me everything I intend to act on before the next time I am scheduled to return.

The key to working with a system like this is to make the whole thing very explicit in your mind, to be clear about the usually short list of different behaviors you need to perform in any given place, particularly around transitions, around comings and goings, around beginnings and endings. Imperative in the use of week maps for planning later activities is the inviolable dictum, "If you can't say when, you can't say yes." What follows that dictum is the statement, "When I get to this place, I'm going to do these things in this particular way, in this particular sequence." If the task sequencing is the same in the same place over and over, time after time, it becomes rote, second nature. It becomes reliable. I don't have to rely on my memory to remember whom I have to call, although I may remember. What I use instead is a system for dealing with a phone calls, a stupid, simple system that involves carrying around small pieces of paper from place to place and putting them in front of me wherever I go. I don't remember the calls; I remember the system for dealing with calls.

The time-map concept calls upon us to get a visual or spatial sense of the rhythms of our activities. The great thing is that it makes everything decidedly finite, involving a relatively small number of sequences that get easier and easier to remember because they are so often the same.

Think about your morning routine. Do you actually remember

to brush your teeth? Probably not. You probably flow through what we call a habit chain, a complex group of actions through which you naturally move because you have repeated them so often. The more we see small repetitive tasks as parts of consciously constructed habit chains, the more reliable we become.

I have found that anchoring my habit chains spatially, giving each routine a physical and temporal location on my time map, makes them very easy for me to remember and perform. I'm continually impressed by the capacity of mental maps to hold associated information. Not only can I draw you a grid of the very complex New York City streets and highway systems I've been driving for most of the last thirty years, but I can also absolutely and effortlessly recall countless details associated with each and every roadway, what time of day the roadways are congested, who lives where, when I last saw them, all the times I was at their houses, the last time construction was done on that road, and so on and so on, ad infinitum.

Socrates said, "An unexamined life is not worth living." For the person dealing with attentional issues, an unexamined life is simply unlivable. The construction and regular use of time maps gives us the chance to examine our behaviors visually and spatially, allowing us to logarithmically increase the efficiency of our reflections.

THE MONTHLY TIME MAP

I am always searching for new metaphors that will help my patients envision the sorts of mental maps I want them to use, particularly for the purpose of assessing the possibility of adding or subtracting repetitive activities. I use rivers, I use roads, I use woven scarves and belts. I have also had considerable success comparing the map of a month to a measure of music written for multiple instruments. All of these metaphors have in common a marriage of time and space, a moved-through when and where.

Everyone has experiences that can be called upon in constructing images of time as space. Musicians have an easy time getting the rhythms of activity when they think about arrangements for multiple instruments. If each instrument's notes are written in a different color ink and only one instrument plays at a time, the written piece of music begins to look just like a woven fabric. Add the ideas that certain instruments come and go in repetitive patterns and that tinkering with these patterns changes the sound of the whole piece, changes the harmonies, and the metaphor starts to take on power. Anyone who does a lot of driving has an exploitable spatiotemporal past. Anyone who makes crafts, any trained athlete, anyone who has ever cultivated a nonverbal pattern-seeing knowing is capable of creating and using time maps, if he or she so desires.

Often, when we have trouble getting ourselves to take on a project, what is stopping us is an intuitive sense that the month map does not have an appropriate repeated or rhythmic slot available. For most busy adults, taking on a new repetitive activity, or behavioral rhythm, requires a concerted, disciplined effort, requires some rearranging and deleting in order to make any sizable chunk of time available on a repetitive basis.

The key phrase here is "rhythms plus one." When we have all of our activities on a rhythm, when we are fully aware of the responsibilities we have accepted, both to ourselves and to others, and of the temporal patterns of those responsibilities, then we are ready to smoothly and easily add a reliable new rhythm to our lives. Rhythms plus one: one new rhythm added at a time.

Humans work most efficiently when using habit chains, a series of actions performed almost automatically once the initial action is taken. People with ADD are capable of forming habit chains. Identifying and locating these habit chains on the time map and then using that time map repeatedly so that its repetitive rhythms become familiar allows the systematic development of new habits and the ultimate mastery of time.

A smoothly working time map is aesthetic, the schedule as art form. An aesthetic schedule will have certain qualities. It will be pleasing to the eye when represented visually. It will have a satisfying click spatially when the pieces fit together. It will be graceful, harmonious, rhythmic, and balanced. An artful schedule will accommodate the physical, the emotional, the spiritual, friends and family, work, and play. The artful, finely wrought but flexible and malleable schedule is the tool by which we fashion our lives, by which we take over the command of our ship. It is the basic mechanism by which we become our true selves. Whether we see measures of music or a convoluted road or a woven belt of fabric, or even if we feel our way through space according to geography and location, when we are aware of the rhythms of our activities, we are empowered and ready to be transformed.

THE TWO LITTLE GUYS

An idea that is implicit in the use of time maps is that we should never begin an activity without knowing when we plan to end it, without knowing when our next transition is scheduled. We need to know our next mark, and we need to keep that mark with us. To put it another way, as we move through time, we need to be aware of ourselves traveling toward our next transition the same way that, as we travel along our route to work, we are aware how long, traffic permitting, we have before needing to make the next turn in our route.

To help myself keep track of my impending transitions, I have created two little people who sit on my shoulders, tiny little guys about six inches big. They look like me, with beards and glasses, matched homunculi. The guy on the right tells me, when I ask him, what time it is and what I'm doing now, and the guy on my left shoulder tells me what I'm doing next and when I'm supposed to start doing it. These little guys are just out of sight behind my ears (I think of them as horsing around behind my back, with the sensibilities of the brothers on Car Talk), but they are ready to help me out at a moment's notice should I need them. I think of them as a kind of spreadsheet. Without any effort on my part, they take the information contained on my time maps and return it to me in a usable form. I think of them as dedicated servers in a computer-science kind of way, little selves who do this and only this, each holding just two pieces of data, three out of four pieces of data changing at each transition, one piece (the current time) changing constantly but, thankfully, in a steady, reliable rhythm.

I try to help out the guy on my right as much as I can by putting clocks all over the place, two or three in every room I work in. Pretty much no matter where I look, I'm going to see the time. I've been doing this for years, all day, every day, and over the years, I've accumulated this detailed time sense. It's an innocuous smidgen of left-brainedness that is with me no matter how absorbed I am in what I'm doing, no matter how right-brained I get, ready to tell me what time it is.

Habits are the linchpins of planning and trusting our behavior, and the two little guys are an important part of my most delicate habit chain, the one I use whenever I am about to move myself from one location to another. My transitional habit chain involves scanning the environment; touching my keys, wallet, appointment book, and phone book; looking at my maps; and especially, talking to the little guys.

The more I use my time maps, the easier it is for me to develop and maintain my two little guys, one on each shoulder, and the easier it is to keep track of what I'm doing and what I'm supposed to be doing.

Let's see what this looks like in practice.

A CASE OF POOR TIME MANAGEMENT

B., a slender Irish-American with dark curly hair, was a merchant marine. He spent his twenties circling the globe on freighters. Now in his thirties, he was married and working out of the Port of New York. B. was an underachiever at school, he came from a large chaotic family that included several men with alcohol problems, he always felt like an outsider growing up, and he was slow to develop relationships with women. He came to see me after having been diagnosed with ADD. His major difficulties revolved around his relationship with his wife, whom he brought with him to his first appointment.

B. is an able seaman. In the very structured environment of the ship, he was able to clearly identify his goals and to follow through on them in a reliable manner, for he was in fact an intelligent and good-hearted fellow. To his wife, a pretty blonde freelance writer, however, he was a constant screw-up.

B. was unreliable, she complained. He was always late. He said he would do things and then he didn't do them. He was disorganized. His things were a mess. They argued frequently, they both reported. She was routinely critical, and he often responded with anger and defensiveness.

B. felt his wife was unfair. He felt he did nothing but pay attention to her wishes, but no matter what he did, she wasn't satisfied. He certainly wasn't lazy. He was always doing something. He just had too many things to do. He said she never let him finish anything anyway. She'd interrupt him in the middle of doing something to tell him he was doing it wrong, doing it in the wrong order, to do it this way and not that way. So he'd stop whatever he was doing to try to accommodate her, but then he'd get all bollixed up and lose track of his own agenda, and pretty soon, she'd be complaining about something else he wasn't doing right.

B. was a very typical person with ADD. He, and certainly his wife, would admit that he procrastinated in the sense that he didn't seem to get around to things in a consistently timely way. But this procrastination was not, as in Arturo's case, a resentful avoidance related to a defiant, underconsulted inner self. Just the reverse. B.'s procrastination was about overcompliance.

What went on with B. was the phenomenon narcissistic overcompensation I mentioned earlier (p. 154), a condition in which subtle insecurities interfere with time and task management in adults with ADD.

Growing up with ADD subjects people to a consistent stream of negative feedback, to messages that they and their behavior are unacceptable, inadequate, not measuring up, not quite what's expected, and so on. This is especially true when the ADD is not recognized or understood, as is the case for the overwhelming majority of adults with ADD.

When we look for the effect of this persistent negativism on the relationship between the inner and the outer selves, we can see a disruption in the response to authority, to external expectations, in a range from passive-aggressive and defiant on one end to a self-negating, almost-fawning compliance on the other. What we see is that dysfunction tends to cluster at the ends of the spectrum. In the case of Alberto, the inner self was alienated, it wasn't trying anymore, it blithely befuddled the outer self until it was politely and properly asked to stop. B. was just the opposite. He wanted nothing more than to please, but it just got him into trouble anyway, because he wound up being unclear, excessively oversensitive, and malleable all at the same time.

Here is how it worked.

B. was a good guy. He wanted to do the right thing. He was always trying. He thought positively, because it sometimes helped, and he was always trying to do more, to do better, to try harder, to get it right the next time. Part of him knew, and he wanted to believe, that he was, in fact, intelligent and competent, but he had been running an approval deficit all of his life. He never got enough praise, never got enough encouragement. He was so starved for approval, he was so raw from the many wounds to his sense of self, even the smallest rejections were inordinately painful. As a result, he had become desperate to avoid them.

When anybody asked him anything, he said yes. He said yes because he genuinely wanted to please, to be helpful. He was only too happy to be asked. He also said yes because he could not tolerate even the small sense of rejection that inevitably accompanied saying no.

Unfortunately, by now, his yes was meaningless. His yes was not a considered yes, not a reliable yes.

A yes is meaningful only if it is connected to a specific activity at a specific time in a specific place. A yes must be anchored in time. Otherwise, a yes is not a yes. It's just another maybe.

In other words, "if you can't say when, you can't say yes." That's a phrase to keep with you. "If you can't say when, you can't say yes."

"Rhythms plus one" is another phrase I like to share with guys like B. when they start developing their nonverbal (read visual and spatial) abilities and apply them to time and activity management. These applied spatiotemporal abilities often lie dormant and undeveloped for the same reason B. always said yes: because the whole topic of prioritizing and organizing time is painful. B. was so raw, he routinely and instantaneously avoided the subject. To avoid the small pain of saying no, B. was always optimistically saying yes B. was always, optimistically saying yes to things he was unlikely to do. He had not created for himself wisdom-based (read right-brain) techniques for keeping track of time and intention. Instead, he frequently generated for himselfar more rejection and pain than he would have encountered if he had said no to begin with.

It was a vicious cycle. The more he failed, the more he was desperate to succeed. The more he tried to prove himself worthy by taking on more and more, the more he failed.

Narcissistic overcompensation is continually creating pain by reflexively trying to avoid it. The compass for gauging behavioral commitments is skewed and unbalanced by past unhealed injuries and the intense urge to avoid reopening the wounds. Which leads to reopening the wounds. And round and round.

What B. got was one of the ever-evolving versions of what I think of as "The Spiel: Dr. Don's Handy Tips on Time Management and Self-Regulation, Hypnotic, and Otherwise." This spiel communicates through metaphors a series of Dr. Don's Dictums, many of which I have already presented in this book. It can be given in trance, or it can be spoken conversationally. The amount of trance versus lecture varies quite a bit depending on the wishes and the abilities of the subject.

B. had already been taught a simple, reproducible trance induction and had had a few encounters with his basic interface inner self, the sum-function, right-brain, nonverbal self. B. had a history of self-mastery in certain situations, particularly at sea, which had created for him a reservoir of positive self-regard. In other words, despite his marital inadequacies, he basically liked and believed in himself. When he met with his inner self, the experience felt familiar and positive. He was also a reasonably good visualizer. These two factors made it possible for him to use trance easily to rework how he experienced time.

The trance I used with B. is presented in full in Appendix II, and you may find reading it to be useful. It consists of several distinct sections: a trance induction, an introduction to the inner self, an orientation to spatial maplike senses, sections on time maps, transitions, and adding new rhythms, and a closing wrap-up. Immediately below is the section on time maps and rhythms, which should give you a flavor of the process. B. was already in a trance when we reached this section.

You're facing east now,
And in front of you is the East River,
Behind you is the Hudson,
And downtown,
Over there,
Is the ferry,
Where you work.
And over there
Is the Statue of Liberty.
And you find that you know
Just where each thing is
In relation to all the others.
You have this map
In your head.
You can almost see it;
Though, it's not quite exactly like seeing.
It's more like a sensing,
But a visual sort of sensing.
And all things have distance and direction.
And time is like that.
See time as space.
Feel yourself in the present,
As a point on a line,
With the past stretching out one way
And the future stretching out the other.
See each day as a rectangle,
About four times as high than as wide.
The weekends can be one color
And the weekdays another.
See the rhythm of time in space,
The way the weekends come up regularly,
Off into the distance in each direction.

You've had trouble with time
And with reliability.
But here's a simple rule
For both of you to learn:
If you can't say when,
You can't say yes.

If you want to say yes,
Then you want to say when.

So use time as space.
See the week now.
Look at the seven rectangles
Laying in a row,
And see that each rectangle
Divides into three equal parts —
Morning, afternoon, evening.
You've been doing it all your life.

If you want to,
You can hover over the seven rectangles
And look at your week
And see the patterns of time
Running through your life.
When you look,
You can see them.

The thing about space
Is that each and every space can contain
Only one single thing.
Space is finite.
So is time.
If you can't say when,
You can't say yes.

You're walking down the street.
You bump into an old friend.
You say, "Let's get together."
You really mean it.
If you don't take out your date book

And pick a time,
It will never happen.
You know it's true.

If you can't say when,
You can't say yes.

When time is space, it has rhythms.
Rhythms of days,
Rhythms of weeks.
Every activity has a rhythm.
Either it's a one-time event
Or it's a multiple event.
If it's a multiple event,
Then the very first thing we have to know is
What rhythm is it on?
There are only eight human rhythms-
Several times a day,
Once a day,
Several times a week,
Once a week,
Several times a month,
Once a month,
Several times a year,
Once a year.
That's it.
Only eight rhythms.
If you want to get something done,
What rhythm is it on?
Here's a not-so-secret secret
That your inner self already knows.
If you tell him to do something,
Something that's a multiple event,
But you don't select a rhythm,
He'll ignore you completely,
Won't he?
B. nods.
He won't waste his time
On something that can't possibly happen.

If you need to get something done,
Look at your week.
Seven rectangles
Divided into threes.
Twenty-one boxes.
That's all.
See the patterns.
Some boxes are always filled.
Some are available
But there are only twenty-one.
It's not an accident
That we use the word "spend"
For both money and time.
To do a budget, you need to know your fixed expenses.
If you want to say yes,
You've got to say when.
When you want to say when,
You can see your week in space.
See the givens,
The fixed expenses.
Life is a puzzle —
See where the task fits in.

Know your rhythms —
The rhythms of work,
The rhythms of play,
The rhythms of chores,
The rhythms of love,
The rhythms of growth.
If you don't see the rhythms,
You'll keep getting lost,
Saying yes without saying when.
When you see the rhythms
You're already living with,
Your yeses have meaning.
So, here's another pithy phrase
To walk around with:
Rhythms plus one.
Think about that one.
Rhythms plus one.

When you see the rhythms
You're already living with,
You can begin to think
About adding a new one,
One at a time.
Rhythms plus one.

This trance was originally written in May 1999. Of course, one trance didn't completely change B.'s time-management style. We continued for a period of months to discuss and reemphasize, in trance and in conversation, his wish to please everyone all the time and how this led him to unanchored, timeless, unlikely-to-be-followed-through-on commitments. After a period of about a nine months, B. had made the changes he needed, was getting along better with is wife, felt much less frazzled, and left therapy. About four years later, in January 2003, I happened to speak to B.'s wife. It seemed that B. had permanently changed his style of organizing tasks and now was routinely quite reliable.

TIME MAPS AND THE INNER SELVES

Everyone has some sort of relationship with an inner self. If and when you try to use the right-brained time management skills we've just finished describing, you're going to bump into that relationship in one way or another. Using time maps means consulting your inner self about the patterns you are proposing, and to do that, you need to have some idea about the type of relationship you have with yourself.

The best way to use time maps and request-handling algorithms is to consult them in a habitual manner, and of course, the right time to do that is during transitions and when you are considering requests. Many people find it useful to spend a few moments reviewing their daily time map at night and in the morning. What will vary tremendously in people who try to use this system or something similar is how important it will be to set up formal meetings with the inner self.

Let's talk about M., a twenty-eight-year-old woman who initially came to see me about insomnia and anxiety. M. was a lovely person, intelligent, personable, hardworking, and responsible, who turned out to have a yearly pattern of hereditary seasonal depression (fatigue, overeating, and crankiness). The seasonal depression was complicated this year by an acquired stress depression (insomnia and anxiety). The two types of depression responded rapidly to Effexor, but it slowly became clear that M. also had ADD.

M. was the type of person rarely recognized as having ADD. She'd been a fairly good student who had always gotten her work done. However, she always felt she had been an underachiever, always felt she could have and should have worked harder and more diligently. She always saved things to the last minute, got bored easily, and had trouble finding what she really wanted to do in life. She currently had a job in an office, which was okay, not too demanding, and she was well-thought-of, but she was becoming progressively more dissatisfied with the job and was having inordinate difficulty in deciding whether to apply herself to something else to generate a new, more meaningful career for herself. She'd tried painting, writing, and music, and had found them all enjoyable for a while, but not consistently compelling enough to stick with.

M. and I talked about the way she managed time. She told me that she loved to play volleyball, and she kept planning on participating in games, but she just didn't, and kind of knew she wouldn't. She basically didn't plan her weekends. They just happened. Even though she had lots of things she would have liked to do, including activities connected to career development, she just didn't do them.

In other ways, however, M. was very responsible, very reliable. She was always on time. If she said she'd meet a friend, she did. She never missed work, always paid her bills. She never let anyone else down, but she always felt like she was somehow letting herself down.

When M. did the inner-self exercises, she met someone with whom she was quite familiar. In fact, M. felt that she got in touch with this part of herself quite easily, and that she knew this self quite well and had no problem describing and predicting how this self was likely to handle a whole range of tasks and requests. Outer M. and inner M. were working together all the time. Formally meeting with inner M. was like taking coals to Newcastle. M. knew, liked, and accepted her inner self, but that in no way meant that the inner M. was likely to do everything, or even anything, that the outer M. thought she should do.

It's interesting to note that M. had suffered from seasonal serotonin depression for a decade before she developed the bad stress depression and finally came for help. Inner M., on the other hand, was quite aware that she often didn't feel like doing anything other than what she absolutely had to do. The result was that, even when M. wasn't depressed, she "allowed" her friend inner M. the luxury of an aimless torpor where growth-related activities were concerned. M. wasn't doing the things she thought she should, but she accepted herself well enough, and she was so grateful that she wasn't really depressed, that it didn't seem to trouble her very much.

By the way, I don't know what happened to M. She had another therapist, and after I got her settled into a medication routine, we lost touch.

The point of all this is that using time maps inherently involves examining the nature of your relationship with your inner self. No change in behavior, or even any effort toward change in behavior, is going to occur unless your inner self agrees to the whole process. Some people routinely try new things and know intuitively whether they (the inner they) are open to the experience. They are able to use the tools described above in a structured, rhythmic manner without having the sorts of inner meetings demonstrated in Chapter 1 and described in detail in Chapter 7. If you want to use the time-map system to address changes with which you've been having difficulty for a while, I suggest that you find some way to have a meeting with yourself. Make the first step an agreement that using these tools is worth meeting on a regular basis, and decide with yourself exactly what that basis will be. Otherwise, you will be just as unlikely to use the time-map system as you have been to follow any of the thousands of other pieces of helpful advice you may have heard before and never used.

———◆+◆+◆———

In Chapter Nine we will pull together a few of the different concepts we've been discussing so far in order to present a robust integrated approach to the treatment of attentional issues.

CHAPTER 9

The Treatment of ADD:
Trance, Meditation, and Brain Training

In Chapter 8, we talked about using trance, visualizations, and right-brained skills to help compensate for a particular accumulated deficit, the ability to reliably manage time and tasks. We might say that Chapter 8 straddles two of our three remedies, psychoeducation and integration. Pursuing our remedy paradigm further, we find a number of wonderful books available for psychoeducation about ADD. A few notable ones are all the *"Distraction"* books by Drs. Hallowell and Ratey, *Healing ADD* by Dr. Amen, and *You Mean I'm Not Lazy, Stupid or Crazy?!* by Kate Kelly and Peggy Ramundo (New York: Scribner, 2006). Although this chapter is, as labeled, largely a consideration of trance, meditation, and brain training — in other words, a more general discussion of integration — please stay with me for a moment while I spend just a page or two speaking about medication for ADD.

MEDICATION

As I hope you can tell by now, I am a vigorous proponent of various specific forms of psychotherapy for certain psychopathological conditions. I am not, however, in any way opposed to the judicious use of medication, which is often absolutely necessary.

Almost all of the techniques I have been describing and will describe — any form of brain training at all — will work better when the patient has already been stabilized with medication for ADD and/or depression, as indicated.

Medicating for underlying ADD certainly works best when all the other neurotransmitter abnormalities, hereditary or acquired, have been addressed. In situations of complex or longstanding imbalances, ADD medication may be entirely ineffective unless antidepressants or mood stabilizers are applied first.

When I set out to explain to patients with ADD what they can and cannot expect from taking stimulant medication, I almost always begin by talking about the difference between "focus" with a little "f" and "focus" with a big F. Focus with a little f involves how well you stay with a clearly chosen task once you have chosen and begun it, or how quickly and easily you can read an assignment once you've sat down to it. Focus with a big F is entirely different. It involves who you are, what matters to you, and what you have chosen to do. It's about how you've developed your executive functioning.

Medicine is immediately helpful with focus because it directly strengthens (stimulates) inhibitory centers, but it is only indirectly helpful with Focus. Focus involves organizing, prioritizing, and planning. Of course, doing these things is easier if your focus is good, if you can easily stay on the task of defining yourself, your goals, and your strategies. Medicine is useful but not sufficient on its own for Focus because, although it improves focus in general, it does not choose for you what to focus on. It will not organize you unless you specifically choose to use improved focus for that purpose. Hence, all our other techniques.

Stimulant medication, methylphenidate (such as Ritalin and Concerta), and dextroamphetamine (Adderall and Dexedrine) are the most commonly used and effective agents for stimulating the prefrontal cortex. Strattera is a new nonstimulant norepinephrine reuptake inhibitor (NRI) that is being marketed for ADD. I commonly use two antidepressants as well, Desiprimine and Wellbutrin. Desipramine (Norpramin) is a tricyclic antidepressant, also an NRI, that has focusing effects in a good percentage of cases. Wellbutrin is a unique dopamine antidepressant that has focusing properties and works on the subtler Type III pleasure depressions that we discussed in Chapter 4.

Each individual has to discover for him or herself the right dosing, timing, and circumstances for the use of stimulants. Over the years, I have noticed that about one-third of patients find stimulants extremely helpful and use them indefinitely; about one-third use them regularly at first but then drift into a more personalized, intermittent, targeted kind of use; and about one-third either find them unhelpful or find the side effects unpalatable.

For the most part, side effects are minor and dose-related, and can be eliminated by varying the dose or schedule or by changing the medication. The most common side effects by far are loss of appetite (which is transient with regular use), indigestion, insomnia, jumpiness, and "rebound." Rebound, which occurs when the medication is wearing off, can present as depression, fatigue, irritability, or even poorer attention. A less common side effect is headaches.

Although you may find the list of side effects ominous, stimulant and most antidepressant medications are not, in fact, dangerous at all. Any unpleasant effects are usually transient if the medicine is stopped, and will be gone within a matter of hours. There are no lasting negative effects from occasional or regular use. Patients on middle to high doses who want to stop stimulants are advised to taper down their dose over a few days to a week. Abruptly stopping a stimulant may lead to a day or so of feeling tired.

The one way in which stimulants can be dangerous is if they are overused, particularly if they are used to postpone sleep over an extended period. Staying awake by using inappropriately high doses of stimulants is a fine way to let go of reality for a while and earn yourself a visit to a psychiatric hospital. Interestingly, I find that very few of my patients wind up abusing stimulant medication. I think this is largely because people with ADD have trouble getting comfortable, and, as a rule, too much speed just does-n't feel that good.

There is one more important caveat in taking stimulants or antidepressants, either together or separately. In a small but significant group of patients, these medicines can trigger a manic or hypomanic response, sometimes with serious consequences. It is not clear whether these situations represent previously undiscovered bipolar illness that would have eventually revealed itself or whether these illnesses would not have occurred in the absence of medication. Most often, this reaction shows up as increased irritability and slightly odd behavior, or as increased confusion or difficulty with focus. It can also present with racing thoughts on just about any topic.

The recent controversy about the prescription of selective serotonin reuptake inhibitors (SSRIs) to children and adolescents was likely caused by a few extreme examples of this relatively uncommon but not rare reaction to stimulating medications. I would suggest that the affected children became hypomanic in response to the antidepressants at a time when they were still quite depressed and, in a mixed bipolar state, committed suicide. (For a discussion of "Suicide and Bipolar Disorder in Children and Adolescents," see Chapter 4.)

What helps the most in avoiding this sort of outcome is to look carefully for any sign of bipolar illness in the patient and in his or her family history before prescribing an antidepressant or stimulant. If there is any hint of bipolar illness, including temper outbursts, irrational anxieties, or unaccountable rapid shifts into deep sadness, a mood stabilizer is required, before other medicines for depression or ADD can be used. Fortunately there are a wide range of mood stabilizers available that are effective in preventing manic or hypomanic reactions to stimulating medicines. If the patient does suffer a manic or hypomanic reaction, one stops the medication and introduces a mood stabilizer, which will rapidly reverse and control the manic or hypomanic symptoms. The stimulant or antidepressant can then be judiciously reintroduced.

In the end, the most important protection against unwanted outcomes is good communication between the prescriber and patient when starting a new medicine, with no lack of hesitation on the part of the patient to contact the prescriber when something unexpected does develop.

These considerations aside, I do not believe that anyone should be discouraged from taking a stimulant or antidepressant by fears about abuse, health risks, or bipolar reactions. Unwanted reactions can be dealt with relatively easily, and the benefits of proper treatment can be enormous.

In general, I encourage people to use as little medicine as they can and to make career choices for which their unmedicated attentional abilities are adequate. Often, people use medication while in school but discontinue it after graduating, or they use it only when they need to accomplish a problematic task.

Although stimulant medication can be wonderful for pure task performance, and also quite good for increasing working memory and presence of mind, it will not be helpful unless the individual has (1) become a connoisseur of his or her own attention and motivation, and (2) addressed the need to integrate his or her left- and right-brain functioning.

This is where trance comes in.

TRANCE

When we study hypnosis as a therapeutic tool, we quickly realize that the techniques of focused awareness that can be used to resolve pathological conflicts and psychosomatic illnesses have much in common with a whole range of spiritual and motivational techniques that are used to enhance growth, creativity, and human development. We originally talked about using trance to deal with the varied manifestations, the accumulated deficits in executive and other functioning, of unresolved posttraumatic left-right brain dissociation. Here we will talk about its use as a way of addressing and training the underinhibited brain in general.

A few years ago, I read an op-ed article in *The New York Times* in which the Dalai Lama talked about how a number of his most senior followers had recently undergone SPECT scanning, the same kind of scanning that Dr. Amen has used to detect the consistent situational prefrontal underactivity in ADD. The brains of these monks showed enormously high activity in those areas correlated with joy, pleasure, contentment, and compassion. These were some happy fellows. The clear implication was that Buddhist meditative training influences the patterns of brain activity in a particular and decidedly positive manner.

The idea that brain-activity patterns change when we learn is not a new one. A SPECT scan of an average person listening to music shows activity in the right brain, but a SPECT scan of a trained musician shows activity in both the left and right brains. The average person is using his right brain for nonanalytically experiencing the music, while the trained individual is experiencing and analyzing at the same time, having over time created a web of neural interconnection between left and right.

The point of these two little SPECT factoids is that brains are not static. They are dynamic; they change all the time. They evolve and function differently depending on the choices we make, depending on the experiences to which they are exposed.

This has many implications in dealing with ADD, both for adults with ADD and for people who care for children and adolescents with ADD. What kinds of experiences are going to strengthen the function of our underperforming inhibitory systems? The answers are everywhere, of course. Almost any sort of human activity will qualify. What all the answers have in common is that they somehow lead to the stimulation of more brain activity in more places at the same time, that they integrate and utilize both left- and right-brain information-processing channels, that they have a healthy emphasis on the timeless, unselfconscious, "flow," "in the zone" land of the right brain and almost all of them, with just a little stretching, can fit into our broadest definitions of trance.

In Chapter 6, we defined trance as focused concentration that decreased left-brain analytic planning functions and increased any of a range of right-brain experiencing functions. It can also be used, as we've seen, therapeutically, in the treatment of a range of post-traumatic dissociative conditions, to create situations in which the right and the left brain are used simultaneously. You may also recall our contention that focus in ADD is not altogether absent but, rather, finicky, requiring higher levels of what we called motivation. To my understanding, when we talk about the extra motivation required to achieve focus in ADD, we are really talking about increased activity in particular brain areas and about increased brain activity in general. Clearly, a threshold of general brain arousal (ADD is about controlling the level of stimulation) exists at which prefrontal cortex inhibitory functioning is adequate to maintain attention. Trance is a state that allows for increased control over a wide range of brain activity.

I think there's little question that the Dalai Lama's SPECT-scan subjects can use their own brand of trances to turn on and off just about any parts of their brains that they desire. So, what exactly are these guys doing?

MEDITATION

Well, they're meditating. . . .

"Meditating" is a big umbrella word for a huge subset of trance. The most basic exercise is called mindfulness meditation. It is a Buddhist technique, but as the Dalai Lama points out in the article in *The Times*, it is a simple exercise that need not be connected to any philosophy or religious teaching. The idea is simply to sit quietly, clear your mind, and watch your thoughts come and go without becoming engaged with or attached to them. Thoughts will come into your mind, seemingly unbidden, about all sorts of things. The instruction given is to "let them float away, like clouds passing before the sun." It really amounts to an exercise at quieting the constant inner commentary created by our judging left-brain selves. Very often, these simple instructions are coupled with an instruction to focus on the sensations associated with breathing (there are many), which increase experiential processing even as we are disconnecting from the judging processes.

Much of what follows is based on your having read Chapter 6

and made some attempt to create an individualized multistep trance portal for yourself. Remember that the left brain developed in order to keep us safe in a complex world, to allow us to label, name, keep track of, and avoid negative outcomes. Getting comfortable enough to turn down those circuits allows us to use a wide range of brain abilities that are usually somewhat obscured behind our often hypertrophied judging dialogue. Remember also that this nonverbal, experiential, right-brain aspect of ourselves may be very powerful, smarter, and faster than the smaller, more careful left brain.

Mindfulness meditation requires that we watch the flow of our thoughts and get some distance from them, that we sit quietly without moving, watching our breath, despite the many little "do this" instructions that emanate from our left-brain thinking.

Meditation has hundreds of variations, and some wonderful guidebooks are available for anyone who is interested in reading about and practicing some of the techniques. *Journey of Awakening* (New York: Bantam, 1990) by Ram Dass, the ex-Harvard psychologist, ex-Timothy Leary/LSD disciple, is very broad and simply terrific. *How to Meditate* (Boston: Little, Brown, 1999) by Lawrence LeShan is much simpler, but it's very clear and useful. In *Full Catastrophe Living*, Dr. Jonathan Kabat-Zinn describes his well-tested, twelve-week, meditation-based stress-reduction program.

As Dr. Kabat-Zinn documents, meditation has a long experimental history of positive effects on health: lowering blood pressure, decreasing the rate of heart attacks, improving ulcers, and irritable bowel syndrome, lowering back pain, and asthma. Transcendental meditation (TM) has been explored the most extensively in this regard. The instructions for this technique are even simpler than for mindfulness meditation: Simply repeat a mantra silently while sitting quietly.

Remember that we are turning down our judging mind and turning up our experiencing mind. What we know about the left brain is that the more repetitive the task, the less possibility for external novelty and stimulation, the safer it feels, the more easily it begins to shut off. When we give the left brain a repetitive instruction, such as watch your breath or repeat a phrase over and over, the left brain lets go. When it does, we become more relaxed. Training your mind to let go of worrying so that your body can carry less tension has obvious health benefits. Unsurprisingly, it also improves focus.

Ram Dass describes walking meditations, dancing meditations, and singing meditations. Buddhist meditations often involve sitting with a particular image, poem, or even idea in mind. Something all meditations and inner trances share is arrival at a state of mental openness, a less left brain-ness, usually but not always including a deep physical relaxation. They vary enormously in terms of whether or not some other right-brain activity is being stimulated. One of the questions that can be looked at in any given trance or meditation is whether we are looking to block or shut down the left brain entirely, to go completely inside, or whether we are looking to create a situation of co-consciousness, where right-brain activity is enhanced but left-brain involvement continues, for instance as in the trance of playing an instrument

The Dalai Lama's followers are, I believe, using this state of mental openness to focus on the deepest, most intuitive levels of pattern-seeing ability, what I would call the spiritual self. At this nonverbal level, we are able to perceive the basic interconnectedness of all living things, and the compassionate parts of our brain turn on and can remain turned on, improving the general responsiveness of our prefrontal cortex and increasing our focus in everything we do.

OTHER BRAIN TRAINING

Quite interesting in this regard are the parallels between the effects of regular meditation and those of various sorts of bio- and neuro-feedback training, which, in some hands, has been reported to be very successful in treating ADD. Some bio-feedback techniques are extremely simple, using sound and a pulse monitor or blood pressure cuff to lower the blood pressure and slow the pulse. In other techniques, brain-wave machines present patterns of auditory and visual stimulation that help train the brain to relax and focus. Bio- and neuro-feedback training hasn't caught on all that much as a common treatment because it's time-consuming, costly, and, although it's pleasant, its effects are subtle and indirect. The harried parents of children and adolescents with ADD rarely seem to find it worth the fight to get their defiant offspring to go to the treatment sessions. I think that bio- and neuro-feedback training causes a trance state variant-focused awareness, immobility, increased experience, and decreased judgment — changing the brain in somewhat the same way that meditation and other trance techniques do.

In addition to meditation and neuro- and bio-feedback training, there are a whole range of Eastern meditative disciplines that I think generally accomplish the same goals and also include much-needed physical activity. These include any of the major strains of yoga, chi gong (Chinese energy yoga), tai chi, and virtually any of the martial arts. Also good are dance and gymnastics — really almost any regular training that involves stretching or moving. Anything that involves absorption in the body in a meditative manner can create rhythms of relative left-brain quiet and can have similar salutary effects.

These sorts of trance-inducing exercise activities are not a cure for ADD, and they are not meant to replace the judicious use of medicine. However, they can help to improve focus in a variety of subtle ways. Practicing becoming aware of and shutting off the judging dialogue encourages becoming more spontaneous, less inhibited, and less weighted by expectations and regrets. It's easier to see clearly what you really want. You become generally less conflicted and therefore less distracted. Most importantly, though, it gives you a way to get centered, a small ritual you can use to clear your mind and relax your body when you are preparing for something that will require your best efforts, something that will require the best use of relatively scarce reflective abilities.

I suspect that many of the effects of this sort of right-brain time rituals work only as long as the activity continues unabated.

(I wonder if the monks have to keep meditating to keep those happy brains humming along. Hard to tell.) I do not for a second think that every child, adolescent, or adult with ADD is going to use neuro-feedback, yoga, or meditation. What I do think is that, given the proven ability of meditative types of activities to alter brain activity, physical health, and focus in general, people with ADD should be on the alert for opportunities for enhancing and deepening activities that have meditative or trance-like aspects.

CREATING YOUR OWN BRAIN TRAINING

Some things about training yourself to clear your mind are, in, fact lasting. At the most basic level, people who are aware that they have ADD and are consciously struggling with it need to know how to arrive at the state of mental openness and physical relaxation, what I like to call the restful feeling of floating, whether they use it all that regularly or not. It's an important skill to have and a relatively easy one to master. In fact, I would say that most people can learn to improve their skill at manipulating their left- and right-brain activity levels and, therefore, their skill at mental and physical relaxation.

Chapter 6 should have given you everything you need to find a way to enter a trance or meditative state. I teach almost everyone with whom I work the basic trances described there. I ask that they spend five minutes twice a day in a state of focused awareness (trance), sometimes just for tension reduction, often to do some of the exercises we talked about in Chapters 7 and 8.

Focus does not occur in a vacuum, and distractibility depends quite a bit on how much we are at peace with the world around us. It's pretty hard to grow up with ADD without having issues with authority and anger. For myself at least, I've found that using trance in the context of Buddhist ideas about compassion and connectedness goes a long way toward taking a whole arena of pointless, dead-end distractions right off the table. In the most general way, I think it's a good idea to reach inside to find the spiritual parts of the brain, the parts that go on when we are feeling most connected to the living universe. As I've said, I think these are parts that can be turned on and stay on, creating a general increase in brain arousal and, in so doing, adding focus and motivation to everything we do.

Meditation is a word that is used mostly in reference to solitary trances that may or may not come with spiritual, religious, or cultural trappings. Hypnosis is a trance that involves another person guiding an individual in the cultivation and use of specific right-brain functions. Self-hypnosis is somewhere in between, a solitary trance guided somewhat by hypnotic understandings. Trance itself, however, is a common, everyday event that occurs naturally all the time. The question is how to recognize it and how to harness it.

We have defined trance as focused concentration, an absorbed experiential state in which judging decreases. Part of the process of mastering yourself when you have ADD is becoming a connoisseur of focus. To me, that means learning to notice your patterns of experiential absorption and using what you've noticed as the key factor in creating your schedule. Just another way of saying "Seek your bliss."

The whole focus on "attention deficit" obscures the understanding that underactivity in inhibitory areas will be most comfortably balanced by overactivity somewhere else. People with ADD are more comfortable at higher levels of stimulation. Focusing on recognizing and cultivating activities with trance-like, right-brained components both provides that comfortable stimulation and gives the poor, overworked, left-brained worriers and planners some much-needed respite.

In this context, let me mention *The 20 Minute Break* by Ernest Lawrence Rossi Ph.D. (New York: Tarcher, 1991). Dr. Rossi is the man who assisted Milton H. Erickson, M.D., the legendary founder of modern clinical hypnosis, in compiling Erikson's written and spoken work into twelve magnificent volumes. In *The 20 Minute Break*, Dr. Rossi talks about the natural rhythms of goal-directed (left-brained) and process-oriented (right-brained) activity present in less industrialized cultures, and he notes a universal ninety-minute cycle of alternation between these two types of activities. He goes on extensively about the range of stress-related human ills that comes from interfering with these rhythms, as western cultures tend to relentlessly demand long, uninterrupted periods of left-brained worry and work of various kinds. Dr. Rossi teaches that we should notice the prompts our bodies give us that it wants to shift rightward (for example, yawning, sexual thoughts, thirst, and stretching) and recommends that, although even he understands how difficult and unlikely this is in the modern world, we go into a twenty-minute trance state once every ninety minutes, up to six times a day if possible.

After reading Dr. Rossi's book, you may be tempted to think of people with ADD as individuals whose left-brain functioning is more easily disturbed by a culture that overuses it. If we are not given the time, opportunity, and skill to enter a full range of productive right-brain states at rhythms that suit us, we become less and less able to use our left-brained executive functions appropriately.

Finding rhythms of right-brained activity and the focus that goes with them is important because of the repeated observation that expertise in any one area over time tends to generalize into better functioning in other areas as well. A master in any one discipline automatically has a leg up in any new pursuit. Therefore, parents should expose their children with ADD to the broadest possible range of right-brained activities, notice their responses, and empower them by engaging them repetitively in those areas in which they demonstrate relatively ready absorption in comfortable rhythms. We need to help our children "seek their bliss," after which they will be much better able to generalize into other, more problematic areas.

Just to be clear here, the underlying idea is to learn to modulate the presence of your left brain, to allow it to be present, looking out for you without dominating you completely. Having accepted that, you will be able to reach other, more experiential parts of your brain and use them to raise your general brain activity to the level where behavioral inhibition becomes adequate.

PUTTING IT ALL TOGETHER: CONTROLLING YOUR MENTAL STATES

One of the more elegant metaphors for what I'm looking to put across here is the yin and yang symbol (see Figure 7). What all the different types of activities we've discussed above have in common is that they can be seen as representing the insertion of the small circles into the opposite field, as in the diagram below:

Figure 7: Dysfunction and Mental Health

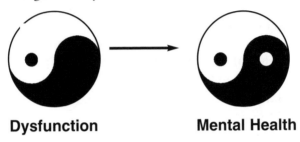

Dysfunction   **Mental Health**

The ancient and powerful yin and yang symbol has enormous resonance because it so deftly represents the ever-present push for humans to integrate their left- and right-brain functioning. Imagine the symbol without the small dots. This represents an uninsightful, uncomfortable, or ineffectual left brain and an angry and heedless or perhaps frightened right brain, each knowing little or nothing about the other. Our goal is to create the mental experiences, to lay down the pathways and the connections, that allow both kinds of knowledge to operate simultaneously, to create those circles in the opposite fields.

The great psychotherapist and theoretician Heinz Kohut, M.D., described the process of mirroring, in which parents empathize with and then label their children's emotions, thereby establishing a basis for gaining control of them. It's not much of a stretch to see this as an early left brain-right brain co-consciousness experience. Placing a piece of the left brain into the right is a safety net that can prevent us from becoming absorbed in experiential states to such a degree that we endanger our health or larger goals. If we wish to explain the self-destructive behavior of people such as the eating disordered, the gambler, or the substance abuser, or the emotional incontinence of the chronically angry, sad, or nervous, we need go no further than to postulate an unleavened right brain.

By the same token, left-brain planners that do not appreciate the larger patterns of social and emotional behavior perceived only by the right brain will be tense and stressed and will severely limit the range of their experience. They will make plans that have no heart, empty sterile plans that reflect only the shoulds and not the realities of the selves, plans that the right brain will be likely to reject, either immediately or eventually.

Once you begin to see the central role of managing the left and right relationship in the human drama, once you accept that it is the goal of the left brain to do its job and then get out of the way, to manage the world so that we can be safe enough to actually turn on the rest of our brains, you can see that guidance for this is everywhere around us. It pervades all cultures, from all times. Almost any tradition of wisdom and enlightenment has at its core some acceptance of a dual way of looking at the world.

When the left and right brains are co-conscious, we can enter a state of experiential intention, we can have the elusive "desire without desire" (a Buddhist idea that captures the essence of left-right co-consciousness), what can be called intention without effort. One of the hallmarks of trance, again quoting Stephen Gilligan, is "effortless expression" — the uninhibited flow of creativity. There is a wonderful book devoted entirely to describing and promoting these timeless co-conscious states that is titled *Flow* by Mihaly Csikszentmihalyi (New York: Harper Perennial, 1991). In it, Csikszentmihalyi describes a broad range of arts, crafts, athletic, and intellectual pursuits that can result in flow states — that is, states that are characterized by an optimal level of challenge, states in which left-brain judgment is suspended just enough to allow uninhibited expression.

It is even quite possible to form flow states around activities with substantial verbal or logical aspects. In my hyperactive youth, my initial trance portals were reading and puzzles. I read stories voraciously, particularly mythology of all kinds. Anyone who knew me for the motorized little buzz saw that I was could easily see the trance-like effect a good book could have. I would go as far as to say that repeated attention to myths and stories in childhood and youth creates a narrative, pattern-seeing sort of right-brained self that is then able to extract the complex wisdom, the blueprints for full, integrated humanity that Dr. Campbell has found at the heart of our narrative traditions. My weary parents also discovered early on that the right puzzle book (words or numbers) could entrance me easily, too, and this served me well later in examination situations. Remember that trance or flow co-consciousness states are characterized by unselfconsciousness and physical relaxation, and that following extended periods of trance, people tend to feel refreshed and invigorated. My puzzle trance popped into place as a teenager, when I took extended examinations like the Scholastic Aptitude Test (SAT). I wasn't at all anxious. I focused intensely, and for a few days afterward, I felt the strange, stimulated sort of euphoria that follows extended trance or meditation. I still use reading (mostly multivolume space operas) and puzzles (nowadays, the double-crosstic word puzzles found at the back of *The New York Times* Sunday magazine) to clear my mind and relax.

As anyone who has employed formal trance in hypnosis or meditation can tell you, the setting and circumstances are critical to initiating and maintaining a state of focused concentration. In people with ADD, understanding and using trance in choosing their activities is a part of becoming connoisseurs of their own focus, of paying attention to their habits of attention. This means not only noticing the circumstances that aid in focus, but becoming empowered to create those circumstances. Youngsters with ADD are routinely and consistently disempowered, made to sit in situations that are extremely socially stimulating and then criticized for not focusing well. Worse yet, even if they have attended properly in a situation in which their preferences are meaningless, with the help of the added motivation provided by a school framework, they are then expected to do homework in a focused and systematic manner once they finally do get free. This is routinely ineffective.

LOVE AS A BRAIN ENHANCER

Individuals with ADD commonly say that they are much better at doing things for others than they are at doing things for themselves. The same way that medication and trancelike activities can raise the level of brain arousal, love — in a generic, nonromantic or nonerotic sense — can cause certain areas of the brain related to interpersonal connectedness to light up. Think of the phrase "She turns me on." Specific parts of the brain are, in fact, "turned on" by love, and this can have interesting effects indeed.

One of my patients is a writer/journalist. She has repeatedly found that when she is in a relationship with someone who likes her writing, she finds it immeasurably easier to sit down and write. I cannot count the number of teenagers with ADD who have told me how much easier it is for them to do schoolwork for teachers they like than for teachers they don't. My belief is that, in the same way that compassionate Buddhist meditation can increase brain arousal in the spiritual centers and therefore improve prefrontal cortex activity enough to facilitate focus, love increases brain arousal in the interpersonal and social centers and has a similar effect on general brain arousal.

Social and interpersonal abilities are both learned and inherited, but when they are present, they offer a very fine route for increasing brain arousal; therefore, focus for individuals with ADD.

THERAPEUTIC TRANCE FOR ADD

The absolute first thing to be said is that the majority of patients I see with ADD have already learned a lot about their own attention along the way. Almost all of them have, in fact, conquered their inattentiveness in at least some areas. The problem is that it's uneven, and it's uneven in all sorts of patterns. By adulthood, most people with ADD have lots of trouble starting things, and that isn't about deficient behavioral inhibition. Rather, it's about your relationship with yourself. If your relationship with your right-brained self is poor, it means that you don't use your knowledge about how to motivate and focus yourself consistently.

A lot of the techniques that I use and recommend to improve motivation and focus have already been discussed in Chapters 6, 7, and 8. All people benefit from enhancing their ability to enter experiential states, as described in Chapter 6. Benefits from the material in Chapter 7 on dissociated ego states or in Chapter 8 on time and task management tend to vary. People usually know what kind of relationship they have with themselves if they think about it. Are they reliable? Are they able to take on new tasks and complete them? Can they do things for others but not for themselves? What categories of things would they like to do but have given up on? In any case, you need some sort of working rapport with yourself even to choose to focus on time maps five minutes twice a day. In the end, I find that both techniques are useful for most people with ADD.

Time maps and the request-handling algorithm are just two tools that can be used to visualize time once you have mastered a state of restful inner focus. Numerous collections of helpful images and metaphors for hypnotists, self-hypnotists, and visualizers are currently available. The broadest and most inclusive of these is D. Corydon Hammond's *Handbook of Hypnotic Suggestions and Metaphors* (New York: W.W. Norton and Company, 1990). Its sixteen chapters include literally hundreds of entries. Most meaningful for people with ADD are Chapter 4, "Ego-Strengthening: Enhancing Esteem, Self-Efficacy, and Confidence," and Chapter 16, "Concentration, Academic Performance, and Athletic Performance." Two other very fine books, *Hypnotherapy Scripts* by Havens and Walters (New York: Bruner and Mazell, 1989) and *Creative Scripts for Hypnotherapy* by Marlene E. Hunter, Ph.D. (Brunner Mazel New York City 1998), have also been helpful to me and are perhaps somewhat more accessible to the average reader than Hammond's gigantic (600 oversized pages with small print) somewhat intimidating handbook.

The range of images and metaphors that can be used once trance is mastered is virtually unlimited. Included immediately below are two metaphors I often use that will be followed by a case study of the creative use of visualized metaphor in a person with ADD.

The Wanting Machine

In this metaphor, you descend into yourself and find the chamber that houses the "wanting machine," a place somewhat akin to the boiler room of a huge ocean liner. Once you arrive there, you look at the machine, which in my boiler room is painted a bright, fire-engine red. It's about the size of an oil tank, looking something like a cross between a vacuum cleaner and an atomic bomb, and it has wires and pipes running out from it in all directions, disappearing into the walls and the ceiling of the chamber.

Stoke up the furnace of the wanting machine to make it chug and huff and pulsate until it's glowing cherry red. It pulsates and burns with energy, desire, libido — with pure, deep wanting — and this energy can be attached to anything you would like. Think carefully, then stoke the machine and send the energy streaming out of the chamber to the places where you need it the most.

The Bull's-Eye

This is a metaphor that is very useful for letting go of negative interpersonal situations. Imagine a huge bull's-eye, alternating red and white concentric circles expanding out as far as the eye can see. You are sitting at the center, and in the circles immediately surrounding you are the people most important to you: your parents, your lovers, your children. Spreading out at ever-greater distances is everyone you know; close friends and colleagues closer to you, older friends further out, acquaintances still further, and, out at the edges, older acquaintances you haven't seen in years.

What is immediately clear is that you have a deep, intuitive, and incontrovertible knowledge of the spatial relationship of any one person to all the others, (A is closer than B but not as close as F), and you can "see" it. The spatial relationship you "see" actually reflects the relative emotional distance between you and all those you know. Perhaps you see people up close to you, in inner circles, but their time has passed; they no longer want or deserve to be held so closely. It is easy enough for you to move those people, watching them walk out to more distant rings, until they are as distant from you as they should be.

When you awake, you will feel much more comfortably detached from the individuals from whom you needed distance.

THE CASE OF V.

V. was an extremely capable, hyperactive man who used trance in an exploratory way over a period of several years. V. had been taking Ritalin and Prozac for a few years before I met him. He stopped the Prozac soon thereafter and never needed it again, but he stayed on the Ritalin.

At the time I met him, V. was working as a church organist. He was about forty years old and had already had two aborted careers, one in the military in which he had risen to become an admiral's right hand and one in the priesthood in which he had been stationed at the Vatican while a senior Seminarian. In both cases, he was fast tracked to advance but became disenchanted and left. He was also gay and had been struggling with that all his life. V. was a guy who functioned perfectly for others — in the navy, in the priesthood, at school — but his room was a mess, he did everything at the last minute, and he could be very impatient. He had suffered from depression in his thirties, which, in my opinion, was due to the added stress of maintaining his high performance in spite of his hyperactivity. V. didn't look hyperactive, but inside, he certainly was. His depressions did not return once he took Ritalin regularly. He felt Ritalin helped him with whatever work he did.

V. didn't need me to teach him how to get things done. His executive functioning was better than mine when he was able to use it. V.'s two issues (which were really the same) were his career and his emotional life. He feared he was unable to love. He had never really had a sustained relationship with either sex. He had dated women early on to fit in, then went through some brief periods of bathhouse promiscuity, but never had anything even remotely like a partnership. Careerwise, he was confused about what he wanted to do. Being an organist felt like no work at all, and he felt he needed to find something more substantial, something that might eventually provide savings, property, a pension — more than just sustenance.

In both aspects of his life, V. was what one might call inhibited. Maybe an even better way to say it is that he was cut off from the deeper, more emotional, and more passionate sides of himself. He was out of touch. V. knew all this, but just talking analytically didn't help him to get in touch any better . Fortunately, V. was an excellent visualizer and an excellent trance subject.

The very first thing I did with V. was to ask him to identify the feeling that prevented him from reaching out to attractive gay men, and then I had him go to the meadow and find a child who also felt that way. Almost right away, V. met a boy of five whose grandmother had just died. He recalled vividly that his grandmother was the warm and caring figure in his life, and that his parents, although they certainly loved him, were rather distant and stoic. What became evident to V. was that no one had consoled him or explained anything about his grandmother's death to him, and that right then, V. had shut off a certain part of himself.

This felt like a breakthrough. Over the next few months, we spent some sessions reworking these experiences, and V. felt more open and more interested in the men around him. However, he still somehow never got around to asking anyone out or dating anyone or sleeping with anyone. He still couldn't decide what to do besides play music. Learn about computers? Go for an MBA? He was unclear.

After a few more months, we decided to try a more exploratory, open kind of trance technique. I asked V. to imagine himself walking down a country road toward a small town and to ask his inner self to help him uncover some clues as to what exactly was stopping him from moving forward in his work and his life.

The very first time he did this, V. immediately realized that, in his trance, he was wearing a military uniform. He became aware that he needed to remove the uniform to be free, and in the trance, he did.

V. proved remarkably adept at returning to the road in the country, and this was only one of a series of images that V. received from his deeper self about what was getting in his way. I gave him very little input other than to ask him to enter the trance (he was so good that that was all it took) and then to pose the same questions: What was stopping him from loving? What did he see? In the second trance, he saw that he was wearing a priest's garb, and he realized that he also needed to be remove this. On another visit, he found he was wearing a suit of medieval armor. This, too, had to go. In other sessions, he saw himself blindfolded, in others shackled, and once, with plugs in his ears. In one fascinating session, we discovered that he could tell with a quick glance who was gay (they glowed pink), who was straight (they glowed blue), and who was sexually available (they sparkled).

A lot of the later images were about his fear of homosexuality and his expectations of discovery and punishment. He soon overcame these obstacles and began to date. Today, V. is living in the suburbs in a committed relationship with his pharmacist partner. His house is even surrounded by a white picket fence. V. realized he loved playing the organ and has managed to combine it with teaching at a local school. He finally feels he is living fully.

Looking back, V. feels certain that the trance walks in the country are what enabled him to love and to find rewarding work; and that may be so. It is certainly not inconceivable that any reasonably skillful conversational therapy might also have produced the same results. Possibly just time and natural maturation could have done the same.

What I think is worth pointing out is that V., who suffered from both ADD and depression, was still not functioning fully once these two conditions were addressed. His dissociation, his being cut off from his deeper emotions, was post-traumatic, and even if the trauma was by some standards mild, it required another level of intervention to be dealt with effectively.

There are, of course, many aspects of the therapy for ADD, and of the therapy for the other conditions that complicate it, and that I have been unable to cover here. Most of the currently available ADD treatments were specifically developed for children and adolescents with ADD — particularly angry and fearful adolescents — and often, unfortunately, they are not too effective. The therapies we discussed in the last two chapters are for motivated adults who are seeking tools to control their partially successful lives. Like trance itself, such treatment requires active participation or it is fruitless.

Treating ADD in mature individuals requires that we look at medication, psychoeducation, cognitive restructuring, relaxation training, and hypnotherapy both for executive-functioning skill acquisition and for integration of the self. At the end of the day, it all comes back to Joseph Campbell and "seek your bliss." Psychotherapy for ADD comes down to productively releasing the hyperactivity, to solving the attentional problem by empowering the individual to find suitable rhythms of activity. Whatever techniques are utilized, this is the underlying core: the confidence that ADD need not be a disability, that needed skills and self knowledge can be absorbed. ADD represents a great paradox and a great public-health challenge. When unleashed, when properly trained, people who are hyperactive or have ADD can be powerful leaders and innovators. My own uncle, for example, Dr. David Shoch, was the president of the American Board of Ophthalmology and chairman of the Ophthalmology Department at Northwestern University for more than twenty years. No one ever said he had ADD, but he was active (hyperactive?) and accomplished enough for several men. Other examples include Lyndon Johnson (read Robert Caro's landmark biography and tell me if I'm wrong); Bill Clinton, whom I someday hope to meet and persuade of the fact; and Howard Stern, the unrivaled, if uncrowned, King of the Hyperactives, whose entire audience, I believe, would likewise be so categorized. I cannot tell you how many extraordinarily accomplished people with ADD I have met. And yet, at the same time, can we deny that our prisons, our divorce courts, our drug and alcohol clinics, our "special schools" are filled with people with ADD who have not empowered themselves? We need to learn what separates the people who do master themselves from those who do not. If we can learn what separates them, we can create effective treatments, and the positive effects can be legion indeed. Millions upon millions of people — far more than is currently acknowledged — are affected by ADD. It is my fondest hope that the material I have presented in Chapters 8 and 9 not only will help the individuals with ADD who read it, but will also stimulate other psychotherapists and hypnotherapists to turn their focus to questions of attention. Their help is sorely needed.

CHAPTER 10

The Treatment of Depression

In Chapter 4, we introduced the idea that neurotransmitter disorders could be divided into four categories. Psychotherapy for these disorders begins with making a distinction between the ones that are hereditary and those that are acquired. Bipolar-spectrum disorders and serotonergic disorders are hereditary, while norepinephrine/stress depressions and dopamine/pleasure depressions are acquired. The acquired disorders are distinguished by the fact that they are potentially entirely reversible; that is, with the proper combination of stress reduction, alteration in attitudes, and lifestyle changes, it is possible to be cured in the sense that medication can be stopped without relapse for a considerable period of time. Such skill acquisition may also be useful in the hereditary disorders, but it is unlikely that the hereditary disorders can be successfully treated without the continued use of medication.

In this chapter, we will discuss the treatment of each of these groups of disorders, as well as their subtypes. The bipolar-spectrum disorders include three subtypes, the serotonergic disorders include five subtypes, and the norepinephrine/stress depressions and dopamine/pleasure depressions each have two subtypes. What holds each group of subtypes together is a common response to a particular class of medicines.

BIPOLAR-SPECTRUM DISORDERS

The bipolar-spectrum disorders include manic-depressive disorder, cyclothymia, and intermittent explosive disorder. First and foremost in the treatment of these disorders are the patient's acceptance of the validity of the diagnosis, the patient's understanding of the role of medication in this condition, and the recruitment of the patient as a cooperative observer of the natural patterns of his or her own particular illness.

For many years, the name manic-depressive disorder conjured up the idea of an obvious and discrete episode of elated or irritable mood accompanied by incredible energy, ranting speech, poor judgment, and even flat-out delusions ("I am the Messiah") that could, at times, be indistinguishable from those of schizophrenia. What we have learned in the past few decades is that there is a wide range of patterns of mood and behavioral alteration that can be affected by a particular class of drugs, in this case the mood stabilizers. Many of these patterns contain little or nothing in the way of classic manic episodes.

Manic-Depressive Disorder

Manic-depressive disorder, also known as bipolar disorder and bipolar affective disorder, is extremely variable in the prominence of manic or hypomanic symptoms. When these manic or hypomanic states are clearly present, antipsychotics and mood stabilizers are the mainstays of treatment. There is also a group of subtle, often treatment-resistant depressions that do not have any clear manic or hypomanic symptoms, yet they appear to be caused by the same underlying mechanism and to respond only to mood stabilizers. This group is characterized by sudden shifts in mood and deep, listless lows that come on suddenly, remit just as rapidly and unpredictably, and seem divorced from any comprehensibly stressful situation. They are also often recognized by the presence of racing thoughts, be they angry, sexual, sad, nonsensical and obsessive, or even suicidal. Very often, these types of depressions, after an initial period of improvement, are made worse by antidepressants. The take-home message here is that people with depression that has been resistant to standard antidepressant treatment would do well to experiment with the mood stabilizers even if they have no obvious manic history.

When manic or hypomanic episodes are clear and persistent, the most important variables that affect outcome are sleep and substance abuse. Patients must get enough sleep and must avoid abusing substances, including pot, coke, alcohol, and, if possible, caffeine and nicotine. This is often easier said than done, but if these two issues are not properly addressed, the chance of a volatile, unruly condition increases sharply. Even one bad night can trigger a manic response, so the patient should have a supply of sleeping pills and should be encouraged to use them.

Research has demonstrated that when people with manic-depressive disorder are taught cognitive-behavioral techniques, their prominent manic or hypomanic cyclings diminish in frequency. I will discuss in detail the combination of techniques I use in the section on the treatment of norepinephrine/stress depressions. Let us say here only that, although these techniques are useful adjuncts in the treatment of manic-depressive disorder, they are unlikely to work well unless they are used in conjunction with appropriate medication.

Medication compliance is a continuing and difficult issue in the treatment of manic-depressive disorder with manic elements. People whose manic elements are mild are often energetic and productive when hypomanic and may be reluctant to blunt the feelings with medication. Unfortunately, such periods are usually followed by depressive episodes that can be quite extended. I therefore advocate tight control of even mild hypomanic symptoms. Even in the absence of pleasant hypomania states, patients with a history of mania are tempted to stop their medications after extended periods of stability. I recommend against this, as the return of symptoms can be subtle and insidious, and mania or hypomania can be remarkably disruptive to work, career, and relationships. It is the rare bipolar patient who hasn't learned the hard way that it is a mistake to take the illness lightly.

I have used lithium, Depakote, Neurontin, Lamictal, Trileptal, Topamax, and Gabitril in recent years. All of these agents are capable of controlling manic and hypomanic episodes. They can also have prominent effects on depression and anxiety. Neurontin is very good for the treatment of anxiety. I most often use it in conjunction with tricyclic antidepressants or Remeron in the treatment of stress depressions. I have found Lamictal to have particularly strong antidepressant effects, and Trileptal to be very good for atypical sorts of manic symptoms.

Cyclothymia

Let me describe two classically cyclothymic patients who responded beautifully to Lamictal. The first was a thirty-year-old man, a TV and film writer with a flourishing career and a happy marriage. The second was a female, a twenty-seven-year-old teacher, again in a good relationship with a fiancé. Both reported the sudden and inexplicable onset of gloom, darkness, and negativity that left just as quickly as it came. Both reported a disconnect between their ideas and philosophy about life and the terrible feelings they reported having from time to time. Both kept their negative feelings largely to themselves but felt that they struggled continuously. "I have a great life," they both said. "Why can't I enjoy it?"

When I asked the female patient about it, she recollected a few periods of unusual energy and productivity. The male patient, on the other hand, had been diagnosed with ADD in childhood. He was always energetic and productive when he felt okay, and often appeared okay to others even when he wasn't feeling well.

Both underwent a rapid and complete change with the Lamictal. They no longer needed to fight off irrational gloom, and they barely even knew they were taking any medicines.

To me, cyclothymia is differentiated from mania by the mild and relatively manageable nature of the hypomania and by a picture of depression that is quite unrelated to situation. In addition, it has a relatively rapid onset compared to the three other types of depressions.

Often, cyclothymic patients require no therapy at all. The two patients we just discussed, for instance, had both been working by themselves for years trying to learn how to deal with their inherited patterns. Once they took the Lamictal, they were like slingshots, finally able to use all they had learned.

A word on Lamictal: In a very small number of cases, serious, even fatal, rashes have occurred with its use. It appears to me that these fatal rashes developed after initial, milder rashes were ignored, and that cautious dosing has greatly decreased the incidence of even mild rashes. The psychiatric dosages of Lamictal are much lower than those for epilepsy, for which it was initially, and is still most frequently, used. I, for one, feel quite safe using it. Depakote, lithium, and Trileptal are all acceptable alternatives.

Intermittent Explosive Disorder

Intermittent explosive disorder is about irrational anger that far exceeds its provocation in both intensity and duration. Again, I'll mention two such cases that I successfully treated with mood stabilizers. Both cases were adolescent boys, one middle class and one working class. The middle-class boy was fifteen. His father was a therapist and his mother a teacher. His parents reported explosive rage at mild provocation. He would scream expletives and sometimes throw things, and he could take hours or days to calm down. Even the boy admitted that it didn't make sense but, once he got into it, his rage seemed to have a life of its own.

The working-class boy, age sixteen, had already been in a series of fights in which he had let go of himself in a truly frightening manner. When I met him, he was intensely aware of his potential to hurt someone seriously. In fact, he was avoiding gym because he felt that he was at risk of attacking someone if they jostled him the wrong way.

Both of these boys actively disapproved of their tempers, and both responded to medication promptly with a significant decrease in their explosive feelings and behavior. The middle-class boy took Depakote. The working-class boy found Depakote too sedating, but did well with Lamictal. Intermittent explosive disorder is more than just the impulsive anger of the person with ADD or the irritability of the person with serotonin depression. The inordinate, intractable quality is what distinguishes the temper of this disorder. There are, of course, many psychotherapeutic techniques for managing anger and many different causes of an anger that can lead to psychotherapeutic intervention. Most anger has to do with the underlying philosophy of the individual, with his expectations about his own rights and the rights of others, and with the rapid, unexamined transformation of fear or sadness into a more psychologically tolerable, externally based emotion. A full discussion of therapeutic approaches to anger is beyond the scope of this book. However, some of the stress reduction techniques that we will discuss shortly may be useful. The take-home for this section is that there are some species of anger that are beyond the psychological and the therapeutic, that are, in fact, related to the same system responsible for the other bipolar-spectrum subtypes, and respond to mood stabilizers.

A considerable amount has been written in recent decades speculating on how the bipolar disordes look in adolescents and latency-age children. Many of the symptoms seem to me to resemble what I am calling intermittent explosive disorder. It remains to be

---

Bipolar-Spectrum Disorders and ADD

Questions have been raised about the relationship between ADD and the bipolar-spectrum disorders. The middle-class boy I treated for intermittent explosive disorder also had ADD. These two conditions seem to operate independently of each other. He took a range of ADD medications (stimulants gave him tics), but finally arrived at Strattera for academic focus. Although Depakote helped his temper, it did nothing for any of his other ADD-related symptoms. Stimulant and other ADD medications didn't help his temper either until he took Depakote.

In the fifteen years that I have treated people with ADD, I have had quite a few patients in whom ADD and bipolar-spectrum disorder overlapped. I have also treated several young men in whom stimulants caused a bipolar response. It is well known that a small percentage of individuals (less than 1 percent) who take antidepressants and stimulants will develop a manic or hypomanic response. In these cases, the addition of any mood stabilizer usually allows the continuation of the treatment for the underlying ADD or neurotransmitter abnormality.

It remains to be seen exactly what sort of relationship exists between ADD and bipolarity. No doubt they coexist. Whether they do so at a rate higher than would be predicted by chance is not yet known.

seen whether such children do or do not progress into full-blown manic-depressive disorder later in life, and whether early treatment influences that likelihood. Such research is in the works. The psychotherapy of the bipolar-spectrum disorders, as we can see, is largely pharmacological. Psychoeducation is also vital, as the illness is characterized by sudden shifts in mood and patients need to become trained observers of their conditions in order to collaborate and communicate with their physicians if disruptive instability is to be avoided. Cognitive behavioral therapy, covered further along in this chapter, may be useful in reducing the frequency of manic or depressive episodes.

SEROTONERGIC DISORDERS

Perhaps the greatest advance in the history of modern psychiatry has been the discovery and widespread use of drugs that specifically address disorders of the neurotransmitter serotonin. Since the release of Prozac in 1987, five more selective serotonin reuptake inhibitors (Paxil, Zoloft, Luvox, Celexa, and Lexapro) and four broader drugs (Serzone, Effexor, Cymbalta, and Remeron) have become available. There are five types of serotonergic disorders — seasonal affective disorder, female hormonal depression, social phobia, obsessive depression, and obsessive-compulsive disorder — and they vary considerably in their clinical pictures and in responses to therapy. It is important to remember that there can be considerable overlap among these five types. They coexist in any and all combinations. Remember as well that any of the five subtypes or any combination of the five types can coexist with any of the subtypes from any of the other categories.

Seasonal Affective Disorder

The classic picture of a serotonin depression involves sleeping too much, eating too much, and irritability. Seasonal affective disorder (SAD) is a clearly inherited biochemical illness. I think it is helpful to think of SAD as a little bit like hibernaton — like a grouchy bear just before winter, eating a lot, growling at everybody, anxiously anticipating a long sleep.

People with SAD may have difficulty falling asleep, especially if it overlaps with obsessive types of serotonin pathology or with stress depression, but the hallmark of the condition is daytime fatigue and trouble getting out of bed. People with SAD may sleep quite a lot, up to sixteen to twenty hours per day, or they may sleep only four to five broken hours, but their sleep does not seem sufficiently restful. They wake up late, they wake up tired, and they have little energy when they are awake.

Seasonal affective disorder is so named because a good deal of the time (at least early in life) it comes on in October or November, when the days become significantly shorter, and it often improves or goes away between March and May, when the days begin to lengthen again. Patients often report having difficult winters as early as ninth or tenth grade, although SAD can begin any time through the late twenties.

The depression of SAD is all about medicine, light treatment, and geography. No amount of psychotherapy or enlightened living will completely eliminate these seasonal changes once they have begun to show themselves. People with the SAD pattern of depression can almost certainly find close relatives who suffer similarly to a greater or lesser degree. This positive family history can often be seen hiding behind the screen of self-medicating substance abuse. Medication is almost always effective in improving, if not entirely eliminating, the fatigue-appetite-irritability triad. If other depressive symptoms remain after trying a few SSRIs or some of their broader cousins, the presence of other, coexisting types of depression should be strongly considered.

It is important to state clearly that the SAD pattern of symptoms (sleeping too much, eating too much, and irritability) is quite capable of being present all year round and does not always worsen significantly in the winter. Occasionally, such a pattern will emerge on a more intermittent basis during life crises, although this is fairly unusual. More commonly, the condition is seasonal or chronic, and I have very often heard patients tell of symptoms that were seasonal in their late teens and early twenties, but that lasted longer and longer as they aged until, by their mid-thirties, they lasted year-round.

Geography is another important consideration in the treatment of SAD. People with SAD who move to a tropical region, where the daylight is constant throughout the year, can sometimes eliminate their symptoms. Light therapy involves using full-spectrum artificial lights. Typical standard light bulbs close in the range of frequencies considerably in comparison to sunlight. These lights are available in manufactured "boxes" on the web (sunboxco.com, for example) or much more cheaply if you construct some timed lights yourself.

Light therapy is an interesting phenomenon. To benefit from it, you do not even need to have your eyes open. However, there have been reports that, just as with antidepressants, it has occasionally caused a manic or, more commonly, hypomanic response when overused. The standard recommendations are to use a light box for a set period of time — say, one hour once or twice a day, and at a level of intensity between 10,000 and 15,000 lumens. Nowadays, many standard home light bulbs are set for full-spectrum. There are even visors one can wear with full-spectrum bulbs in the brim, so intensity and duration can be varied enormously.

In practice, light therapy often turns out to be a bit of a hassle. The vast majority of sufferers seem to prefer pills, but the therapy can be very useful in conjunction with medication for people who have reached a dose of serotonergic drugs beyond which they experience unpleasant side effects (agitation, insomnia, indigestion, and decreased sexual function are the most common).

Irritability is the second most prominent symptom of SAD after the increased need for sleep. Increased appetite is often present, but it is the least consistent of the three key symptoms. Other serotonin-related symptoms, such as obsessive thinking, interpersonal hypersensitivity, and social performance anxiety, are all potentially present in patients with a classic seasonal picture of pronounced fatigue, but all three of these symptoms can also exist alone — that is, without marked fatigue.

Female Hormonal Depression

Female hormonal depression can actually be broken down into two further types: late luteal phase dysphoria (LLPD), more commonly referred to as PMS, and depressions resulting from larger hormonal insults, specifically post-partum, post-abortion, post-miscarriage, and peri-menopausal depressions.

In PMS, the most prominent feature is irritability, just plain crankiness. Increased appetite is the second most common feature. The terrible fatigue of SAD is not nearly as obvious. The most striking aspect of PMS is the timing. The women with this condition begin to feel awful anywhere from three to ten days before they bleed, and they feel significantly improved in mood, far less irritable, the day that bleeding begins. PMS can show some variability from month to month, but again, these episodes appear to be relatively unrelated to the life situation at the moment. They seem so biological that they defy any specific psychotherapeutic intervention. Therapy can be very useful in learning how to best manage feelings of irritability when they occur and in minimizing their negative impact on familial relationships, but the underlying neurophysiological patterns and the resultant cyclical mood changes do not change with therapy.

The decision about whether to treat this condition with medication depends entirely on how many days the symptoms last versus the negative effects of the medication. When the symptoms last more than seven to ten days, many women feel it is worthwhile to eliminate the irritability with the help of an SSRI.

The other type of female hormonal depression, the one that results from insults such as pregnancy, miscarriage, abortion, and menopause, can be among the most profound and debilitating depressions and is also among those most likely to include psychotic features. Post-partum depression can involve the profound fatigue of SAD, but it also frequently has an obsessive ruminative aspect and a profound sense of being overwhelmed and incapable. While many people with SAD are able to function in both the work and the family spheres in spite of their illnesses, women with female hormonal depressions resulting from larger hormonal insults often experience a profound practical dysfunction as well. When psychosis is present, it is mood-congruent. The delusions are depressive — for instance, of bodily decay or insidious illness. If hallucinations are present, they are negative and hostile, and may go so far as to instruct the woman to kill herself.

Psychosis has affected a much smaller percentage of women with female hormonal depression since the dawn of the serotonergic age. All hormonal depressions require at least serotonin support, and many mild hormonal depressions respond to SSRIs alone. With considerable frequency, however, hormonal depressions are complicated by the symptoms of stress depression (insomnia, panic, decreased appetite, and poor concentration) or psychosis. When a woman has such a complicated depression, she also needs to be medicated with a norepinephrine drug or antipsychotic, respectively.

Psychotherapy in these cases is, again, supportive. It helps the woman to recognize the symptoms and to return to functioning with relative speed after the medication becomes effective. This kind of supportive treatment may be extensive and vital. Every mental illness includes emotional disturbance, therefore, it is important that patients learn how to interpret their emotions, how to tell depression the mood from depression the illness. For this purpose, there is no substitute for warm and regular contact with a knowledgeable person who conveys actual concern. Medical-management visits are inadequate for this task; real integrated psychoeducational and skill-based treatment is required.

Social Phobia

"Social phobia" is a catch-all phrase for a fascinating and complex spectrum of disorders that ranges from stage fright over infrequent public speaking to profound and pervasive socially avoidant behavior that is the central focus of a person's existence and informs and limits that person almost totally. Also called social anxiety, it can be found in an enormous percentage of substance abusers, since alcohol is a common self-medication for the socially phobic.

Although social phobia has been clearly shown to respond to SSRIs and is, therefore, by inference related to serotonin metabolism, it quite frequently exists without any other serotonergic symptoms, such as a SAD picture or obsessiveness. What unifies the broad category of social phobia is the nature and context of the anxiety symptoms.

The anxiety attack of the socially phobic can be similar to a panic attack, but it also has some prominent differences. While a norepinephrine-mediated panic attack makes people feel as if they are going to die with its symptoms of a tight chest and shortness of breath, the serotonin-mediated social-phobia attack involves things such as sweating or freezing in front of others, dizziness, and trembling. People with panic disorder need to go to the bathroom; the socially phobic are more likely to throw up. Social-phobia attacks often resolve as soon as the specific feared stimuli is successfully avoided, whereas untreated panic disorder tends to become more and more generalized. Social-phobics rarely have the sleep and appetite disturbances of people with norepinephrine-mediated panic attacks. People with panic disorder are afraid something terrible is going to happen. Social phobics are afraid that they won't be able to do something that they are expected to do and that they will be judged, found wanting, and rejected by others. Panic disorder is danger anxiety. Social phobia is stranger anxiety.

Both kinds of anxiety are evolutionary adaptations that served humans well in earlier periods. The human anxiety response of "fight, flight, freeze, or faint" increases arousal in challenging situations. The increased heart rate and agitation of panic disorder ready us to flee or to fight. Social phobics tend more to the freeze or faint half of the equation.

A wide range of effective treatment approaches that work well in conjunction with medicine are available these days both for social phobia and for panic disorder. Rarely are they applied in an appropriately integrated manner.

The first issue is designing any effective treatment for social phobia is to assess the specific nature of the anxiety. Under what circumstances does it occur? Does it always occur in the same situation in the same way? Many people are socially phobic only in response to sexual situations. Others experience anxiety in response only to new people and are fine with known people. The more specific the stimulus, the easier it is to design an integrated intervention.

The anxiety of the socially phobic is a good example of a self-fulfilling prophecy. The fact is that people don't like us if we are nervous. We are correct to be afraid in the sense that if we are nervous, we will, in fact, lose something of value. The paradox is, of course, that we often get other people's approval only if we appear not to need it. This doesn't mean that people who aren't needy are never rejected. It simply means that the most effective interpersonal strategy is to genuinely care much less about controlling outcomes, to genuinely believe that no one bats a thousand, that no matter how "good" or "appealing" or "acceptable" we are, many people will reject us for reasons that have little or nothing to do with us. This strategy can be adopted successfully by shifting the emphasis away from being everyone's cup of tea to being some people's cup of tea. With the proper perspective, we can detach ourselves from needing to gain the approval or interest of any one person to instead focusing on correctly identifying the people who are likely to be interested in and approve of us willingly. Seeing that a no is just one more step to an eventual yes is not at all difficult.

In my practice, the therapy for social phobia and related anxieties is some tailored combination of five elements: medication, psychoeducation, progressive desensitization, cognitive restructuring, and hypnotherapeutic reframing.

Medication
Unlike in the treatment of seasonal affective disorder or intermittent explosive disorder, medication alone is only very rarely fully effective at removing the uncomfortable physical sensations and the behavioral avoidance that characterize social phobia. SSRIs usually somewhat dampen the hyper-responsiveness of the stranger reflex. They essentially reset the trigger point at which fear (the perception of threat) turns into anxiety (the physical response to fear). They do not, however, overrule the reflex entirely, and if the stimulation is strong enough, the reflex will begin to fire in spite of the medication.

I recently treated a young Catholic school teacher who suffered from social anxiety. He had always been a shy boy, and he himself had attended a boys-only Catholic school. He was twenty-four and single, and he had very limited experience with women. He routinely froze up verbally and felt awkward and nervous whenever a woman was present. When he began teaching at a boys-only Catholic high school, he began to experience social anxiety attacks in the classroom. His symptoms included sweating, some nausea, and a sense of difficulty at speaking smoothly — overall, a frozen, jerky quality. He consulted a psychiatrist, who prescribed Effexor, a good choice, as it covers both serotonin and norepinephrine mediated anxiety, both stranger and danger anxiety. Within a few weeks, his symptoms abated, and he became more comfortable teaching. He received no psychotherapy.

This young man, let's call him H., compensated for his shyness in unfamiliar situations by having a stubborn, pushy side that emerged when he was around people he did know and with whom he did feel comfortable. He got into a power struggle with his dean over the discipline of a student on the last day of exams, and he wound up needing a job. Over the summer, he found another teaching job, this time at a coed Catholic high school.

Within a short time, the Effexor was no longer working. By the time I met him, H. was having severe, protracted anxiety attacks in school and increasing difficulty with getting himself to go to work. I increased his Effexor and added Neurontin, a mood stabilizer that is often good at lowering anxiety. Because he was so insistent, I even temporarily added Klonopin, a minor tranquilizer. None of this proved sufficient, however, and at H.'s adamant insistence that he simply could no longer tolerate the stress of teaching, he filed for disability and quit his job within three weeks of meeting me.

The medications for social phobia and for panic essentially offer windows of relative relief from unwanted, overactive anxiety reflexes, but unless the socially phobic work at changing their ideas and understandings and at retraining their reflexes, they might very well find anxiety or panic breaking through the medicine.

Not all social phobics respond to medication. As a general rule, the more reasonable and justified the expectation of rejection, the less likely medicines are to affect it. To put it another way, people with obvious deficits who are, in fact, ostracized by peer groups they can't escape, avoid, or replace are less likely to let go of their social anxieties than people who are afraid for no good reason of people they have never met and are unlikely to see again.

Psychoeducation

The psychoeducation of the socially phobic is like a college course in social psychology with a smattering of psychophysiology and Zen Buddhism sprinkled into the mix. Recently, I have begun assigning an excellent out-of-print textbook that I used in an interpersonal communications class I took as a junior in college in 1974. Written by Zick Rubin, it's called *Liking and Loving* (Austin, TX: Holt, Rinehart and Winston, 1973), and the material inside is timeless, just as applicable today as it was then. I also ask social phobics to purchase and read the Stephen Mitchell translation of the *Tao Te Ching* (New York: Harper Perennial, 1992). Poem 6 reads: "Seek others' approval and you will be their prisoner." Mostly, though, I just talk. What follows are points I've emphasized repeatedly over the years, points that I think underpin any willingness or ability to participate actively in the "homework" parts of the therapy of social phobias, which are so essential to success.

The Effects of Nervousness. The second noble truth of Buddhism tells us, "Desire is the root of all suffering." For the socially phobic, the desire is for validation, for acceptance. The paradox, as we've mentioned, is that the more approval and validation we need — not just want, but feel we need — particularly in unstructured, purely social situations, the less likely people are to give it to us.

Why is this? Why don't people just reassure us if we need it? Here are four obvious reasons.

The first is what Dr. Aaron Beck the cognitive therapist calls the see-do reflex. Humans are innately imitative. We copy what we see. This has tremendous evolutionary advantage. It's why children smile at their parents. It's how we learn to speak. It's how we gradually shape our gestures and expressions.

What this reflex means functionally is that if two people in different moods come together in the same room, pretty soon they will be in the same mood. This happens because, unless we are very aware of ourselves on several levels, our bodies and our voices unconsciously mimic. It takes a trained person not to scream at someone who is screaming at him or her. The reflex is to match the screamer. When someone matches a person with social phobia, the matcher becomes nervous and unhappy, and rejects the person who is making him or her feel that way.

Of course, for the socially phobic, the immediate tendency is to feel that the rejecting party has seen entirely through them, knows their deepest fears and flaws, and has judged them harshly. Really, the socially phobic just make the rejecting party nervous.

So, there's one good reason why it's a bad idea to need someone's approval badly enough to be nervous about it. It makes the other person nervous.

Second, people naturally tend to dislike those who fear them. Why is this? Well, simply put, we are all still, on some level, animals. See how quickly we can become savage if, for instance, someone attacks our spouse or child or we are starving. The veneer of civilization has dropped all too quickly in Africa, South America, Asia, the Middle East, and the old Communist Bloc in recent decades for anyone to doubt our underlying nature. Even as we must acknowledge our animal nature, we yearn to be more than that, to be comfortable, to be safe. Most of us seek to minimize conflict, to avoid and control our savage side. We cling tenaciously — we must — to our view of ourselves as civilized men and women, and we are not always happy to be reminded otherwise.

When people fear us, they challenge our civilized veneer. When people fear us, we don't like them because they are holding up to us a mirror that shows us we are animals, that we are dangerous, threatening beasts. We don't want to know that, so we reject it, and we reject the person showing it to us.

So, the second reason it's a bad idea to require approval and to fear its being withheld is that it makes people angry.

Third, people generally do not want responsibility for someone else's mental state. Nor do they want the guilt that goes with that responsibility. Everybody has obligations — to their parents, their children, their job. Approval of you before you can relax is a burden they don't want, a power they didn't ask for, a responsibility they reject.

Three reasons: nervousness, anger, and guilt.

One more: What message are we sending when we fear the disapproval of someone who does not claim nor want that authority? They become suspicious. They want to know what you want and why you are so afraid of not getting it. They wonder what you know about yourself that they don't know. You are telling the other person that he or she shouldn't trust you because you don't trust yourself.

Whose Head Are You In? We have been talking about why the social phobic needs to let go of the need for immediate and constant success in every social contact, about how and why to decatastrophize rejection. We've spent a few pages talking about how our nervousness creates unwanted mood states — specifically, anxiety, anger, guilt, and suspicion — in those we seek to please. What we are looking for is the replacement of a frantic effort to read the mind of those around us with a relaxed willingness to respond appropriately to any clearly sent messages. We should do this largely because it is virtually impossible to accurately predict or explain our own motivation and actions, let alone those of people we haven't even talked to yet.

What I am defining as the central, early task in the treatment of social anxiety is coming to the understanding that we need to get out of other people's heads and into our own, that we have to stop being a supplicant and start being a knowledgeable consumer. We need to see the process of choosing ongoing social arrangements as more about fit, like looking for the right puzzle pieces, than about judgment. Pieces that don't fit aren't bad; they're just not as useful in a particular part of the puzzle.

The moment socially phobic people encounter someone else, be it a stranger, a potentially available member of the opposite sex, or a member of a peer group, they anxiously scan for and prematurely react to an expected rejection. Here come the frantic attempts at mind-reading. These attempts, however, will obviously never work. We cannot reliably predict the ideas, attitudes, preferences, and life situations of the people we meet casually, and our excessive efforts to do so are bound to be met less than enthusiastically.

All this is about being in the wrong head. We shouldn't be overly concerned with knowing other people's preferences, although we should be glad to hear about them if the other people choose to discuss them. Instead, we need to be aware of our own preferences and how to communicate them. In short, we shouldn't worry about whether other people like us. Rather, we should worry about whether we like them, about what we would like from them and we can go about getting it.

There are lots of reasons why getting out of other people's heads is so vital. Our responsibility is to effectively communicate to the world what we are after. Otherwise, we are certainly less likely to get it. To put it another way, it's hardly clever to assume as a basic stance that people in this polyglot, Internet world will accurately intuit our wishes in a reliable way if we don't take the trouble to learn how to express ourselves clearly.

We shouldn't feel that we have to do the work of figuring out what other parties in social situations want unless they take personal responsibility for explaining themselves. Even if we are able to correctly guess the desires of uncommunicative people, are these really the kind of people whose approval we desire? If they do accept us, we have to keep guessing correctly forever without any help from them. How likely is that to succeed indefinitely?

Liking Yourself. When we talk about getting into our own head, clearly we are talking about our relationship with ourself. Do we even need to point out that we cannot love anyone else if we don't first love ourself?

Ultimately, getting into your own head means knowing yourself, your preferences, and your limitations, and demonstrating your approval of yourself by giving weight to those preferences and boundaries when deciding whether to accept or initiate social contact with others.

The cost of disliking yourself, of denying yourself the right to act upon your preferences, is all too obvious: Others often don't like you either. Think about how quickly we tend to form our own impressions of others. How do we do that when we know so little about them? Although we may not be aware of it, what we appreciate so quickly at first glance when we look at others is what they think of themselves. If you like yourself, all things being equal — that is, you have no grossly obvious stigmata of unacceptability — others, depending on their own state, of course, may well like you, too. If they see at a glance that you don't like yourself, you will have a much tougher time.

I believe it is possible to quickly learn and master a philosophical approach to life that allows us to like ourselves pretty much no matter what we've done or thought about ourselves in the past. The approach is as follows:

There are only two kinds of evil in the world: the exploitation of others and the disrespect of the self. Being a "good" person, a person worthy of consideration as a social ally of any sort, is the opposite. It is being willing to carry your own weight and being committed to your own development. When I say, "willing to carry your own weight," I mean that you aren't looking to get over on anyone, you don't want something for nothing, you are willing and anxious to work for what you get. Being "committed to your own development" means that you are willing to invest in yourself both by learning new skills and by committing to open-ended relationships.

Liking yourself means that you don't want anything from anyone that is not willingly and knowingly given. It also means being willing to look at and clarify your values and attitudes about your relations with others so that you can define a stance toward them that will be reliable and consistent. Defining and articulating your stance toward others is vital for several reasons. First, it frees us to treat others well regardless of how they treat us. We choose to treat others well because that is how we choose to be, who we are, and because it feels good to us to be ourselves, not because the other people have done anything to deserve it. Even more importantly, when we present a consistent, reliable stance toward others, their reactions to us tell us about them, not about us. Let's pursue this idea for a moment. The tendency of the socially phobic is to give the power to judge to people who don't want it or deserve it. They even go so far as to give this power to people they have only just met. This is not useful. I've known myself for fifty years. I've known you for ten minutes. Why are you the expert on me? Why are you the judge?

Of course, you shouldn't be. If one has developed and worked at presenting a reliable stance for interacting with others, then each encounter is like an experiment in which one variable is held constant (your stance) and the other (the response you get) gives you information about the other person.

Liking yourself doesn't mean you have to be happy with everything about yourself or your situation. But as long as you are willing to work for what you get and you are devoted to understanding and improving yourself, you can see yourself as decent and legitimate, and you can define a stance toward others that reflects these ideas and that offers the possibility for ongoing, satisfying social interactions.

The Proper Stance. The stance I use for myself and that I teach to patients can be summed-up as "fine without you, better with you." Another phrase I like is "available, flexible self-reliance." What these two phrases mean, in practice, is that we are perfectly willing to respond actively to clear requests (unless we don't want to), and that we are equally perfectly willing to, without resentment or rancor, go off and take care of ourselves.

Being willing to go off and take care of ourselves takes us back to one of the prerequisites for self-acceptance: the willingness to invest in our own development. This entails cultivating the ability to be alone and to devote our solitary attention to long-term projects in our own interests.

I cannot overemphasize the necessity of developing a reliable commitment to your own interests in providing secure footing for an appropriate and effective interpersonal stance. Knowing what you enjoy and being able to productively use your alone time, together, take social interaction off a need basis and put it where it belongs, as a purely voluntary act.

A basic aspect of a useful stance is realizing that nobody owes you anything and that all you owe anybody else is to live up to your own idea of civility and good citizenship. I owe it to others to respond politely when something is requested of me. I am not required to comply with the request. No one should have to endure resentment or rage for saying no, nor is anyone entitled to be full of rage or resentment upon hearing no.

A stance that is willing but undemanding, that is appreciative of a yes but comfortable with a no, that is fine without other people but better with them is bound to be more comfortable than one in which every encounter is with a judge and every verdict is a tragedy.

Back to Buddhism. There is a terrific little movie called *The Tao of Steve* that is basically the love story of an overweight man who gets a girl. The story is wrapped up in some Buddhist ideas, which are presented as the heavy fellow gives lessons to his more attractive, younger friend about how to get women. The Steve of the title is not, by the way, the heavy guy. He's Steve McQueen, an actor, whom, if you are of a certain age, you will remember for his unquenchable coolness in *The Great Escape* or *Papillon*.

With Steve as his guide, the heavy guy imparts three rules over the course of the movie: (1) Desire without desire, (2) do something excellent, and (3) move away. The idea of desiring without desire is what I want patients to understand, what is so central to the psychoeducation of the socially phobic. Many people with social anxieties let go entirely of ever wanting to be with other people. They settle for small, constricted, lonely lives. The trick is to recover the desire for all the lovely possibilities of social contact without having excessive attachment, without focusing on the goal so much that it becomes altered in a negative way. Simply put, it involves letting go of outcomes and staying in the present. It means enjoying the smile and the voice of a pretty girl even if you might not ever get to see it again.

When I give my Buddhist spiel, I invariably talk about the "four noble truths." The first noble truth is "Life is suffering." I expand as follows: "Life is inconstant, ever-changing, unreliable. Everything that lives will die. You will die. Your body will betray you before you die. Everyone you love will die, or you will die first. Five minutes after you die, nobody will give a rat's ass what you did or didn't do in life. Everything you buy will break; everything you build will fall down. Nothing will ever stay the same; you can't count on anything, and you can't do anything about any of this."

For people who have never thought like this or had it presented to them in just this way, this understanding can be quite a mouthful. It can certainly help in letting go of all the desires, the attachments, the shoulds and musts that so often make us edgy, distract us, and take us out of being in the moment. Such ideas can also go a long way toward helping us take other people's behavior less personally.

Another central Buddhist tenet is that anger and aggression are more accurately seen as unenlightened responses to the suffering that all of us will endure. If we see someone on the ground yelling in pain because of a broken leg, we don't kick that person. When we realize that all anger comes from pain, when we can see rejection, anger, aggression, and all of the negative emotions with which people greet us as signs of that pain, then we can forgive them and soothe them. We can know that, whatever the nominal cause of bad or negative or aggressive behavior by others, it is not about us, it's about them. The people who express their anger and pain ungraciously are stuck with themselves, and they suffer much more than we do, since we can walk away from it, ending it for us if we so desire.

One of the poems of the *Tao Te Ching* includes the phrase, "Embrace death, and then you can truly live." Many people never accept death and all the sense of limitation it implies. They remain angry and anxious about the pain they have experienced and expect to experience. Again the Tao: "When you know where you come from you naturally become tolerant, amused, as kindly as a grandmother, as dignified as a judge." I take this to mean that when we have accepted that we are all in the same leaky boat, that we are all going to die, that no one will get out alive, that no one will get out unscathed, then we can forgive our fellows their anguished responses even as we hope they will grow toward a more peaceful acceptance. Once we have forgiven the people around us for their pain and the ways they express it, what is there to fear? Psychoeducation as presented here, or even much more extensively presented, is seldom enough to eliminate such a complex problem completely. Fortunately other useful techniques exist.

Progressive Desensitization

Progressive desensitization, also called systematic desensitization, is a well-tested, effective, and perhaps underutilized treatment for phobias that works by coupling training in deep relaxation with a hierarchy of progressively more disturbing stimuli. The treatment is based on the understanding that the nervous system accommodates, that it cannot remain aroused and overstimulated in the face of continued exposure. This technique was popularized by one of its developers, a psychologist named Joseph Wolpe, and it is most useful when the phobia is clearly circumscribed. I remember reading an article in *The New York Times* many years ago about a reporter with a phobia to blood. She spent years in analytic therapy for the problem without being cured. She then completely conquered the phobia in just a few sessions using this type of treatment.

The treatment consists of devising a hierarchy of troubling images — for example, imagining someone with a drop of blood on the next block, then slowly getting closer, then adding more blood to the image, and so on. The patient is taught a deep-relaxation technique, and after mastering the technique, the patient is instructed to imagine the least disturbing stimuli on the hierarchy until he or she begins to feel the first stirrings of an anxiety reaction. At that point, the patient returns to the relaxation technique until he or she is again comfortable. The process is repeated over and over until the initial, mild stimuli no longer causes anxiety. It's then repeated with each successive level of stimuli until eventually, even the most troublesome stimuli no longer elicits an anxiety response.

Ultimately, the success of the treatment depends on the skill used in constructing the gradual hierarchy and on the courage of the patient in exposing himself or herself to the offending situation. Using these techniques for social phobia again works best when the anxiety is circumscribed — a fear of public speaking, let's say, or of speaking to strangers in dating situations. The treatment, of course, is ultimately based on exposure. The reality is that many social phobics rarely allow themselves to get into frightening situations in the first place or they already would have learned to fear them less.

Albert Ellis, the creator of the cognitive therapy technique called rational emotive therapy, tells how he conquered a paralyzing fear of women. He says that for one hundred days in a row, he forced himself to go to Central Park and sit down on a bench next to a woman and ask her to sleep with him. He says he never had sex, but he stopped being afraid. Dr. Beck says that when we find ourselves in a fearful, anxiety-provoking situation, we have two choices: We can move away from the situation, or we can stay put and wait for the anxiety to pass. If we move away, the anxiety lessens but the fear grows. If we stay, the anxiety lessens eventually (people don't stay strangers forever) and the fear also lessens.

Systematic desensitization requires that, at some point, the leap is made from imagination to reality. Eventually, the person who fears public speaking needs to give a speech. Anxiety about public speaking is a good example because quite a number of highly successful behavioral programs use some combination of relaxation, imagination, and exposure to gradually retrain the reflexes. They work well, and they are often given in a classroom setting. What I've noticed is that some people require medication to calm themselves enough to tolerate going through such a program, and others decidedly do not.

One of the interesting things about people who have some degree of social phobia is the great lengths to which they will go to in order to (1) stay comfortable, and (2) hide from themselves the idea that what they are doing is in any way unusual. I know many socially anxious people who associate only with their immediate and extended family, and consider this normal. Sometimes, anxiety about public speaking is the tip of a socially avoidant iceberg. Individuals who are forced to confront this as a key job demand may, upon examination, reveal a whole range of avoidant behavior around interpersonal relations. A lifetime history of general discomfort across quite a few situations usually indicates that medication will likely be needed to help the person tolerate specific behavioral interventions. In contrast, other folks with speaking anxieties really do have much less general anxiety, and for these people, systematic desensitization or a variant is more than adequate.

In the same vein, a phobia about speaking with attractive or eligible members of the opposite sex may also be just tip of the iceberg. Difficulty in speaking with the opposite sex is very common, and yet, it is a phenomenon that can be either intimately tied up with neurotransmitter abnormalities or have nothing to do with them whatsoever. Systematic desensitization and other similar behavioral techniques can be quite effective when social anxiety is confined only to potential sexual partners, and there's a big role here, too, of course, for insightful psychotherapeutic conversations that look at how these things are influenced by familial relationships.

Cognitive Restructuring

Cognitive restructuring has been most widely popularized by David Burns, M.D., in his best-selling book *Feeling Good* (New York: Avon, 1999). It involves capturing, examining, and altering the constant flow of self-talk, the internal dialogue of comment about ourselves and our feelings, and what we ought to be doing.

This type of thing involves written homework. The central feature is something called the triple-column technique. In the first column, you write down what is called the automatic thought, the negative self-statements you've noticed during the day. In the second column, you list the cognitive distortions contained in your statements. Cognitive distortions are errors in the form or the "grammar" of your usual, and typically emotionally tinged, self-statements, errors that make the statements highly unlikely to be true. In the third column, you record rational responses. Rational responses are basically more "grammatically correct" versions of your concerns that address the three questions, "So what?" "What's the evidence?" and "Is there another way of looking at it?"

Dr. Burns includes a diagram of the triple-column technique, in his book *Feeling Good*. I advise anyone who has either social phobia or panic disorder to get a copy of *Feeling Good* and to master this simple but very useful technique.

The intellectual heart of this technique are the cognitive distortions. Dr. Burns lists ten, some of which overlap quite a bit. Dr. Beck describes what he calls primitive (distorted) thinking as absolutist, moralistic, invariant, irreversible, and character-based, and he contrasts it with mature (undistorted), relativistic, non-judgmental, variable, reversible, behaviorally-based thinking, which is the kind of thinking we get after we weed out all the distortions.

Figure 8: Triple Column Technique

PRIMITIVE (DISTORTED)	MATURE (UNDISTORTED)
absolutist	relativistic
moralistic	non-judgmental
invariant	variable
irreversible	reversible
character-based	behaviorally-based

Some typical distortions include all-or-nothing thinking, predicting the future, reading other people's minds, labeling, overfocusing on the negative, excluding the positive, and should statements. Dr. Burns and Dr. Beck are both quite good at explicating these concepts further. The main idea is that if you repeatedly tell yourself something that fits into one of these distorted formats, it's pretty darn likely that this deformed statement is untrue, and it's certainly not worth making yourself miserable about.

I think the key to using this technique is to write everything down every day for a period of two to three months. Having a cognitive-behavioral discussion with a therapist is just fine, but without the repetitive written exercises, its much less likely to stick. I'm reminded of the time, as a third grader, that Mrs. Perry, an angry, imposing sixth-grade teacher, told me to write 100 times, "I will not talk during fire drills." I never did talk during a fire drill again. Doing the triple-column technique for even a few weeks makes it clear that the same small number of concerns come up over and over. By the time you have written 500 rational responses, you are no longer capable of thinking the negative thought without its overlearned rejoinder trailing along behind.

Cognitive therapy is easy to learn and easy to use. It takes three to five psychotherapeutic visits to implement, and anxious folks ought to learn it.

Hypnotherapeutic Reframing

The cure for social phobia lies ultimately in genuinely reducing the fear of negative social outcome. Meditation and progressive desensitization work directly on bodily feelings and may break the cycle of fear and anxiety. Cognitive restructuring works on the verbal and logical left brain. Hypnotherapeutic reframing involves a change in context within a nonverbal representational system, zooming the camera in or out from different angles so that the same material takes on different meanings. Reframing, like so many therapeutic techniques, involves learning to enter a state of relaxed and focused awareness, in this case to allow openness to suggestions that can stimulate the use of nonverbal information in novel ways, to create new meanings, and to let go of old ones.

Dr. Gilligan tells the story of a girl who always felt that people were looking at her and who was, therefore, always uniformly self-conscious. While she was in a trance, Dr. Gilligan asked her to look into the eyes that were watching her. Their gaze was cold and appraising, she said. Dr. Gilligan then asked her to instead see a pair of kindly eyes that would gently watch over her and protect her. She was able to do this and felt immediate relief.

The key here is that, often, nonverbal transformations (think morphing) are much faster and more powerful than painfully slow, detailed, verbal ones.

We've been talking about hypnotic metaphor on and off in these pages for quite some time, and we've been discussing social phobia for a while now, too, so I'm not going to try to provide a more extensive illustration of reframing at this time. Many of the inner-child and inner-parent exercises can be usefully modified here. The utility of these types of experiences are limited only by the skill of the person in mastering trance and in the creativity of the hypnotist in devising appropriate metaphors.

Apart from medication, psycho-education, cognitive-behavioral or hypno-therapeutic techniques, a case can also be made that the best approach for the training of social skills and the treatment of social anxieties is ongoing group therapy. Unfortunately such groups are very difficult for therapists to arrange and maintain, and consequently they are very difficult for patients to find.

What clear is that there are a range of useful approaches that can be used here and that the socially phobic patient needs to be aggressive in pursuing them. Often a combination of approaches is best. Medication alone will rarely treat the full range of socially anxious difficulties.

Obsessive Depression and Obsessive-Compulsive Disorder

Although obsessive depression and OCD are two distinct, if related, subtypes of serotonergic disorders, I am going to discuss them together because I think the contrast will be instructive. By and large, obsessive depressions are temporary and reversible, whereas OCD is a lifelong, inherited disorder. Obsessive depressions tend to cluster with other serotonin symptoms, such as irritability, hypersomnia, fatigue, or performance anxiety. Pure OCD can be complicated by any subtype of depression, but it often stands alone, without any mood changes or sleep, appetite, or energy disturbances. Obsessive depressions tend to be a deviation from baseline in which the mind gets stuck in an unusual way at a time when other symptoms of depression or stress are also present. OCD tends to be stable and lifelong once it develops, although it also tends to worsen if any sort of depression develops alongside it.

Many people are familiar by now with the classic description of OCD. Constant hand washing is the most common symptom, but other cleanliness issues, repeated checking of doors, faucets, and stoves, and the need for the precise arrangement of objects are also common. Compulsive counting is also often seen, and obsessive hoarders collect and cling to any of a range of relatively worthless objects. An obsession is essentially an idea that is stuck in a loop, a thought that may or may not lead to action (a compulsion) but that is repeated over and over, long past the point of usefulness. An obsession can be focused on just about any human activity. Some eating disorders are fundamentally obsessive and respond to SSRIs. I have seen sexual addicts whose behavior ceased when treated for OCD. I recently treated a man whose obsessive thought concerned the way people felt about his gaze (he believed that they thought he looked crazy), and another who couldn't drive because he became obsessed by the thought that he would get lost, panic, and crash. Both of these men found their obsessions diminishing quickly when they began taking an SSRI.

Some OCD patients have very stable obsessions. Some find their obsessions significantly shifting over time. I have one OCD patient who has a whole range of cleanliness obsessions and compulsions when he is at his parents' home, but at his girlfriend's house, where he first went after being on medication, he has no symptoms whatsoever.

In contrast, there is a type of obsessive depression that is characterized by something called rejection hypersensitivity, in which the obsessive thought revolves around slights and perceived slights, usually from emotionally significant individuals. This symptom, the inability to let go of interpersonal disappointments, may be the only or most prominent complaint, and it may or may not be present all the time. It can accompany seasonal or hormonal depressions, including premenstrual depression, in which case it will most likely disappear when the other symptoms do. It is, of course, possible to be what my mother used to call an injustice collector solely on the basis of personality and character.

What distinguishes people with obsessive pathology from people with character issues is that even when the obsessive realizes how useless and counterproductive the whole thing is, when they know it's not justified, when they really want to let go of it, they find that they just can't. The symptoms become what are called ego dystonic — that is, alien to the self. By contrast, people who are injustice collectors are ego syntonic. They think they should be upset. This particular symptom, obsessive interpersonal rumination, turns out to be very responsive to medication. After a few weeks, those who truly want to be more accepting and forgiving find that they can be.

Obsessiveness as a new symptom in an already depressed, anxious person is often a sign of multi-neurotransmitter-system dysfunction and of a dangerously worsening depression. I recently treated a man with a lifetime of worrying about everything but without overt OCD who began obsessing about an upcoming audit at work and about the masses of paperwork he would never finish in time. Within weeks of finding out about the audit, he lost his appetite, began having panic attacks, and could no longer sleep through the night — all symptoms of a classic norepinephrine/stress depression. I saw him at this point and gave him Effexor, but he kept ruminating and obsessing about the paperwork, and then about his own worthlessness, and then about suicide, and he wound up making a thankfully unsuccessful suicide attempt with pills. As is often the case when obsessions become psychotic, the man improved considerably with a brief hospitalization and the addition of antipsychotic medication.

In the last paragraph, I used, in passing, the word "ruminating" to describe a type of obsessive thinking. A ruminant is an animal that has several stomachs and regurgitates its food and then swallows it again. A cow is a ruminant. Rumination in psychiatry is an endless, continual chewing of the same issues. It is, perhaps, the best way to understand the difference between the obsessiveness seen in obsessive depressions and the obsessiveness of OCD. Rumination tends to be more complex, to involve protracted internal conversations of justification and blame apportionment. OCD obsessions are simpler, consisting of single sentences: Do this or that. Avoid this or that. Even when the compulsion is not obvious, the obsession of OCD is about a relatively neutral act, like counting or arranging or what's called undoing. Rumination is less about taking a particular action and more about thinking about it. It's about the endless chewing and chewing and chewing.

The tendency to ruminate, as a lifelong trait, about interpersonal slights or other issues is often medication-sensitive in the sense that the patient will feel much less pressure to enter the maze of complex contemplation when the idea occurs and will be able to move on to other, more useful thoughts.

To be sure, there are those who would be called obsessive by friends and family, who might be called control freaks, who are inflexible and rigid in ordering the world around them, but who do not have an underlying neurotransmitter-based obsessiveness. Conversely, people with neurotransmitter-based obsessiveness are just as able to develop an obsessive personality as anyone. By the way, cognitive restructuring and Buddhist philosophizing can be just as useful for the socially controlling as for the socially anxious.

Medication
Serotonergic medications have been a tremendous breakthrough for the broad range of people who suffer from OCD symptoms. It is, however, vital that people with OCD understand that these medications will not stop obsessive thoughts from occurring. They will simply make it far less difficult and unpleasant to resist the impulses.

When people with OCD are prevented from acting in their typical manner in response to an obsessive thought — say, if a hand washer was tied up and couldn't wash or a door checker was prevented from returning to check the door — they usually feel a powerful and painful sense of panic that seems to be centered right in the middle of the chest. Serotonergic medications do not keep people with OCD from having the idea of washing or arranging, but if they can be persuaded to resist the impulse, they will notice that they won't have the panic and terror in the middle of the chest.

Psychoeducation

I recommend that everyone with OCD read three books. The *Boy Who Couldn't Stop Washing* by Judith L. Rapoport, M.D. (New York: Signet, 1991) describes the range and breadth of OCD symptoms. Dr. Rapoport is an OCD expert from the National Institutes of Mental Health. *Shadow Syndromes* by John J. Ratey, M.D. and Catherine Johnson, Ph.D. (New York: Bantam, 1998) has a very fine chapter on how OCD symptoms present in the mildly affected, who may also benefit from medication. Lastly, and most relevant to treatment, I ask patients to read a book called *Brain Lock* by Jeffrey M. Schwartz, M.D. This book provides a simple, effective method for dealing with obsessive thoughts either before medication or, more commonly, alongside it.

Brain Lock, like *Feeling Good*, is a long book with a few basic ideas and many examples written in simple language so as to be accessible to the broadest population. *Brain Lock* offers a four-step mantra. The mantra is even provided on a cut-out card for your wallet: "Relabel, Reattribute, Refocus, Revalue." Again, I strongly urge anyone with OCD or anything like it to purchase this book. The basic strategy is to extend the obsessive thought to include a new tail — a caboose to the train, if you will — the four-step mantra. Ordinarily, an obsessive thought leads to some particular action or is repeated in the mind, over and over, until the action is taken. Once the new "tail" is added to the obsessive train of thought, it has a different ending, a refocusing, which leads to a more useful place.

DOPAMINE/PLEASURE DEPRESSIONS

The dopamine/pleasure depressions, the third group of neurotransmitter disorders, are acquired. This means that they involve choices and experiences, and as such, they can be changed by making new choices and creating new experiences. They can sometimes be "cured."

The two subtypes of dopamine/pleasure depression are defined by their response to the drug Wellbutrin (buproprion), which is, so far, unique as a drug that addresses a group of dopamine neurons that are involved in a certain type of depression. One of the subtypes is post-substance-abuse depression, with the abused substances most typically being alcohol, pot, or cocaine, and the other subtype is what I call denial-of-the-self/under-"fun"-ded depression, experienced by people who have not successfully "sought their bliss." First, missed bliss.

Pleasure Depressions

When I try to describe this sort of denial-of-the-self/under-"fun"-ded depression, I use the words "pleasure," "interest," "energy," and "motivation." In its purest form, this type of depression leaves sleep and appetite unaffected. Rather, people talk about not enjoying things they had always loved. Several runners have told me that they knew something was off when they stopped looking forward to the pleasure of the run. This depression is often missed because it is in the shadows of its two more obvious cousins, the serotonergic or the stress depressions. Very often, people with this depression who are on other medications feel better but not completely well. When dopamine-based Wellbutrin is added, the missing ability to enjoy oneself returns. Dopamine neurons are strengthened by peak experiences, by moments of joyful, absorbed concentration, and they are taxed by long periods of depression, chronic pain, or just plain stuckness.

I've taken the liberty of labeling the excessive taxation of these populations of neurons as "denial of the self." I never cease to marvel at the enormous importance to human health of time spent communicating with and catering to your own deepest perceptions and wishes, of how vital it is to make your own enthusiasms, interests, and growth a legitimate focus of time, energy, and attention. And I never cease to marvel at the endless variety of ways in which people can rationalize and justify their repeated failure to do so.

Joseph Campbell sums up these ideas as "seeking your bliss." Seeking your bliss doesn't mean the short-sighted hedonism of heroin or sexual addiction. It means knowing yourself well enough to see what it is inside you that can power your growth, what it is inside you that seeks nurturance and experience like a plant reaching toward the sun. When people ignore that part of themselves, whether they know it or not, they are risking this type of depression.

G., age sixty-four, was a modestly successful businessman, a guy who was into computers early on but somehow missed out on a few chances to make his bundle. He had a few regrets, but he was a peaceful sort of guy, and he didn't blame himself too much for living modestly. His wife, on the other hand, did.

Mr. and Mrs. G. lived in a nice co-op in Manhattan, and most of Mrs. G.'s friends and the couple's neighbors were wealthier than they. In fact, most of them had already retired. They'd done so in their own time, on their own terms, and had been able to maintain their lifestyles. Mr. and Mrs. G., already in their mid-sixties, were not yet in a position to retire and wouldn't be for several more years at best.

Mrs. G. was unhappy with her lot, disliked her job, and resented having to continue to work at it. She had been quite angry for a number of years.

G. came to me to satisfy his wife, who complained that he was depressed and withdrawn. G. had to admit he wasn't enjoying himself much lately, and he was one of the guys who said he had noticed a significant change in his attitude toward running.

G. was an interior kind of guy. He liked to read, and when he wasn't working at his dead-end but stable job, he escaped into books. He wasn't too unhappy, but he always felt uncomfortable around his wife because he believed she was mad at him most of the time.

To begin with, I gave G. Wellbutrin. Within a few weeks, his mood was better, and he once again looked forward to his running high. Then we spent a year or so talking, a few sessions early on with Mrs. G. and then many more without her, during which she was often, nevertheless, the focus of the conversation.

Mrs. G. was angry with G. for not earning more. She was also just plain unhappy overall. She was sad that he was distant, and was unhappy when he withdrew. But when they were together, she complained constantly about many things, including him. For his part, G. felt responsible and guilty. He always tried to be reasonable, always tried to please her, but never succeeded.

We had Mrs. G. in to talk with us several times, maybe five or six, and G. and I tried to address her concerns. G. was less listless and more proactive, but his wife still felt very put-upon and unhappy with him, and complained of his passivity.

The breakthrough for G. was realizing that he couldn't please his wife no matter what he did, and he gradually stopped caring so much about it. He did what she said she wanted him to do, and he became clearer and less conflicted about what he wanted. He was polite and perhaps more responsive, but he didn't try to guess what would make her happy if she didn't make it clear. He stopped working so hard for her, and when she complained, he made a few sympathetic noises and stopped there. He learned to be the willow that bends with the wind instead of the oak that breaks.

G. stopped taking Wellbutrin after about nine months and is without relapse after more than a year. His wife is still often unhappy, but a lot less often with him. He feels freer and happier than he has in a long time.

People who deny themselves consistently enough to tax their dopamine system usually tell themselves they are doing it because of their responsibilities to others or for survival, which usually means for money, job, or career reasons. People who deny their deeper selves do so mainly because they have always done so, because of some set of rules that someone else taught them.

G. was raised in a culture where a man was responsible for the happiness of his woman. Before he could pay attention to himself, he needed to let go of that deeply held belief. Therapy is almost by definition an affirmation of the deeper self and its right to be heard and heeded. There are any number of therapy approaches that will work on this type of depression. I employed no special techniques with G., just a repetitive process of asking him what he really wanted, what was stopping him from getting it, and what he was going to do about it.

I think it is possible that G. would have gotten well without Wellbutrin. With the drug, however, I believe that he felt better faster and that he was less distracted from and had more energy for the work of therapy. In other contexts, where Wellbutrin addresses one component of a complex depression, I believe that its addition can be very important and often makes the difference between full recovery and a chronic, lingering, partially treated depression.

Post-Substance-Abuse Depression

The internal system that allows us to experience pleasure is affected by many of the "pleasurable" substances that are available in modern society. When we repeatedly use external substances to stimulate our pleasure systems, our bodies begin to produce the internal biochemical substances at lower levels or not at all. Marijuana is the most directly dopaminergic substance of abuse, but cocaine, alcohol, and caffeine are all active there as well. When people who have used these substances in a habitual manner cease to use them, they suffer a distinct period of pleasurelessness, which can be of variable length.

Wellbutrin has been marketed successfully for smoking cessation under the name of Zyban. I have found it to be similarly effective with the other substances I have mentioned. Often, by the time I see them, alcohol and pot abusers also have signs of norepinephrine dysfunction, so I've found tricyclic antidepressants are often useful as well. Desiprimine, a tricyclic that also has stimulant properties, is particularly helpful in diminishing the craving for cocaine.

What often occurs with chronic substance abuse is that, after a while, the abuser begins to experience symptoms of depressive withdrawal even while actively using the substance — that is, the self-medication no longer works. At that point, the person finds it very difficult to abstain from using the substance without an appropriate antidepressant. In milder cases, when sobriety occurs earlier in the cycle, the person may be an initial sense of well-being with abstinence, but develops a pleasureless or agitated depression anywhere from three to twelve weeks later.

I am not terribly satisfied with a substance-abuse treatment system that expends large resources on relatively brief inpatient stays (thirty days) and stints on long-term follow-up care. The good news for people who stay sober is that they are often quite able to get off the antidepressants they are taking without relapse (of their depressive symptoms) after a period of four to nine months.

Knowledgeable experts attribute a very high percentage of substance abuse to self-medication by people with learning disabilities, attention deficit disorder, and social phobia. Persistent substance abuse in these people despite the obvious negative consequences can be seen as related to exactly the kind of left-right brain dissociation we have been talking about as the result of chronic childhood trauma. What I have seen repeatedly is that people with substance abuse are rarely treated in a comprehensive manner that addresses not only the addiction, but also addresses both whatever other underlying conditions exist as well as the effect these conditions have had on the developing left-right brain relationship. No wonder success rates are so low.

A closing note: Although Wellbutrin is the best direct dopamine mediator, some people cannot use it, either because of the risk of seizures (less of a problem now that the extended-release version is available) or because of rashes or other allergic hypersensitivities. Some other drugs are available that seem to stimulate some of the same populations of neurons: Lamictal, the mood stabilizer; Provigil (modafnil), the narcolepsy drug; and Geodon, an atypical antipsychotic. I've used all of these in cases in which I've had to discontinue Wellbutrin.

NOREPINEPHRINE/STRESS DEPRESSIONS

The norepinephrine neurotransmitter system is responsible for our ability to arouse ourselves to adapt to the changing stressors in the world around us. It is also responsible for our ability to relax. The way in which we tend to our cycles of arousal and relaxation is what determines how much pressure is exerted upon this system.

You may recall a diagram that I presented in one of the early introductory chapters to explain the distinction we are making between dissociative and affective disorders. Let's look at this diagram again.

Figure 9: The Effects of Trauma in Adults and Children

	Adults	Children
Acute	PTSD (Post-traumatic Stress Disorder)	MPD/DID (Multiple Personality Disorder/Dissociative Identity Disorder)
Chronic	Panic Disorder/Agitated-Stress Depression	Right/Left Brain Dissociation

Children do not seem to get stress depression, or at least, they do not get it nearly as frequently as adults do. From time to time, I have seen truly depressed children as young as eight or nine, but the depressions in these children tended to involve hereditary conditions, either serotonergic or bipolar or both. Children respond to stress by dissociating before they respond with neurotransmitter imbalance.

One of the goals of this book is to make it clear how subtle sorts of dissociation between left- and right-brain aspects of functioning are on a continuum with the more well-known dissociative disorders, such as traumatic amnesia and multiple personality disorder. Post-traumatic stress disorders, panic disorders, and anxious-agitated stress depressions all involve similar sorts of alterations in autonomic nervous system function, but PTSD also involves dissociative pathology. All these conditions respond very well to a wide range of specific and not-so-specific psychotherapies (to my mind, the more specific, the better), and all respond much more quickly and thoroughly if both medication and psychoeducation are part of the mix.

Panic Disorder and Anxious-Agitated Stress Depression Psychoeducation

Of all the material that I teach to my patients about their illnesses, there is none I repeat more often than the following, since panic disorder and anxious-agitated stress depression are all-too-common results of the constant double binds of modern life.

We can begin by acknowledging that anxiety is a normal, healthy response that is very useful under the right circumstances. Anxiety, which we define as the physical response to fear, is a set of adjustments that our bodies make to help us respond to threats of various sorts. Anxiety is really just a word that we use to describe one way of looking at the extreme end of a continuum of arousal.

Please take a look at Figures 10, 11, and 12. Figure 10 is a visual representation of the relationship between fear, anxiety, and panic. Panic results when we respond to an anxious feeling with fear of the anxiety symptoms themselves. More fear creates more anxiety, and that vicious cycle is what we call panic. Figure 11 is an arousal continuum from 0 to 100. Along this continuum, arousal levels of 20 to 80 are sustainable, while a level above 80 without respite creates stress depression. Figure 12 is what I call the Fear-o-Stat, a graph that measures how much fear is required to turn on an anxiety response.

The genesis of panic

We constantly adjust our level of arousal. We do this in several complementary ways. We have a rapid and a delayed hormonal response (adrenaline and steroids, respectively), both of which are centered in the adrenal glands and work on multiple systems directly at the end-organ level. We also have a brain-and-nerve-mediated system, which relies on adequate norepinephrine functioning.

Individuals perceive arousal in general and hyperarousal in particular in a variety of ways that depend on context. The same feelings that are described as exciting by a rollercoaster fan can be described as panic by someone else. Research has clearly and

Figure 10: Fear, Anxiety, Panic Relationship

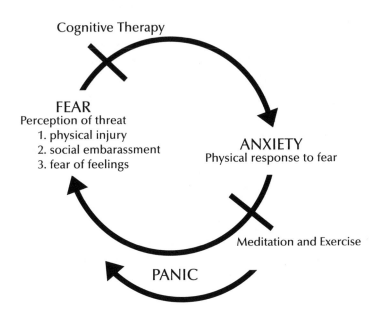

Figure 11: Arousel Continuum

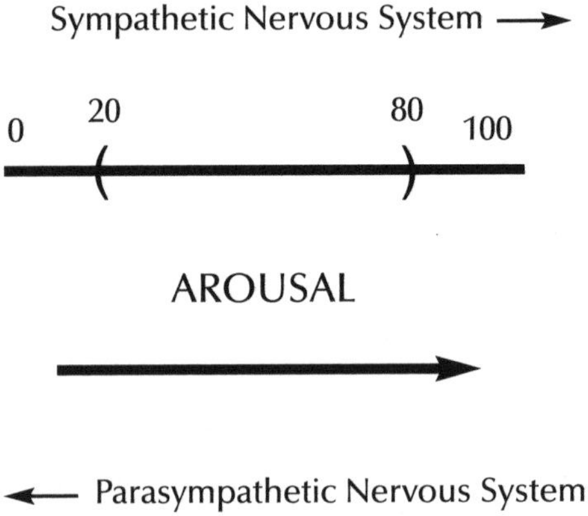

Sympathetic Nervous System ⟶

0   20   80   100
(   )

AROUSAL

⟵ Parasympathetic Nervous System

Figure 12: Fear-o-Stat

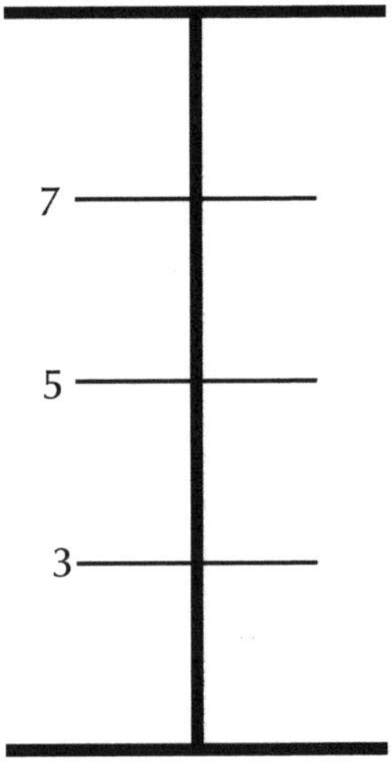

7

5

3

repeatedly proven that the increased arousal states that we call anxiety, rage, and ecstasy all result in the exact same sorts of physiological changes (increased heart rate, increased blood pressure, increased rate of breathing, increased intestinal motility, increased muscle tension, increased sweating, and on and on.)

Simply put, panic disorder and stress depression are caused by chronic hyperarousal. As already mentioned, healthy arousal is anything between 20 and 80 on the scale presented in Figure 11. If necessary, we can run ourselves over 80 for quite some time without a problem. If we do that only intermittently, with a lot of time spent well below 80, we can do it pretty much indefinitely. If we chronically run ourselves hot, we risk a number of unintended consequences. The four most common results of chronic hyperarousal are insomnia, poor digestion, impaired concentration, and changes in the fear-o-stat.

As we go through life, we develop deeply held beliefs about when it is acceptable to feel certain kinds of emotions. (It's okay to cry at a funeral but not over a flat tire.) Some of this programming concerns when it is acceptable to be anxious. If we are anxious when we expect to be — for example, the night before our wedding — we are not upset about it. If someone points a gun to our head and we pee in our pants (one possible result of extremely sudden arousal), we don't call the urologist. It makes sense to us to wet ourselves when there's a gun to our head. What really frightens us is feeling out of control in situations in which we previously felt comfortable.

The Fear-o-Stat is a graph of how much fear it takes to create noticeable feelings of anxiety. We have all sorts of low-probability fears every day. ("I'll lose my job." "I'll get yelled at." "I'll get sick." "I won't get my way." "My children will get hurt." "My spouse will leave me.") These fears do not cause physical anxiety. If we subject ourselves to chronic hyperarousal, we lower the level of fear required to create an anxiety response (a 7, say, becomes a 3), and now, all of a sudden, we are anxious in a bunch of situations in which we used to feel just fine. This is the genesis of panic.

Lead Symptoms

People whose norepinephrine neurotransmitters respond to stress by disturbing their sleep patterns and altering the regulation of the arousal of their autonomic nervous systems tend to be diagnosed as having either major depression or panic disorder. Which one depends on which symptoms are more prominent and how tolerant and experienced the person is with states of increased arousal. In panic disorder, the scarily sudden attacks of hyperarousal are often accompanied by anticipatory anxiety (worry about getting an attack) and by avoidant behavior (avoiding certain stimuli associated with the attacks). I find that most people with long-term panic disorder also sleep and eat poorly, although they may never mention it. Patients who are extremely bothered by insomnia and decreased concentration and work function often have chronic anxiety when they wake up in the morning. They may even have attacks. However, they may not mention these symptoms unless they are questioned about them. Although the lead symptoms in panic disorder and stress depression may be different, I am thoroughly convinced that these two conditions are, in essence, the same disorder.

Three Ideas

Where does this information take us? First, for people with panic disorder, the immediate task at hand is to decatastrophize and reframe the anxiety as a useful signal from the body and the inner self that we need to pay attention to arousal in general. To break the cycle shown in Figure 10.1, we need to normalize anxiety, to make it a known, familiar quantity that may annoy or disappoint us, but should not scare us. The second important task is to learn that arousal can be lowered relatively easily regardless of the cause of the anxiety. (If you are in Chicago, Detroit is in the same direction no matter where you were before). The skill of decreasing arousal, of altering the sympathetic-parasympathetic balance at will, is widely known and easily mastered. In a few pages, I will serve up my own easy-to-learn version. When we can take anxiety as a signal and feel confident that we can relax ourselves at any time as needed, we are able to short-circuit the cycle of panic.

The symptoms of norepinephrine neurotransmitter dysfunction do not develop overnight. Considerable pressure is required to use up the natural reserves of this often quite resilient system. Panic disorder with avoidance develops in the context of a sudden panic attack, which then initiates a desperate search for the cause. Although the underlying cause is always chronic stress, panicking people give unwarranted significance to whatever they may seize on as the likely cause at the moment of panic. From then on, they get anxious about that same cause over and over. The third important idea in the psychoeducation for panic disorder is helping people to focus on the bigger picture of their rhythms of exercise, work, relaxation, and particularly arousal and overarousal, and realizing that the cause lies there, in lifestyle and habit, and not in whatever cause they have chosen to avoid. Once we notice the role of chronic hyperarousal, we can then accept that changes in attitude and activity are necessary.

The Incurious Rats

When addressing avoidant behavior in people with panic disorder, I almost always tell the story of the rats in the two connected cages. The first cage contained lab rats and the second contained food and an electrified floor. When the door between the cages was opened, the hungry rats scrambled for the food, only to be shocked by the electrified floor. After a few shocks, the rats no longer tried to go into the second cage. The experimenters then turned off the electricity and waited for the rats to eat. They didn't. They continued to stay put. It turned out that the rats actually chose to starve to death rather than try to re-enter the electrified cage.

The important point here is that even when the electricity was turned off in the second cage, the rats never found out. For people with panic disorder, the shock of panic attacks can be turned off with medications that reset the Fear-o-Stat, but they also then need to make themselves go back into their "cage" and prove that the "shock" is gone. There's no getting around it.

So far, we've discussed how three excellent ways to combat the symptoms of panic disorder and stress depression are to reframe anxiety as a useful response, to master how to decrease arousal, and to let go of erroneous ideas about the causes of arousal and the resulting avoidant behaviors. Once these ideas have been mastered it becomes far easier to begin to manipulate the rhythms of exercise, meditation, and relaxation to lower arousal. Nothing is more effective or more broadly useful as an intervention in arousal disorders than regular, vigorous exercise. I have seen countless people in very stressful situations maintain minimal symptoms simply because they engaged in a regular regime of vigorous physical activity. Many people just naturally get more exercise when they feel the symptoms of hyperarousal coming on, and they bounce back out right away. So, too, regularly practicing deep relaxation or meditation minimizes, and can even sometimes effectively treat, stress-related symptoms.

Medication

The medicines I use most often for resetting the norepinephrine system are the tricyclic antidepressants, particularly nortriptyline and desipramine. Nortriptyline is better if falling asleep is a problem. Desipramine is preferable if ADD is present or if alertness is a particular concern. These medicines take ten days to three weeks to work, although small changes in sleep pattern or the intensity of anxiety can be seen within four to seven days. SSRIs take longer (four to six weeks) in these depressions, if they work at all, and they create more side effects in people with norepinephrine symptoms than they do in people who have obvious serotonergic symptoms. Remeron is an excellent alternative if tricyclic antidepressants are ineffective or poorly tolerated. It works very quickly, aiding with insomnia almost immediately and decreasing anxiety at five to seven days. The drawbacks of Remeron are weight gain and extreme daytime sedation during the first few days of use.

I do not routinely teach my patients the self-hypnosis relaxation exercise until after their sleep has improved or their anxiety has decreased. Self-hypnosis works much more dramatically once norepinephrine functioning has been restored. It can then help the person get off the medicines easier and quicker, and can also help prevent relapse.

Medication for panic disorder and stress depression needs to be taken for variable lengths of time. Depressed people with insomnia but without panic or avoidant behavior often find that it works completely in four to six weeks. After six months or so, they can begin to slowly taper off the medication without relapse, especially if they've dealt with the more severe stressors or have passed the developmental crisis, and especially if they've begun a regular exercise and relaxation routine.

Panic disorder patients often require longer periods of medication and more extensive therapy to clarify and eliminate their cognitive distortions, to master relaxation, and to let go of their avoidant behavior. After several years of work, they can also often go without medication, if they do not have any other complicating hereditary depressions.

The great trap of psychiatric treatment for stress depression is the mistaken chronic use of minor tranquilizers such as Klonopin, Ativan, and Xanax. Some of the most difficult psychiatric work I have ever done has included weaning anxious patients from their addictions to their minor tranquilizers. Antidepressants and minor tranquilizers can be compared to antibiotics and aspirin, respectively. If you have a fever, aspirin will lower it right away, but when the aspirin wears off, you still have the infection. Antibiotics won't lower the fever right away, but they will cure the illness.

Minor tranquilizers lower anxiety immediately. However, in the same way that alcoholics develop tolerance and then have seizures (the ultimate hyperarousal) when they abruptly stop drinking, the body adapts to the tranquilizer's depressant effects on the central nervous system by becoming more excited. Minor tranquilizers are really little more than alcohol in a pill, and their chronic use is clearly counterproductive. Antidepressants, on the other hand, are stimulants. The reason they take weeks to work is the body reacts to them, adjusting to the chronic stimulation by relaxing.

Minor tranquilizers and sleeping pills are wonderful for occasional use. However, with chronic use, they very quickly become part of the problem.

BSLHB

BSLHB (pronounced BUSH-el-hub) is the acronym for the relaxation exercise I teach almost everyone. It stands for Breathing, Stairs, Light, Hands, Beach.

The exercise is a simple, five-step process that anyone can learn, and it's based on the principles described in Chapter 6. When I do it in person, I embroider in a lot of helpful, relaxing suggestions, but they aren't really necessary. Someday, a companion tape or CD might be available with this book and will contain a version with all the bells and whistles. For now, you can read some of the following into a tape recorder and play it back for yourself. Like all trances, it's boring to read (you can skip it if you like), but it sounds good if it's read aloud properly.

1. Breathing. Start by concentrating your awareness on the sensation of air moving in and out of your body at your mouth or your nostrils (you can use either one). There is a place where the skin changes to the moister mucus membrane inside. Focus your awareness there, and feel the air moving in and out. This is called one-pointed breathing. It is a restful, yoga way of breathing. While you are doing that, you can also slow your breath down, stretching out the inhale and the exhale. You can also begin to notice the changes in your body, how it moves as you breathe, your shoulders, your neck, your head, your chest, your abdomen. Feel the breath inside as it slides down into your chest and your abdomen. Feel the breath arrive at a soft center, and feel the walls of your stomach softening.

Then imagine there is a balloon between your belly-button and your spine. Breathe in slowly, filling up that balloon. That is called diaphragmatic breathing, another restful, yoga way of breathing.

When you start one-pointed breathing and gradually become aware of all the different aspects of your breath, you will, at the same time, begin to feel your body relaxing. You'll experience a restful feeling of floating.

2. Stairs. With a part of your mind still on your breath, imagine a staircase in front of you. Any kind of staircase will do. I prefer a black, spiral staircase. It really doesn't matter whether you see yourself going down the stairs, an objective camera catching you descending, or maybe you just look out of your eyes and see your feet on the stairs. Maybe you simply feel what it's like to shift your weight from one foot to the other, to slide your hand down the cool, metal banister. Maybe you hear the sound of your footsteps on the stairs as you go down. What does matter is that you go down the stairs, down, down, down. The farther down you go, the more relaxed you become and the less aware you are of your surroundings.

If thoughts come into your mind, let them float away like clouds passing before the sun or raindrops sliding down a windowpane. Your mind is clear, your breathing is easy, and your body is comfortable. Keep going down until you reach the bottom of the stairs, then go through an archway into a cavern.

3. Light. As you go through the archway, you see a hallway off to one side with a pulsing light at the end. This is the life force pulsing inside you. When you are in touch with the life force pulsing inside you, you feel a great sense of peacefulness and contentedness, a sense of connection to all the living rhythms of the universe, to the sun rising and setting, to the seasons changing, to the children being born and the old folks dying, to your own breath, to the hummingbird's racing heart, to stars going nova and dark over millions of years. When you are in touch with the life force pulsing inside you, you find that you can slow it down, slower, and

slower, and slower, until you find a rhythm that is soothing and comfortable for you.

4. Hands. Even as you see the life force pulsing in the hallway, you can feel it in your hands — a warmth, a buzzing, a pulsing, a tingling, a fullness in the pads of your fingers that moves back and forth, back and forth, getting clearer and stronger, clearer and stronger.

5. Beach. And then feel yourself on the beach, your favorite beach. Really be there in all your senses. See the way the blue of the sky meets the blue of the sea, smell the salt air, feel the sun on your face, hear the waves crashing on the shore, the children playing, the birds crying. And then close your eyes and feel the relaxed familiar sensation of your favorite beach. And then . . .

At this point, go back to step 1 and start the five steps all over again. Continue repeating the steps, going round and round, deeper and deeper.

This relaxation exercise is enormously effective at providing people with the sense that their anxiety is manageable, not catastrophic, and that, with just a little practice and a little focus, they can relax themselves. However, it doesn't work if you don't use it, and it takes some time and persistence to realize the full benefit. Many people find it helpful to make an agreement with themselves, set a timer, and give themselves this deep relaxation for five minutes, three times a day.

Post-Traumatic Stress Disorder
Post-traumatic stress disorder consists of three clusters of symptoms that occur after a profound acute trauma: increased autonomic nervous system tone, dissociative flashback experiences, and emotional numbing and withdrawal. Many of the symptoms in the autonomic nervous system cluster look very similar to those of panic disorder or stress depression, and they respond to the

same medications: tricyclic antidepressants and Remeron. The other two clusters are better treated with established hypnotherapeutic and experiential techniques.

The military has, in fact, been at the forefront of PTSD treatment and, even more importantly, PTSD prevention. Very often, as was evident in many of the people affected by the September 11 terrorist attacks, people who go through a trauma can experience a period of relief at being spared or saved and then have PTSD symptoms gradually develop later. The initial period of relief can extend for weeks or months. In the recent military campaigns in Iraq, psychiatrists were present and available virtually immediately to victims of battle trauma. Early treatment lowers the rate of eventual PTSD dramatically.

All PTSD treatment involves the telling and retelling, the controlled re-experiencing, of the trauma. Repeated exposure and systematic desensitization to the traumatic material is essentially a "trance" sort of treatment, whether it is overtly described as hypnosis or not. When flashbacks are associated with calming and distancing images, they eventually become just like any other memory that is less than pleasant but not very powerful. Emotional numbing can be profound and chronic, and its treatment can be very difficult. Hypnotherapy can sometimes be helpful here, as can good-quality, clarifying-and-challenging conversational therapy. A number of specific hypnotherapeutic techniques are well described in the excellent, though somewhat challenging to read, *Healing the Divided Self* by Philips and Frederick. It is beyond the scope of this book to discuss these techniques in detail, but again, PTSD is another condition in which the proper combination of medication and psychotherapy is essential to an optimal outcome.

———◆◆◆———

Clearly, much more can be said about psychotherapy for the treatment of neurotransmitter disorders. It is my hope that this chapter makes the case for the need to integrate medication and psychotherapy, and for the need to create more specific therapies for specific diagnostic entities. What I have offered here is just a beginning — my thoughts on a few common entities. What is really required to allow the consistent application of the broad array of modern therapeutic techniques is a corps of dedicated therapist/prescribers.

CHAPTER 11

Dr. Don's Dreams

I have tried to make the case in these pages that an integrated understanding of the genesis of under functioning adults requires us to look at depression attention and the effects of trauma. We also need to look at the ramifications of this approach for the delivery of care, for the training of therapists and psychopharmacological prescribers, and for educational policy.

THE PROBLEMS

In Chapter 1, we talked about a mental health system in our country that is just as fragmented as the individuals it is supposed to assist. The reality is psychiatrists don't do therapy anymore, therapists can't prescribe, and the patients suffer.

And that's only part of it. Health insurance companies, in their often frantic efforts to economize, have created, at least for psychiatrists, jobs that no sane person would want. Certainly, they have created jobs that very few American medical school graduates seem to want.

To demonstrate some of the problems confronting an outpatient mental health practitioner, I am going to talk a little bit now about my practice in New York. I have offices in the Greenpoint/Williamsburg section of Brooklyn — a currently gentrifying working class and artists' neighborhood right across the East River from the United Nations — as well as in downtown Manhattan, between Chelsea and Murray Hill. Until recently, I also had an office in Pleasantville, a small suburban town in central Westchester, about thirty-five miles north of the city.

I belong to a number of different managed-care panels, each of which is organized along different lines and all of which have different sorts of rules, often with several different subsets of rules within each panel. I am on a panel for city employees and for state employees. I am on panels for specific insurance companies, such as CIGNA, and I am on panels for large mental health managed care organizations, such as Magellan Behavioral, Value Options, and MHN, which sell their services to several insurance companies.

The rules are all about payment and authorization, number of visits allowed, co-payments, steps for authorizing treatment, and authorization renewal. Just to discover and then keep abreast of these ever-changing rules is villainously time-consuming, involving multiple telephone numbers, long holds on the phone, and uninformed staff (high turnover there, surprise, surprise).

The most onerous aspect of the whole operation is the authorization process, which is, of course, different for each company and often for each contract within each company. Thankfully, some companies have been moving away from this demeaning, alienating process, but for about half of my patients, I need to fill out complicated but ultimately useless forms three to five times a year.

Thankfully, I have staff that bills for me, helps me with the authorizations, and chases down the money when the authorizers and the payers manage to muck things up. You would be amazed at how often that happens (another big surprise).

I am mentioning all this because I want you to understand why it is so difficult for the average consumer to find reasonable psychiatric care. To begin with, managed-care fees are, at best, roughly only 45 to 60 percent of the fees charged by psychiatrists who do not accept insurance. Most psychiatrists do outpatient work only part-time, if at all. They tend to have day jobs. Even more discouraging, psychiatrists are generally not even allowed to join these panels until they have six years of experience.

By the time psychiatrists have six years of experience, they have jobs and small to medium-size noninsurance practices. They have neither the time nor the inclination to take anywhere near enough insurance patients to make it worth hiring assistance or figuring out how to manage these complex systems by themselves. So, they just don't join the panels.

In my section of Brooklyn, a neighborhood of 150,000 people where I work two days a week, I am the only outpatient psychiatrist. An outer borough of Manhattan, Brooklyn itself, at 2.5 million people, is the fourth largest city in the nation. It even has its own medical school. Yet, I do not believe there are even ten private-practice, American-trained, prescriber-therapist psychiatrists who routinely take insurance in the entire borough.

Every week, I get between ten and twenty people calling me for services. I can't even call most of them back. It's too painful to say no, and I have nowhere to send them. It so happens that, because I interrupted my training between internship and residency for three and a half years, and because I returned in the middle of the year — in January instead of July — I trained with three different classes of residents. Each class had twenty or more psychiatrists; a total of over sixty psychiatrists who finished their residencies between 1984 and 1989. Of these, only a handful are in full-time private practice, and I don't think any take insurance.

There's a problem out there.

For those who feel themselves unable to function in a manner commensurate with their natural gifts, for those who are "stuck" in the way we have been discussing, it is indeed the best of times and the worst of times. It is the best of times because never have we had better, more effective medications to treat biochemical and neurophysiological states. Never before have we understood the structure of the mind, its left- and right-brain modes and their interaction, as well as we have in the past few decades. And never before have we had such a wide range of therapeutic techniques available to deal with this left-right brain relationship.

Unfortunately, it is also the worst of times. For although there has never been more of a need to integrate the medical and psychotherapeutic aspects of mental health treatment, never have our therapists been so unlikely to acquire the broad training necessary to do so. The result is patients continue to have difficulty finding adequate, appropriate, effective treatment.

Much of this failure to effectively train therapists and to make integrated effective treatment available can be attributed to the pernicious economic and political interaction between large health insurers and academic institutional psychiatry.

Right now, the psychiatric community as a whole is failing to produce an adequate supply of broadly trained physicians. The vast majority of those who are being trained see themselves primarily as psychopharmacologists and are not proficient in (if they are even acquainted with) the psychotherapeutic techniques we have been discussing in this book. Academic psychiatrists are reproducing themselves, and most of them are very broad based. A wide range of institutions is legally mandated to retain psychiatrists, and these institutional administrative jobs are also by and large being filled. What is not being provided are solidly and broadly trained practitioners to go out into the thousands upon thousands of middle-class neighborhoods scattered around our nation. The average working person, union member, corporate employee, or participant in a small business does not have access to, nor can he or she afford care from, a broadly trained professional. What should be done?

THE SOLUTIONS

As a boy, I indulged myself in what I now look back on as utopian fantasies. In these fantasies, I would somehow have accumulated enormous power (of course, without becoming corrupt). I would then set about using this power in some clever and benevolent fashion, depending, of course, on the particular human failing I was attempting to correct at the time. Nowadays, my utopian fantasies often revolve around the state of modern psychiatry.

So, if I were king, I would:

• Make drug companies and insurance companies support the training and development of outpatient-based therapist prescribers.

• Create a standardized mental health authorization and benefit policy across all entities.

• Create a subspecialty board in affective attentional and obsessive disorders.

• Revamp our educational and penal systems for early recognition of ADD and learning disabilities, and for the use of right-left brain integration techniques.

I want to expand on each of these somewhat.

A Training Program
It is easy for me to imagine a program in which an entity funded partly by the government and partly by the companies that profit from providing mental health care (insurance and pharmaceutical companies come to mind) would select high school students and feed them through a streamlined track of undergraduate social sciences, medical school, and tailored residencies. The students would, upon graduation, make a three-to five-year commitment to moderate wage work as prescribers/therapists in clinics set up specifically for the uninsured and the underinsured. At the end of the required time, these practitioners would be automatically enrolled in fee-for-service managed-care panels.

Although it would take some time — say, ten or twelve years — to bear fruit, such a program would eventually be more than cost effective in providing the much-needed practitioners. Medical schools would be happy to have the additional spots that such a program would fund. Such training is far more likely to produce the brief, time-limited, cost-effective therapies the insurance companies say they want than does the current system of empty panels and doctorless patients.

Perhaps this is the place to mention that I would wholeheartedly support a mechanism by which psychologists and social workers could also somehow become outpatient precribers/therapists. The medical schools and hospitals have not, I believe, earned the right to keep these privileges to themselves. I, for one, would like to see the birth of a new profession, the mental health therapist/prescriber, created by calling upon the medical, nursing, psychological, and social work establishments to come together to create a new comprehensive, efficient curriculum that could create the needed practitioners in the briefest period of time.

In any case, we need some mechanism for increasing the number of mental health prescribers in our communities. To my mind, only a combined government, corporate, and academic coalition can be expected to do the job. And here's a tip: The most likely outcome in the near-term is the use of psychiatric nurse practitioners, as these professonals are the only ones, besides psychiatrists, of which there will never be enough and who can legally integrate medication and psychotherapy.

A Rational System

The training program we just discussed would be predicated, of course, upon a rationalized mental health insurance system. Clearly, the people drawn to become mental health practitioners are rarely interested in paperwork and office systems. If we want to attract our finest young people to enter a profession that requires at least twelve years of training after high school, we can't ask them to be clerks as well. Obviously, legislation is required — and all I can think to say is that if every person who has one of the conditions discussed in this book and every person who is related to someone with one of these conditions put their political power behind such legislation, it might have a chance.

A New Subspecialty

There are subspecialty boards in geriatric and substance-abuse psychiatry. It seems to be appropriate to create a subspecialty in neurotransmitter and attentional disorders, which would include ADD, depression, anxiety, and OCD, and which would center on outpatient treatment. Insurance companies could use such a subspecialty to award higher fees and institute less-restrictive authorization policies. Certainly, such an academy would promote the creation of specific therapeutic techniques like the ones we have been discussing herein.

A New Educational Approach

There is no question that many enlightened educators throughout our country understand the relationship between the left and the right brains and recognize attentional and learning problems at appropriately early stages. Still, many classroom teachers don't recognize common problems and don't know what to do if they do recognize them. Many feel constrained about making diagnoses, and few solid resources are available for kids with ADD anyway.

My own son, a bright boy with mild ADD and considerable behavioral problems, floundered in several high schools before we found the Hyde School. It is not at all a coincidence that I am ending this book with a few comments on my recent experiences with the Hyde School, because if everyone went to a school like Hyde, a lot of people wouldn't need to do all the work I have described in the pages that precede these.

Hyde is a boarding school with two campuses. It specializes in what it calls family-based character education. It does not sell itself as a school for ADD, although many of its students do carry this diagnosis.

You may or may not recall that at the end of Chapter 9, when summing up the treatment for ADD, I mentioned that most of the work done with therapy for ADD had been directed at children, and adolescents in particular, and that it was not very successful. I myself have, in the past several years, often refused to take on angry high school students. The amount of therapy I can provide is simply not sufficient to the task.

I do not want to attempt to summarize the Hyde philosophy here. Its founder, Joe Gault, has written very well on his own behalf. What Hyde did for my child was to provide a comprehensive, easy-to-understand structure that challenged him repeatedly and held him accountable. What made Hyde so perfect for my kid, and for so many other kids with ADD, is that part of its structure is a repeated, in-your-face demand that children do their best, that they find and explore their unique potential. If you are doing what you love, with passion, the school is happy. If you are not, you are held accountable.

This is so great for kids with ADD because it makes them seek their bliss or answer why not. Remember, it is not really an attention deficit disorder. Rather, it's an attention modulation disorder. At Hyde, they know this, and they know that when you seek your bliss, attention deficits are beside the point.

The secret about Hyde is that they really know the kids and they have control over the environment. Outpatient therapy for defiant, angry, dissociated kids just isn't enough when they aren't "known" and when there are so many incentives for kids to dull the pain and avoid the hard work of mastering themselves. It seems to me that our educational system needs to reflect the tendency for youths to dissociate and also to address the need for ongoing right-brain training of all sorts. The trend toward less and less art, music, and sports at school is damnably short-sighted because every child needs the right brain cultivated as well as the left. When it's not, children are cut off from themselves and become stuck adults.

Well, well, well. We've reached the end.

For the last dream, more than anything else, what I want is to share what I know, to help those like myself, the hyperactive, and those not so like myself, too. In the coming years, I will be working to turn this book into a series of seminars. I am hopeful that, rather quickly, I can take this material out to mental-health professionals. In the middle term, I will work on developing a seminar for young adults on using the right brain; a seminar, in group format, that would teach the trance skills we have discussed in this book. The knowledge and insights I gain through these seminars will form the basis of my next book.

I expect that many of you who read this book will want help using some of the material. Find a hypnotist and make him or her read it. He or she will know what to do.

APPENDIX I

Cathy's Trance

I listen to Cathy for a while, and then I ask her if she's a visual person, if she can see things easily in her mind's eye. She nods.

> If you close your eyes, can you see your mother's face?
> *Cathy nods.*
> Then close your eyes
> And focus on your breathing.
> Be aware of the feeling of the air as it moves
> In and out of your nostrils.
> That's a restful yoga way of breathing,
> A way of breathing that turns on
> All the relaxational systems in your body.
> That's right,
> Breathing so easily.
> And I'd like you to imagine yourself in a meadow.
> See the grass.
> Can you see the grass, Cathy?
> *Cathy nods.*
> Good.
> Even in this restful state, you can nod your head, can't you, Cathy?
> *Cathy nods.*
> And you do feel restful, don't you, Cathy?
> *Cathy nods.*

And you'll find that you can speak
Without disturbing this restful state
Of focused concentration.
Can you see the grass, Cathy?
Cathy says, "Yes."

What color is it?
Cathy says, "Yellow-green."
And how tall is it?
Cathy says, "About two feet."
Are there trees?
Cathy says, "Around the edges."
And flowers?
Cathy says, "Some."
And now, with another part of your mind,
I'd like you to think about the feelings
We were talking about —
The fear,
The sadness,
The sense that you'll always be alone.
And I'd like you to look over to the side of the meadow.
And there's a fallen tree.
And sitting on the tree is a little girl,
A little girl who feels that way.
Can you see the little girl?
Cathy nods.
Walk over to her.
What's she wearing?
Cathy says, "A jumper."
Can you see how her hair is cut?
Cathy nods.
How old is she?
Cathy says, "Five."
Do you know her?
It's you, isn't it?
Cathy nods.
Little Cathy.
Go over to her.

Sit down next to her on the log.

Introduce yourself.

Tell her you are her all grown up.

Ask her how she feels.

Cathy says, "All alone, scared."

Is it something with her parents?

Cathy says, "No, it's the other children. They won't play with her."

They don't like her?

Cathy says, "She doesn't fit in. She moves around too much. Talks too much. Bothers them. She's too much."

(A light goes on in my head.)

Were you a very active child?

Cathy says, "Yes."

Some trouble learning and following the rules?

Cathy nods.

Trouble concentrating in school?

Cathy says, "Some."

Always being told you could do better if only you tried harder?

Cathy says, "Always."

(Now I was almost sure.)

Okay,

Look into the little girl's eyes.

Take her on your lap.

Stroke her hair.

Tell her she's a good girl.

She is a good girl, isn't she?

Cathy nods.

She tries so hard.

She means so well.

Tell her she's a good girl.

Now, the thing is, Cathy,

That you didn't stay lonely,

Did you?

Cathy shakes her head no.

And you learned.

You learned to control yourself,
To move around less,
To speak less,
To think more
About what people wanted.
You learned to give it to them,
Didn't you?
Cathy nods.
You had friends.
Cathy nods.
And you discovered men.
Cathy nods.
And that became the measure,
Didn't it?
Cathy nods.
So, as long as you had one,
This girl was quiet,
She felt okay,
She was sort of sleeping.
Cathy nods.
But now, she's woken up.
Cathy nods.
And she needs your help,
Your love,
Your acceptance.
She's sweet, isn't she?
Cathy nods.
She deserves love and understanding.
Every child deserves love and understanding,
Don't they?
Cathy nods.
Can you give her your love?
Cathy nods.
Think of your love like a radiant energy,
An aura surrounding you.

Envelop the girl in your love.
Turn up the volume.
Turn up the heat.
Can the little girl feel your love?
Cathy nods.
That feels better, doesn't it?
When she feels better, Cathy,
You feel better, too.
So, look her in the eye.
Tell her you accept her.
Tell her you'll be there for her.
Look her in the eye and say,
Now . . .
Cathy says, "Now . . ."
We're in this together.
Cathy says, "Now we're in this together."
Tell her you'll be back.
Give her a hug.
Cathy says, "Now we're in this together."

B.'s Trance

Close your eyes
And focus on your breathing.
All your awareness
On the feeling of the air
As it moves in and out of your nostrils.
A restful yoga way of breathing.
A way of breathing
That turns on
All the relaxational systems in your body.
As you listen to my voice
And you sit in that chair
And you focus on your breathing,
You can begin to relax,
So that part of your mind
Is aware of the air
Moving in and out of your nostrils,
And another part of your mind
Can see in front of you

A black spiral staircase.
And it really doesn't matter
Whether you see yourself going down the stairs
From an objective point of view,
An objective camera catches you descending.
Or maybe you're just looking out

And seeing your feet
Out of your eyes,
The way we do.
Maybe you just feel what it's like
To shift your weight
From one foot to the other,
To slide your hand
Down the cool, metal banister.
What does matter
Is that you go down,
Down,
Down,
Down,
Deeper and deeper into yourself.
The further down you go,
The more relaxed you become,
The less aware you are of your surroundings.
My voice is not even recognizable
As a separate voice,
Just part of your own mind
As you go down the stairs,
Down,
Down,
Down,
Deeper and deeper
Into yourself.
When you get to the bottom of the stairs,
There's an archway,
And through the archway
Is a cavern.
The cavern of yourself.
You can already begin to be curious
About all the things you might find there.
And off to one side
Is a conference room
With a table and two chairs.
And you sit down in one chair.
And sitting opposite you
Is you,
Your inner self,

The one we've met before.
He's your friend,
Isn't he?
B. nods.
Can you see him?
B. nods.
Do you know him?
B. nods.
He's got a lot of different parts,
This one.
He can do all sorts of things,
Can't he?
But he has to be asked
Nicely.
He can be sidetracked.
He can be frightened.
He hates it if you don't like him.
He needs to be talked to,
Doesn't he?
B. nods.
Not yelled at.
When you've had trouble with time
And responsibility,
You've often berated him
Instead of finding ways
To use his talents.
There's so much he can do.
Ask him if he's willing
To show you what he can do.
He will, won't he?
B. nods.
For example, now
Take a moment
And think about yourself in space.
He does that easily, doesn't he?
You are him and he is you,
So you can feel what he feels,
Sense what he senses,
Can't you?

B. nods.
You're facing east now,
And in front of you is the East River,
And behind you is the Hudson,
And downtown,
Over there,
Is the ferry,
Where you work.
And over there,
But not quite as far down,
Is the World Trade Center.
And you find that you know
Every place that is important.
Specifically,
Just where each thing is
In relation to all the others.
You have this map
In your head.
Maybe you can almost see it,
Although maybe it's not quite like seeing —
More like a sensing,
But a visual sort of sensing.
And all things have distance and direction.
And time is like that.
See time as space.
Feel yourself in the present
As a point on a line,
With the past stretching out one way
And the future stretching the other.
See each day as a rectangle
About four times as high than as wide.
The weekends can be one color
And the weekdays another.
See the rhythm of time in space,
The way the weekends come up regularly,
Off into the distance in each direction,

You've had trouble with time
And with reliability.
But here's a simple rule

For both of you to learn:
If you can't say when,
You can't say yes.
If you want to say yes,
Then you want to say when.
So use time as space.
See the week now.
Look at the seven rectangles
Laying in a row,
And see that each rectangle
Divides into three equal parts —
Morning, afternoon, evening.
You've been doing it all your life.
If you want to,
You can hover over the seven rectangles
And look at your week.
See the patterns of time
Running through your life.
When you look,
You can see them.
The thing about space
Is that each and every space can contain
Only one single thing.
Space is finite.
So is time.
If you can't say when,
You can't say yes.
You're walking down the street.
You bump into an old friend.
You say, "Let's get together."
You really mean it.
If you don't take out your date book
And pick a time,
It will never happen.
You know it's true.
If you can't say when,
You can't say yes.

When time is space, it has rhythms.
Rhythms of days,
Rhythms of weeks.
Every activity has a rhythm.
Either it's a one-time event
Or it's a multiple event.
If it's a multiple event,
Then the very first thing we have to know is
What rhythm is it on?
There are only eight human rhythms —
Several times a day,
Once a day,
Several times a week,
Once a week,
Several times a month,
Once a month,
Several times a year,
Once a year.
That's it.
Only eight rhythms.
If you want to get something done,
What rhythm is it on?
Here's a not-so-secret secret
That your inner self already knows.
If you tell him to do something,
Something that's a multiple event,
But you don't select a rhythm,
He'll ignore you completely,
Won't he?

B. nods.

He won't waste his time
On something that can't possibly happen.
If you need to get something done,
Look at your week.
Seven rectangles
Divided into threes.
Twenty-one boxes.
That's all.
See the patterns.
Some boxes are always filled.
Some are available

But there are only twenty-one.
It's not an accident
That we use the word "spend"
For both money and time.
To do a budget, you need to know your fixed expenses.
If you want to say yes,
You've got to say when.
When you want to say when,
You can see your week in space.
See the givens,
The fixed expenses.
Life is a puzzle —
See where the task fits in.

Know your rhythms —
The rhythms of work,
The rhythms of play,
The rhythms of chores,
The rhythms of love,
The rhythms of growth.
If you don't see the rhythms,
You'll keep getting lost,
Saying yes without saying when.
When you see the rhythms
You're already living with,
Your yeses have meaning.
So, here's another pithy phrase
To walk around with:
Rhythms plus one.
Think about that:
Rhythms plus one.
When you see the rhythms
You're already living with,
You can begin to think
About adding new ones,
One at a time.
Rhythms plus one.
So now you're beginning to see
Just how easy it can be
To know things about time,
About your time.
When you ask your inner self to see it,

He doesn't mind, does he?
As long as you're not yelling at him.
As long as you ask him nicely.
As long as you ask him regularly.
You're starting to get the idea.
If you can't say when,
You can't say yes.
When you want to say when,
Rhythms plus one.
We're getting there.

Now here's the next big thing:
Transitions.
Think about transitions.
Reliability means smooth transitions,
Transitions that make sense
When you look at time in space.
Look at the transitions in your day.
When are you going to move
From one place to another?
When are you going to change activities?
These transitions
Are the most crucial moments in the day,
The vulnerable moments
When things can go awry.
When are you going to move?
And how are you going to go about it?

So, listen carefully,
Both of you —
The outer self,
Who makes the plans,
Who knows the deadlines,
Who always seems to be overloading himself
With just a few too many details
To really keep in mind.
And the inner self,
Who knows how to store it all,
Doesn't lose a thing
Because a picture is worth a thousand words,
Which is just another way of saying

That a picture can hold
An infinite number
Of pieces of data.
But each word holds only one —
You have to work together.
You have to meet regularly,
Several times a day,
Morning and night.
Together, you can see the rhythms
And make them work for you.
Oh, how rare that's been,
Eh?
So, listen carefully,
Both of you.
A transition is a chord.
The chord has three notes.
You can't play just one note.
It won't sound like a chord.
It doesn't come out right.
So, listen to the notes.
All three.
When do I have to get there?
When do I have to leave?
When do I have to start to get ready to leave?
If you want to be at Dr. Kerson's office
At five o'clock,
You can't just tell yourself
Five o'clock,
Because by the time you look up from what you're doing,
It will be almost five o'clock,
Or close enough to five o'clock
That you can't possibly
Get your shit together
And get there
By five o'clock.
That's only one note.
Play the second note, too.
When do I want to get there?
Five o'clock.
When do I have to leave?

Well, that depends.
How long does it take?
Ask your inner self.
He has an answer.
He has parts of him that keep track of time.
You're going to have to get to know those guys better.
We'll get back there in a bit.
All the same,
He can give you an estimate
Give or take.
And now, stop a minute
And reflect.
Are you an optimist
Or a pessimist?

Look at a bell-shaped curve.
Everything in nature
Is a bell-shaped curve.
It's symmetrical.
One side matches the other.
Draw a bell-shaped curve
Of your travel times.
Draw a line down the middle.
That's thirty minutes.
At the opposite ends
Are fifteen and forty five minutes.
How long do you leave yourself?
Are you an optimist?

Or a pessimist?
Do you assume the best?
Just because you sometimes can
Get there in twenty minutes
Means that you usually will?
Then you're an optimist.
A late optimist.
A pessimist assumes the worst.
He's on time.
Play a pessimistic second note.
When do I want to get there?
Five o'clock.
When do I want to leave?

Pessimistically speaking,
At four ten.
You can always bring a book.
Then there's the third note.
It's a whole chord in itself,
That third note.
When do I want to start to get ready to leave?
The crucial third note.
When do I want to start to get ready to leave?
Let's put it another way.
It takes time to get your shit together.
Everyone knows that phrase.
We have to get our shit together.
What does that mean?
We have to stop and reflect,
Go through our next few transitions,
And make sure we bring with us everything we need.
It's also not a bad idea
To make sure you haven't left some inconsiderate mess

For some unsuspecting loved one
Who may not feel so loved
When walking in on your dirty dishes
And your strewn papers
And your underwear
For the nine-thousandth time.
In fact, here's where we introduce
Another chord.
A subchord, you might say.
Three notes for the third note:
What did I bring here?
What do I have to take with me?
Did I leave this place the way I found it?
That's getting your shit together.
How long does it take?
Well, that depends on what you were doing.
How long does it take
To think about and gather and tidy?
To play the third note?

When you make a transition,
You have to play the chord,

All three notes.
When do I want to get there?
Five o'clock.
When do I want to leave?
Four ten.
When do I have to stop what I am doing and
Start to get ready to leave?
Say, three forty-five.
Now, that's a harmonious transition.

So, look down on your week,
Hover over the seven rectangles,
Divided into three parts each —
Morning, afternoon, evening.
The weekdays can be one color
And the weekends another,
Or maybe not.
But you can pick a color for transitions.
See where the chord needs to be played.
It's not a line,
One note at five o'clock.
It's a block of time,
A chord of time.
When do I want to get there?
When do I want to leave?
When do I have to start to get ready to leave?

So, you're sitting with yourself.
He's you, and he's not you.
He's familiar, but he can surprise you.
He's part of you, and he's separate from you, too.
You need each other.
He can store enormous amounts of information
If only it's shown to him properly,
Respectfully.
Can you see him across from you?
B. nods.
Did he hear everything we said?
B. nods.
Did he show you time as space?
B. nods.

He knows about rhythms and patterns,
Doesn't he?
B. nods.
Did you see the patterns in time?
B. nods.
You need each other,
And you have to meet regularly.
Twice a day,
Every day.
Look at the rhythms.
See the transitions.
Review what you've learned.
If you can't say when,
You can't say yes.
When you want to say when,
What rhythm is it on?
When it's all on a rhythm,
It's rhythms plus one.
Think it over.
He'll meet with you, won't he?
B. nods.
But you must accept him.
You must want his opinions.
He will show you the patterns
If he is asked for them.
Look into his eyes.
Grasp his hand.
Tell him, "Now,
We're in this together.
B. says, "Now, we're in this together."

So, take a minute
And review what you've learned.
And promise to meet each other,
To review your intentions,
To find unity
And clarity of purpose.
It's so easy to find him.
Just close your eyes

And focus on your breathing.
Go down the stairs,
Into the conference room,
And there he is.
He'll meet with you,
Won't he?

B. nods.
Because now,
You're in this together.
Now, you're in this together.
So, take a minute
And review what you've learned.
Promise to meet each other
Twice a day,
Morning and night.
And then slowly count backward
From three to two to one.
When you say "three," get ready.
When you say "two," open your eyes.
When you say "one," wake up.
Are you ready?

Three.
Get ready.

Two.
Open your eyes.

One.
Wake up.

References by Author

Akhtar, A. (1977). *Psycheye.* New York: Brandon House.

Akhtar, A. (1989). *The Eidetic Parents Test.* New York: Brandon House.

Amen, D. (2001). *Healing ADD.* New York: G.P. Putnam.

American Psychiatric Association Press. (1994). *Diagnostic and Statistical Manual of Mental Disorders* DSM-IV. Washington, D.C: Author.

Barkley, R. (1997). *ADHD and The Nature of Self Control.* New York. The Guildford Press.

Beck, A. (2005). *Anxiety Disorders and Phobias: A Cognitive Perspective.* New York: Basic Books.

Burns, D. (1999). *Feeling Good.* New York: Avon Books.

Campbell, J. (1972). *The Hero With A Thousand Faces.* Princeton: Princeton University Press.

Campbell, J. (1993). *Myths to Live By.* New York: Penguin.

Dass, Ram. (1971). *Be Here Now*. New Mexico: Lama Foundation.

Dass, Ram. (1990). *Journey of Awakening*. New York: Bantam.

Frederick, C. & Philips, M. (1995). *Healing the Divided Self*. New York: W.W. Norton & Company.

Gilligan, S. (1987). *Therapeutic Trances*. New York: Brunner/Mazell.

Gilligan, S. (1997). *The Courage to Love*. New York: W.W. Norton & Company.

Hammond, R. Corydon. (1990). *Handbook of Hypnotic Metaphor and Suggestion*. New York: W.W. Norton & Company.

Havens, R.A. & Walters, C. (1989). *Hypnotherapy Scripts*. New York: Bruner/ Mazell.

Hunter, Marlene E. (1994). *Creative Scripts for Hypnotherapy*. New York: Brunner/Mazell.

Lamas, Surya Das. (1997). *Awakening The Buddah Within*. New York: Broadway Books.

Landis, R. (1991). *Interactive Imageries for Habit Feeling and Behavior Change (Vols.1-2)*. Los Angeles: Orange County Society for Ericksonian Psychotherapy Publications.

Leguin, Ursula. (1997). *Tao Te Ching*. Boston: Shambala Publications.

LeShan, Lawrence. (1999). *How to Meditate*. New York: Little, Brown and Company.

Mitchell, S. (1988). *Tao Te Ching*. New York: Harper Collins.

Rhawn, J. (2001). *The Right Brain and the Unconscious Discovering the Stranger Within*. New York: Basic Books.

Rapaport, J. (1991). *The Boy Who Couldn't Stop Washing His Hands*. New York: Signet/Penguin.

Ratey, J. (1998). *The Shadow Syndromes*. New York: Bantam.

Ross, Ernest. (1991). *Twenty Minute Break*. New York: Tarcher/Penguin.

Rubin, Zick (1973) *Liking & Loving*. Austin: Holt, Rhinehart & Winston.

Schwartz, J. (1997). *Brain Lock*. New York: Regan Books.

Soskis, D. (1986). *Teaching Self-Hypnosis*. New York: W.W. Norton & Company.

Watkins, J. (1987). *Ego States: Theory and Therapy*. New York: W.W. Norton.

References by Chapter

Chapter 3

1. American Psychiatric Association Press. (1994). *Diagnostic and Statistical Manual of Mental Disorders* DSM-IV. Washington, D.C: Author.

2. Barkley, R. (1997). *ADHD and The Nature of Self Control.* New York. The Guildford Press.

3. Amen, D. (2001). *Healing ADD.* New York: G.P. Putnam.

Chapter 5

1. Watkins, J. (1987). *Ego States: Theory and Therapy.* New York: W.W. Norton.

2. Frederick, C. & Philips, M. (1995). *Healing the Divided Self.* New York: W.W. Norton & Company.

3. Rhawn, J. (2001). *The Right Brain and the Unconscious Discovering the Stranger Within.* New York: Basic Books.

Chapter 6

1. Soskis, D. (1986). *Teaching Self-Hypnosis.* New York: W.W. Norton & Company.

Chapter 7

1. Landis, R. (1991). *Interactive Imageries for Habit Feeling and Behavior Change (Vols.1-2).* Los Angeles: Orange County Society for Ericksonian Psychotherapy Publications.

2. Gilligan, S. (1997). *The Courage to Love.* New York: W.W. Norton & Company.

3. Gilligan, S. (1987). *Therapeutic Trances.* New York: Brunner/Mazell.

4. Akhtar, A. (1989). *The Eidetic Parents Test.* New York: Brandon House.

5. Akhtar, A. (1977). *Psycheye.* New York: Brandon House.

6. Campbell, J. (1972). *The Hero With A Thousand Faces.* Princeton: Princeton University Press

7. Campbell, J. (1993). *Myths to Live By.* New York: Penguin.

8. Leguin, Ursula. (1997). *Tao Te Ching.* Boston: Shambala Publications.

Chapter 9

1. Dass, Ram. (1990). *Journey of Awakening.* New York: Bantam.

2. Dass, Ram. (1971). *Be Here Now.* New Mexico: Lama Foundation.

3. LeShan, Lawrence. (1999). *How to Meditate.* New York: Little, Brown and Company.

4. Ross, Ernest. (1991). *Twenty Minute Break.* New York: Tarcher/Penguin.

5. Lamas, Surya Das. (1997). *Awakening The Buddah Within.* New York: Broadway Books.

6. Hammond, R. Corydon. (1990). *Handbook of Hypnotic Metaphor and Suggestion.* New York: W.W. Norton & Company.

7. Havens, R.A. & Walters, C. (1989). *Hypnotherapy Scripts.* New York: Bruner/ Mazell.

8. Hunter, Marlene E. (1994). *Creative Scripts for Hypnotherapy.* New York: Brunner/Mazell.

Chapter 10

1. Beck, Aaron T. (2005). *Anxiety Disorders and Phobias: A Cognitive Perspective.*

2. Burns, David. *Feeling Good.* (1999). New York: Avon Books.

3. Frederick, C. & Philips, M. (1995). *Healing The Divided Self.* New York: WW. Norton & Company.

4. Mitchell, Stephen. *Tao Te Ching.* (1992). New York: Harper Perennial.

5. Schwartz, Stephen. *Brain Lock.* (1997). New York: Regan Books.

6. Rapoport, Judith L. *The Boy Who Couldn't Stop Washing.* (1991). New York: Signet/Penguin.

7. Ratey, John. *The Shadow Syndromes.* (1998). New York: Bantam.

8. Rubin, Zick. *Liking and Loving.* (1973). Austin: Holt, Rhinehart and Winston

Index

Journey of Awakening (Dass), 178
Jung, Carl, 86

Kabat-Zinn, Jon, 64
Kohut, Heinz, 184

Lamictal, 57, 61, 66, 198-199, 231
    side effects of, 199
Landis, Richard, 109-110, 132
late luteal phase dysphoria (LLPD). *see* PMS
left brain, 7-8, 13, 44, 77, 80-90, 97, 105, 138-141, 177-179
LeShan, Lawrence, 178
Lexapro, 64, 201
light therapy, 203
Liking and Loving (Rubin), 209
lithium, 61, 198, 199
love and ADD, 186
Luvox, 64, 201

manic depressive disorders, 66-67, 196-201
    intermittent explosive disorder, 201-203
    treatment of, 197-201
marijuana, 65, 66, 70, 230
Maslow, Abraham, 95
medication, 2, 4, 6, 9-10, 12-13, 58, 60, 62, 67, 68, 74-75, 98, 108,
    171-175, 187, 193, 195, 209, 218-232, 239, 243, 247, 250
    serotonergic, 195, 201-205, 222, 225, 227, 232, 238
    side effects of, 173, 203
meditation, 81, 87, 96, 99-101, 117, 143, 177-187, 221, 234, 238
melancholia, 62-63
mental health system, 9
    problems with, 245-252
mental states, controlling, 184-189
methylphenidate, 12, 172
mindfulness meditation, 177-179
mirroring, 184
Mitchell, Stephen, 140, 209
mood, 36, 58-59, 66
mood stabilizing drugs, 66-67
Morrison, Van, 62
motivation, 10, 17, 36, 39-42, 45, 47-48, 53-55, 58, 61, 65, 71, 175,

Order *Getting Unstuck* online at www.theattentiondoctor.com

OR Complete this form to order *Getting Unstuck: Unraveling the Knot of Depression, Attention and Trauma* by mail.

Quantity	Unit Cost	NY State Residents Only Tax (8⅜%/0.0838	NY State Residents Price Including Tax
1	$24.95	$2.09	$27.04
2	$24.95	$4.18	$54.08
3	$24.95	$6.27	$81.12
4	$24.95	$8.36	$108.16

(indicate other quantities) _____ @ $24.95 $_____

Subtotal $_____

Sales Tax: New York State residents only:

add 8⅜% (0.0838) tax per book to total (see prices above). $_____

Shipping & Handling (U.S.: $4.95 for the first book. Add $2.00 for $_____
each additional book. International: $9.00 for the first book. Add $5.00 for each additional book.)

TOTAL ENCLOSED $_____

SHIPPING INFORMATION

Name _____

Address _____

City _____ State/Province _____ Zip _____

Telephone _____

PLEASE INDICATE AMOUNT AND PAYMENT METHOD.

Total Cost of Order $_____

❑ Mastercard   ❑ VISA   ❑ Check Enclosed

Card # _____ Expiration _____

❑ Check box, if billing information is same as shipping. If billing information is different, please enter below. Credit card users, be sure to sign below.

Billing Name _____

Billing Address _____

City _____ State/Province _____ Zip _____

Billing Telephone Number _____

*Cardholders Signature (Required) _____

Please return completed form, with payment or credit card information, in a stamped envelope to: Greenpoint Psychiatric Press, 861 Manhattan Avenue, Brooklyn, NY 11222

All orders sent via U.S. Postal Service Priority Mail Service.

Thank you for your interest in *Getting Unstuck*. Visit www.theattentiondoctor.com for more great stuff from Dr. Don, and to give him your feedback on the book!